THIRD EDITION

A SHORT GUIDE TO ACTION RESEARCH

ANDREW P. JOHNSON

Minnesota State University, Mankato

PEARSON

Boston ■ New York ■ San Francisco
Mexico City ■ Montreal ■ Toronto ■ London ■ Madrid ■ Munich ■ Paris
Hong Kong ■ Singapore ■ Tokyo ■ Cape Town ■ Sydney

Senior Editor: Arnis E. Burvikovs
Editorial Assistant: Erin Reilly
Marketing Manager: Erica DeLuca
Editorial Production Service: Omegatype Typography, Inc.
Composition Buyer: Linda Cox
Manufacturing Buyer: Linda Morris
Electronic Composition: Omegatype Typography, Inc.
Cover Administrator: Elena Sidorova

For related titles and support materials, visit our online catalog at www.ablongman.com.

Between the time website information is gathered and then published, it is not unusual for some sites to have closed. Also, the transcription of URLs can result in typographical errors. The publisher would appreciate notification where these errors occur so that they may be corrected in subsequent editions.

ISBN-13: 978-0-205-50931-7   ISBN-10: 0-205-50931-2

Printed in the United States of America

10   9   8   7   11   10

ABOUT THE AUTHOR

Dr. Andrew Johnson is Professor of Holistic Education in the Department of Educational Studies: Special Populations at Minnesota State University, Mankato. Here he specializes in gifted education, holistic education, literacy instruction, academic and professional writing, and spiritual intelligence. He worked for 9 years in the public schools as a second grade teacher, wrestling coach, and as a gifted education coordinator before moving into higher education. His most recent books include *Making Connections in Elementary and Middle School Social Studies* and *The Inner Curriculum: Classroom Activities to Develop Emotional Intelligence.*

Dr. Johnson can be reached for comment at: andrew.johnson@mnsu.edu. For information related to workshops and professional development opportunities go to: www.teachergrowth.com.

CONTENTS

CHAPTER NINE

METHODS OF ANALYZING DATA   100

CHAPTER TEN

QUANTITATIVE DESIGN IN ACTION RESEARCH   112

CHAPTER ELEVEN

DISCUSSION: YOUR PLAN OF ACTION   128

CHAPTER TWELVE

SAMPLE ACTION RESEARCH PROJECTS   141

CHAPTER THIRTEEN

PRESENTING YOUR ACTION RESEARCH   169

CHAPTER FOURTEEN

WRITING AN ACTION RESEARCH REPORT   176

CHAPTER FIFTEEN

ACTION RESEARCH AS MASTER'S THESIS   183

PREFACE

The most important variable in determining the quality of our children's educational experience is the teacher standing in front of a classroom. As such, it is a wise investment to spend time and resources to help teachers become knowledgeable practitioners and to create the conditions whereby they are able to make informed, research-based decisions. Action research is one of the most practical, effective, and economically efficient methods to achieve this. This book takes you through all phases of the action research process. My hope is that it can be used as an agent of change as well as a vehicle for teacher empowerment.

Action research is a systematic inquiry into one's own practice. The process can be an important part of the professional growth and development of practicing teachers. This book describes how to conduct and report action research. I have endeavored to write in a style that is concise, informative, reader friendly, and to the point. In so doing, I am modeling the style best used in writing action research reports.

This is the third edition of this action research book. I have made some significant changes that I believe make this a much better and more usable book. However, like the first two editions, I have tried to keep things as short and as straightforward as possible. Too often in education, quantity and complexity are mistaken for rigor and effectiveness. I do not want to make this mistake.

NEW TO THIS EDITION

In this third edition I have made the following changes or additions:

- **Possible research questions** for action research projects have been included at the end of the chapters in the first half of the book. These should give you some ideas for possible action research projects that you might conduct. Also, I have included tips to help you think of and formulate your own action research questions.
- Chapter 1 has been expanded to include a section describing what a theory is, how research is used to create theories, and how theories are used to help educators become better decision makers.
- I have included many more practical examples throughout the book and have focused much more on the practicing classroom teacher.
- Chapter 2, Research Paradigms and the Nature of Reality, has been revised and simplified. I have also included some practical, illustrative examples with this chapter.

- There are many new graphics and forms included that can be downloaded for your use from our website, www.ablongman.com/johnsonAR3e.
- Chapter 5, Strategies for Professional Growth and Development, has been revised to include many more ideas and practical examples for using action research for your own professional growth and development.
- I have significantly **expanded the section on descriptive statistics.** In doing so, I have endeavored to write in a way that makes the basic principles of statistical analysis fairly easy to understand.
- New **samples of students' action research projects** have been included.
- Examples of two full master's theses have been included on the website along with a research proposal form for a master's thesis and a checklist that describes the criteria for a thesis or an action research report.

MyLabSchool

ĉmylabschool is a collection of online tools for your success in this course, on your licensure exams, and in your teaching career. Visit www.mylabschool.com to access the following:

- Video footage of real-life classrooms, with opportunities for you to reflect on the videos and offer your own thoughts and suggestions for applying theory to practice
- An extensive archive of text and multimedia cases that provide valuable perspectives on real classrooms and real teaching challenges
- Allyn & Bacon's Lesson and Portfolio Builder application, which includes an integrated state standards correlation tool
- Research paper assistance using Research Navigator™, which provides access to three exclusive databases of credible and reliable source material: EBSCO's ContentSelect Academic Journal Database, The *New York Times* Search by Subject Archive, and "Best of the Web" Link Library
- Career Center with resources for Praxis exams and licensure preparation, professional portfolio development, and job search and interview techniques

ACKNOWLEDGMENTS

I thank editor Arnis Burvikovs for his suggestions and work on this project, as well as editorial assistant Erin Reilly, and the reviewers for this edition: Joyce Logan, University of Kentucky; Sandra McCune, Stephen F. Austin State University; Carole Milner, Minnesota State University; and Rodney White, Eastern Kentucky University. I also thank those graduate students and teachers who have allowed me to use their fine work in this text. Finally, I want to acknowledge all classroom teachers who have embraced the ideas in this text and put them to practice use. Your dedication to education and your determination to move the field of education forward does not show up on standardized tests results, yet it exists nonetheless and it is truly inspiring.

CHAPTER ONE

SCIENCE, RESEARCH, AND TEACHING

This book describes how to conduct action research in an educational setting. This chapter contains a description of the nature of science, research, and teaching, all of which are complementary parts of the same pursuit of truth.

SCIENCE

Ask somebody what he or she associates with the term *science*. That person is likely to respond with something like biology, astronomy, physics, or chemistry. However, science is not solely a body of knowledge or a particular content area; rather, it includes the processes used to examine and organize the world around us (Johnson, 2000). To engage in the process of science means to look, to seek to understand or know, to guess and test guesses, to create order from chaos, and to develop concepts. Science is "a way of thinking about and observing the universe that leads to a deep understanding of its workings" (Stanovich, 1992, p. 9).

Scientists are simply those who ask questions and find answers. In fact, we all use science in some way each day. Our questions might be as grand as, How did our universe begin? or as mundane as, Which line at the grocery store checkout is faster? or, I wonder what kind of response my new haircut will generate? Teachers are natural scientists. They engage in a form of science when they ask questions such as, How will this new teaching technique work? How are Sally's reading skills coming along? How can I help Billy learn long division?

Science and Pseudoscience

As consumers of scientific inquiry related to education, we must be aware of the differences between science and *pseudoscience*. Science uses perceived reality to determine beliefs. That is, data are collected to determine what is

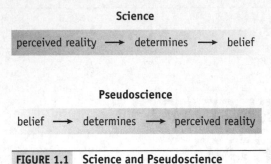

Science

perceived reality ⟶ determines ⟶ belief

Pseudoscience

belief ⟶ determines ⟶ perceived reality

FIGURE 1.1   Science and Pseudoscience

believed. Pseudoscience uses beliefs to determine perceived reality. One starts with a strong belief, then looks for data to support that belief (see Figure 1.1). Pseudoscience is often used by companies, groups, or individuals to demonstrate that their product, method, or ideology is the most effective or best. Science provides an honest analysis of the situation and is much preferred to pseudoscience.

An example of pseudoscience is the type of "research" that is included with some of the phonics programs advertised on television, which are guaranteed to improve children's reading scores, usually with some snappy, new method. Before you believe these claims, however, consider this: More than a million teachers in our country and thousands of professors have been looking for effective ways to teach children to read for years. If some secret key or magic method were superior to all others, the mathematical odds alone dictate that one of us would have found it by now and published many books and articles describing it.

An example of real science in education is the information published by the National Assessment of Educational Progress (NAEP), which is a part of the U.S. Department of Education. A representative sample of 30,000 students across the United States is selected at random for study (National Center for Educational Statistics, 1998). The kinds of tests, measures, and interviews given to this group are held constant across time and region. That is, a standardized math test given in 1970 in Georgia is similar in content, form, and length to one given in California in 2006 so that comparisons can be made. Thus, we are able to track the progress of U.S. students with some accuracy over time and place.

It is interesting to note that although many improvements are still needed for our schools, they are not in the miserable state of decay that some groups claim (Allington, 2006; McQuillan, 1998). When looking at basic skills, scores have remained constant or even risen slightly over the last 25 years (see Table 1.1). This is rather remarkable when one considers the influx of cultures and the many changes in our society, which have included an increase in drug use and violence. On the whole, U.S. teachers are doing a good job. However, NAEP shows that although basic skills have remained constant over the years, scores on tasks calling for higher-level thinking have dropped (Routmann, 1996). This contradicts the call

TABLE 1.1	Average Scores on Standardized Test (500 points possible)							
	SCIENCE		MATH			READING		
Age	1971	1999	1973	1999	2004	1970	1999	2004
9	225	229	219	232	241	208	212	219
13	255	256	266	276	281	255	259	254
17	305	295	304	308	307	285	288	286

for schools to get back to the basics, to have a standardization of process and product in education, and to engage in more testing. However, these are the kinds of remedies that are thrust on our children when pseudoscience is used to make important educational decisions.

RESEARCH

Scientific knowledge is a body of knowledge generated by research. *Research* is a way of seeing, a procedure used to view and re-view the world in order to understand it. Research is the systematic method used to collect data to answer questions. The systematic method used by the researcher is the lens through which the world is viewed. Different research methods or lenses provide different views of reality. A variety of scientific methods are used to study the unknown (Hodson, 1988; Stanovich, 1992); however, these methods tend to be put into two broad categories: quantitative and qualitative. *Transcendental research methodology,* a third type of research method, is mentioned in Chapter 2, but a full examination of this topic is beyond the scope of this current text.

Quantitative Research

In *quantitative research,* sometimes called *experimental research,* the researcher takes an active role in setting up an observation or experiment to isolate a variable. A variable is the quality or condition about which the researcher wants to draw conclusions. The goal of experimental research is to figure out what the effect of a particular approach or treatment (variable) might be. To make an accurate prediction or to demonstrate a causal relationship, the researcher creates an environment that isolates a particular variable by controlling all the extraneous variables. Some important terms in understanding quantitative research follow:

1. The *independent variable* is the treatment or factor that the researcher manipulates to determine a particular effect. It is what is done or not done to a group of people, animals, plants, or things.
2. The *dependent variable* is the particular result or the effect of the treatment. An easy way to remember the distinction between these two variables is to think

of the dependent variable as depending on the treatment or independent variable.

3. The *treatment group* or experimental group is the group of subjects, participants, or objects that are exposed to the particular treatment.

4. The *control group* is a group as similar as possible in all characteristics to the treatment group; however, this group is not exposed to the particular treatment for the purposes of comparison.

5. The *research question* is what the researcher hopes to find an answer for.

6. The *hypothesis* is a tentative statement that can be supported if the outcome of the experimentation is as expected. If a number of different tests continue to support that hypothesis, it may be elevated to the status of theory.

7. A *theory* is an interrelated set of concepts that is used to explain a body of data (Stanovich, 1992). Most hypotheses never make it to the level of theory because it takes a great deal of evidence to support a hypothesis before it can be viewed as valid. Hypotheses and theories are described further in the following sections.

To better understand this process, I have created a mock experiment. This mock experiment is purposely simplistic and exaggerated to demonstrate clearly the salient aspects of quantitative research.

The Coffee Study.   I wanted to find out whether drinking coffee (independent variable) would lead to higher student test scores on standardized achievement tests (dependent variable). To do this, I set up an experimental world in which two relatively similar groups of people had the same experience except for the independent variable. I randomly selected 200 college students and put them into two groups: Group A was the treatment group; Group B was the control group. Group A students were administered the treatment, which in this case was five cups of coffee each day. Group B students were not given coffee. The research question was, Does coffee improve students' performance on standardized tests? My hypothesis was, Drinking coffee improves students' ability to perform on standardized tests. The goal of this study was to prove or disprove my hypothesis.

A standardized test was given as a pretest measure to both groups to determine whether they were relatively equal at the beginning of the experiment. (If all the smart people happened to end up in the treatment group, this would confound the experiment and lead to a false conclusion.) For this experiment to be valid, I needed a sample size that was large enough to conclude that the results were not due to coincidence. The number depends on the research question, but in education, 30 is often seen as the minimum number of subjects needed in each group for a quantitative research study. Of course more subjects are usually better than fewer subjects.

Next, I created a controlled environment in which everything about the two groups was exactly the same except for the independent variable (coffee). In this way, the independent variable (coffee) could be isolated, and I could say for certain that coffee did or did not affect the dependent variable (scores on standardized achievement tests). For this to happen, I put the subjects in a biosphere and gave each group controlled doses of study time, food, sleep, television, social interaction, and emotional stress.

In this exaggerated experiment you can begin to see one of the problems with controlled experimental research dealing with human subjects: Manipulating reality makes it nonreality. By controlling the environment I created an unreal world. Data from this unreal world are then used to make conclusions about the real world. This is not to suggest, however, that empirical data from quantitative research studies are not valid, but rather that the research method used should be determined by the research question. In this case, the research method is the best possible one to use in specifically answering my research question. However, if I wanted to understand why, when, or where college students drink coffee, I would need to use qualitative methods (discussed in the next section).

In this make-believe coffee experiment, I kept the two groups in their controlled environments long enough for the treatment effect to show up. In this case, it was 2 months. At the end of the treatment, I tested the two groups. These posttest scores were then compared to see whether one group's average was significantly higher than the other's. I also looked at the difference between pretest and posttest scores to see whether one group's gain score was significantly greater than the other's. Statistical procedures were then used to figure out whether the difference between the two groups was statistically significant, which means that the difference was larger than could reasonably be expected by chance or that it could not have happened by coincidence. Table 1.2 shows the results of this experiment.

The results show that the treatment group outperformed the control group by 17% on posttest measures. We will assume this difference is statistically significant. (I do not want to get into a description of statistical analysis here.) It appears that coffee does have a positive effect in students' ability to perform on standardized achievement tests. These results may transfer into other areas of academic performance. However, even in experimental research with the strictest controls, we can never claim absolute certainty. Maybe coffee has this effect only on college students. Perhaps the coffee effect is negated by a particular study method. Would coffee have the same effect on a group of elementary students? Are there maximum and minimum levels after which there is no effect or a negative effect? Certainly, more research is needed in these areas.

TABLE 1.2   Effects of Coffee on Achievement Test Scores

	PRETEST AVERAGE	POST-TEST AVERAGE	GAIN
Treatment Group A	78%	95%	17%
Control Group B	77%	78%	1%

Qualitative Research

As demonstrated, *quantitative research* uses numbers to reach a state of knowing. Controlled environments are created to isolate one particular aspect of reality. The questions are stated up front and only data related to the research questions are observed and recorded. A cause-and-effect paradigm is used to make sense of the world.

Qualitative research, on the other hand, uses systematic observations to reach understanding. Researchers take the world as they find it instead of trying to manipulate conditions to isolate variables. The questions are more open ended and less defined, with plenty of room to collect a variety of data through collateral observations. Also, qualitative researchers sometimes begin a study with only a focus or area of interest and allow the specific research question to form or begin to be defined with early observations. To demonstrate the differences between quantitative and qualitative research, I include another mock study. This mock study also is purposely simplistic in order to highlight the salient elements of qualitative research.

The Coffeehouse Study.   When I went to college in the 1970s, beer and bars were an integral part of the college culture, often the prime areas of socialization and interaction between genders. Many campuses even had a beer bar in their student union. Times have changed. The legal drinking age has gone up, awareness of the negative effects and dangerous situations created with the use of alcohol has increased, and most campuses today are alcohol free. This is something we could not have imagined in the 1970s.

On the campus of Minnesota State University, where I work, coffee and coffeehouses seem to have replaced beer and bars in the social milieu of the college culture. I wanted to see whether this was so. I was also interested in the nature of the interactions found in both types of environments.

Getting at my research questions meant going beyond numbers. I began my research spending a great deal of time observing the people and social interactions that took place in the coffeehouses and bars found near our campus. I did not try to control or manipulate the environment; rather, I observed individuals within their natural environment. After several observations, I developed a systematic method for collecting data that initially included taking detailed field notes and interviewing students on campus and in the bars and coffeehouses. (Data collection methods are described in detail in Chapter 8.) After my initial observations, certain patterns of behaviors began to emerge. I created a checklist of these behaviors and put tally marks every time I saw them displayed. This checklist allowed me to quantify what I was seeing and provided me with a sense of the frequency, time, and gender related to each behavior.

In this study I became the lens through which this bit of reality was observed. My goal was to describe the quality of those things observed to help understand the nature of these places. What I found was that beer and bars were still an integral part of the social culture of this particular college campus. The types of interactions that occurred seemed similar in kind to what I remembered from the 1970s. The music was loud and affrontive, the atmosphere was highly sexual, conversation tended to be short and light, groups that came together tended to splinter and mix, and there were many instances of initial intergender interaction (III); that is, boy meets girl or girl meets boy. A sort of mating dance was going on here, complete with colorful plumage, strutting, dancing, and establishing territory. All that was missing was two bucks charging at each other and locking horns. But I am sure that had I stayed longer, I would have observed this in some form.

In the coffeehouses, the music tended to be quieter and more a part of the background. The general atmosphere seemed more subdued and cerebral without the sense of heightened sexuality. Also, conversation was on a much deeper level conceptually and of longer duration; groups seldom splintered off or mixed with other groups; and initial intergender interactions rarely occurred.

It appeared as if beer and bars were still an integral part of college social interactions; however, because the age of legal alcohol consumption is 21 in Minnesota, most students found in the bars were in their junior and senior years. In this study I was not able to find out much about the socialization of younger students, but this is perhaps worthy of consideration for future research. It appears as if coffee and coffee houses have not replaced beer and bars in the college culture at Minnesota State University; rather, they have provided an additional outlet for a different kind of socialization.

Quantitative or Qualitative?

Is one type of research "better" than the other? No. Both are to be used to answer different kinds of questions. However, of these two categories of research, action research most often falls in the realm of qualitative research because action researchers study the world (their schools and classrooms) as they find them. And even though quantitative data may be collected, action researchers generally do not manipulate the environment to isolate variables. I often tell beginning action researchers to think of themselves as Jane Goodall studying a group of gorillas in the middle of the jungle.

TEACHING

Teachers and scientists are similar in many respects. Gallagher and Gallagher (1994) describe seven essential activities of a scientist. Each of these, in various forms, is also an essential part of teaching.

What Scientists and Teachers Do

1. *Scientists develop content expertise.* The process of science is highly dependent on having a well-organized knowledge base (Armbruster, 1993; Gallagher & Gallagher, 1994; Hodson, 1988; Thelen, 1984). Knowledge helps the scientist structure and assimilate new information. Scientific inquiries are built on accepted theories

and previous research. New data make sense only when they are grounded in what is familiar. Thus, methods of science involve generating relations between prior knowledge and new knowledge (Johnson, 2000).

Effective teaching also requires knowledge related to subject matter, the learning process, and pedagogy. A sound knowledge base enables teachers to make thoughtful decisions about the teaching and learning process. Professional journals, workshops, conferences, and graduate courses are some traditional ways for teachers to expand their knowledge. Action research is one of the best ways to link theory to practice and expand teachers' knowledge base. This is described in more detail in Chapter 3.

2. *Scientists detect problems or ask questions.* As described above, scientists are continually asking questions about the universe and trying to solve problems (Stanovich, 1992). Teachers reflect on teaching experiences, looking for problems or ways in which to improve. They question and probe to see whether learning is occurring or whether students are grasping a particular skill or concept. The reflective teacher is continually asking, How is it going? How well and to what degree is learning taking place? What other strategies might I use? How is this new technique working?

3. *Scientists observe.* Scientists use observation in a variety of forms in collecting data. Kenneth Goodman (1986) tells us that effective teachers are kid watchers. They watch their students as they work with new skills and concepts and listen to them as they engage in small-group discussions to see how learning is taking place and what skills need to be taught. Observation and reflection are skills that are used naturally by teachers as they monitor students engaged in the act of learning (Erickson, 1986).

4. *Scientists organize and classify data.* Scientists use forms of categorization such as phylum, classes, and divisions to put order to the natural world. Using authentic assessment techniques, teachers often record their observations using anecdotal records. These data are then organized by looking for patterns and put into context so that they can be used to inform instruction or to evaluate and report students' progress.

5. *Scientists measure or collect data.* Teachers measure and collect data when they give any form of standardized tests or use other forms of authentic assessment and evaluation. They monitor assignments, record scores, make anecdotal records, give standardized tests, and create checklists, all to help them answer the question, How well is learning taking place with my students? Measurement takes place as teachers determine how far students have progressed. Portfolios are used to show growth over time.

6. *Scientists hypothesize or make predictions.* Hypothesizing occurs also when teachers say, "I think this technique or this new teaching idea might work in my class." It also occurs when teachers try to understand a particular student or learning problem.

7. *Scientists experiment.* Experimenting occurs when teachers try a new technique or methodology, or implement a new solution to a problem.

USING RESEARCH IN EDUCATION: THEORIES, HYPOTHESES, AND PARADIGMS, OH MY!

So why should educators be concerned about educational research? What relevance does it have to our everyday practice? We have all heard the common litany: "It's just a bunch of theory. You can make research say anything you want. Ivory tower researchers don't know what it's like in the trenches. It doesn't work that way in the real world."

Sigh.

Let me address some of these.

Theories and Hypotheses

Educational research is used to create the theories on which we design educational policies and practices. Theories help to organize relevant empirical facts (*empirical* means they can be observed or measured) to create a context for understanding phenomena. Sometimes people try to dismiss an idea or practice with which they do not agree by saying it is just a bunch of theory, meaning that the theoretical realm is somehow far removed from the practical realm, perhaps even having a different set of laws that govern it. But this would be a misunderstanding of what a theory is.

A theory is a way to explain a set of facts. Put another way, if reality were a dot-to-dot picture, a theory would be a way to connect a set of data dots (see Figure 1.2). However, varying theories connect different data dots in different ways resulting in a wide variety of pictures and practices. Thus, varying theoretical perspectives, although based on a set of empirical data, can often advocate different practices or practical notions. An example is behavioral learning theory and cognitive learning theory (see Chapter 2), both of which are based on solid empirical evidence.

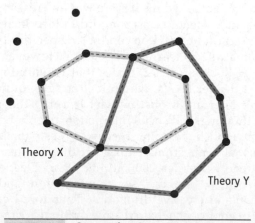

FIGURE 1.2   Connecting Data Dots to Create a Theory

- Theory of cognitive dissonance
- Constructivist theory
- Holistic learning theory
- Drive reduction theory
- Behavioral learning theory
- Information processing theory
- Levels of processing theory
- Multiple intelligence theory
- Triarchic theory of intelligence
- Social learning theory
- Situated learning theory

FIGURE 1.3   Common Education Theories

Theories are not meant to be eternal entities. They are designed to exist only as long as they continue to explain facts or connect the relevant data dots. When an abundance of new data are shown to conflict with established theories, the data are discounted or restructured. (You cannot put new wine in an old wineskin.) A list of common education theories are listed in Figure 1.3.

A theory is often confused with a *hypothesis*, which is an untested conjecture. A hypothesis is the first part of a study or experiment. Here the researcher says, "I think that _____," or, "What will happen to X when Y is present?" or, "I wonder about _____." This thinking is then put in the form of a research question or questions. In a formal quantitative experiment this becomes the basis of a null hypothesis, which is then either supported or rejected by data collected during the experiment. However, in qualitative or descriptive studies data are collected to answer or explore the question.

Finally, theories can often be used to justify a practice or procedure for which there may not be direct research-based evidence. For example, in one of my undergraduate classes students are taught how to use creative dramatics to enhance learning, not only in language arts but also in science and social studies classes as well. One day a student asked me if there was any research to show that using creative dramatics in a science classroom did indeed increase learning. Now I do not know if any studies have been conducted specifically to examine the effects of creative dramatics and learning in science. However, the levels of processing theory (Craig & Lockhart, 1972) states that when information is manipulated or processed at deeper levels, we are better able to understand, remember, and retrieve it for later use. Constructivist learning theory tells us that creativity, higher-order thinking, and social interaction all enhance learning (Sternberg & Williams, 2002). Holistic learning theory suggests that when students are able to make personal connections with what they are learning they learn more and learn more deeply (Kessler, 2000; Miller, 1996). Deeper levels of processing, creativity, higher-order thinking, social interaction, and personal connections are all components of creative dramatics. Therefore I can tell my students with a fair amount of confidence that creative dramatics can be used to enhance learning in science.

Paradigms

A *paradigm,* as you will see in the next chapter, is a shared worldview based on one or more theories. It includes a set of beliefs or assumptions that (1) establishes boundaries and principles within a particular field, (2) guides perception, and (3) describes a particular view of reality. Paradigms are useful in providing a form of cognitive scaffolding to guide understanding or new learning. However, if they become too rigid, they prevent more growth than they promote. That is, if we automatically discount all data or events that fall outside our particular paradigms, we become parochial in our thinking and locked into old ways of doing things. Progress and innovation become stymied.

An example of this paradigm-induced rigidity can be found in education in which a *positivistic paradigm* predominates (see Chapter 2). From this view, the only things that are valued are those that can be observed, weighed, or measured. Logic and knowledge reign while emotion, intuition, creativity, and altered states of consciousness are ignored, demeaned, or dismissed. Yet these last four qualities have been instrumental in all the great human innovations and breakthroughs in science, the arts, the humanities, and other areas (Csikszentmihalyi, 1990; Harman & Rheingold, 1984). Thus it would seem logical that an education system that seeks to fully develop the potential of all its students to create a better society would address or cultivate these areas. Yet a paradigm gets in our way.

Better Decision Makers

The main point here is this: Educational research is a key factor in enabling school administrators, principals, teachers, and parents to make sound decisions (Marzano, 2003). Teachers and schools have a tremendous effect on student learning and achievement (Marzano, Pickering, & Pollock, 2001). This effect is more likely to be positive if the decisions related to policy, curriculum, and teaching practices are made based on what a body of research has determined to be best practice. Unfortunately, this is not always the case. Following are some general approaches that are often used to making educational decisions.

   1. *Personal experience or anecdotal evidence.* Educational decisions are sometimes made on personal experience. You may have tried a strategy or approach or had a particular experience, and this becomes the basis of all future decisions. For example, "I tried cooperative learning once and it didn't work." This is called *anecdotal evidence,* and although it is very powerful, (because of the personal connection) it is not a sound approach to making decisions.

   2. *One or two studies.* Here an educator starts out with a personal opinion or preconceived idea, then locates one or two studies to support this view. This also is not a sound approach to decision making because of the possibility of selecting studies that are limited, flawed, or biased. This is similar to pseudoscience described previously. Can you make research say anything you want? Not if you look at the broad spectrum of research. But it is likely that you can find one or two incomplete, poorly designed, or outlier studies to support a particular point of view. However, this is more likely to happen if a study has not been peer reviewed. Indeed, science is not science without the review of one's findings by a group of peers (Stanovich, 1992). For this reason, one should always be skeptical of "scientific studies" presented by companies or corporations that are intent on selling a product, political organizations, or any group that has an agenda.

3. *Famous person.* Sometimes decisions are made based on the statements of a well known person. For example, William Bennett, the former secretary of education under the Reagan administration, received a bachelor of arts degree in philosophy from Williams College, a Ph.D. in philosophy from the University of Texas, and a law degree from Harvard. With this background he was named secretary of education by Ronald Reagan in 1985. He has had much to say about education over the years, all of which should be taken with many grains of salt because they are statements based on philosophy and ideology, not on research-based theory. His recommendations should not be considered research based or set in a solid theoretical context. Similarly, the statements of politicians, newspaper columnists, TV commentators, famous scientists, world leaders, or even action research textbook writers are all of interest as general statements but should not be used as the sole basis for making educational decisions. In all things you must say, "Show me the data."

4. *Tradition and folklore.* With the tradition and folklore approach, a decision is made or a particular practice is continued because "We've always done it this way." A case in point is the weekly spelling test that is given in most elementary schools every Friday. From Monday to Thursday students study a list of words in isolation (outside any meaningful context) that are selected by the textbook company. On Friday they are asked to recall the exactly spelling of these words. This process is supposed to improve students' ability to spell; yet, there is no research evidence to show that doing this improves students' ability to spell under real-life conditions (Gentry, 1992), what Donald Graves calls "game conditions" (Graves, 1992). Although this idea seems to makes sense, there is no research to support this over other methods used for developing students' spelling. Why is it done? "Because we've always done it this way."

Likewise the common sayings that a teacher should not smile until Christmas or that student behavior problems can be solved by "getting tough" are both bits of folklore that are often repeated as truth. These are based on the assumption that an effective teacher has a stern demeanor and is able to control students. Control and manipulation are valued over relationship, shared goals, synergistic learning, community building, and cooperation. But if there were any research to suggest that simply being stern and getting tough actually worked, we would certainly be writing about these in our books and journal articles. We would also be teaching get-tough techniques to our students in all our teacher preparation courses. But they do not work. As behavioral learning

Best Practice: New Standards for Teaching and Learning in America's Schools (3rd ed.) (Zemelman, Daniels, & Hyde, 2006)

Classroom Instruction That Works: Research-Based Strategies for Increasing Student Achievement, (Marzano, Pickering, & Pollock, 2001)

What Really Matters for Struggling Readers: Designing Research-Based Programs (2nd ed.) (Allington, 2006)

What Works in Schools: Translating Research into Action, (Marzano, 2003)

FIGURE 1.4   Books Describing Research-Based Teaching Practices

---

theory describes, simply getting tough is not effective in changing behavior, whether one is dealing with mice in a Skinner box or humans beings in a second grade classroom, because the mouse or students simply learn to avoid the punishment or aversive conditioner, and when the punishment disappears the behavior reappears.

5. *Magic bullets and flashy new packages.* Sometimes pedagogical decisions in schools and classrooms are made based on the claims of for-profit manufacturers of educational materials. Do not believe what is written on the outside of the package even if you see the word *research.* Again, research is not research without peer review. Even though commercial programs may claim to have the ultimate answer for teaching a particular skill or subject, there are no magic bullets (Allington, 2006). There is not one miraculous cure or single best method for teaching anything. Rather, there are many research-based strategies and pedagogical techniques, all of which should be intelligently adopted and adapted to meet the needs of particular teachers and learners in particular situations. What are these research-based strategies? The books listed in Figure 1.4 will give you a sense of some research-based strategies.

6. *Research-based theory and a synthesis of peer reviewed studies.* This is the optimal decision-making approach, in which schools and teachers look at a body of research or make decisions that are solidly supported by research-based theory. This reinforces the need to have well-educated teachers, principals, and administrators with a substantial body of knowledge related to teaching and learning. Indeed, experts in any field have at their disposal a large body of knowledge to solve problems and make decisions (Sternberg & Williams, 2002). It is not possible to provide all the knowledge that teachers need in two years of an undergraduate teacher preparation program. That is why it is so important to have a plan for continued staff development activities for both teachers and administrators. Action research can be a part of this plan (see Chapter 5). Figure 1.5 contains Internet sources for teacher professional development.

National Staff Development Council:
www.nsdc.org/standards/researchbased.cfm

Professional Development for Teachers:
www.teachergrowth.com

Annenberg Media: www.learner.org

Tapped In: http://tappedin.org/tappedin

FIGURE 1.5   **Teacher Professional Development Websites**

SUMMARY

- Science is a body of knowledge generated by research.
- Science is the process of asking and answering questions.
- Research is the systematic method used to collect data to answer questions.
- Quantitative or experimental research manipulates the environment to isolate a variable so that a cause–effect relationship can be determined.
- Qualitative research looks at the environment as it is and uses systematic methods to understand things happening there.
- Action research is a form of qualitative research.
- Teachers and scientists engage in many of the same kinds of activities.
- Educational research is used to develop the theories that underly educational policies and practices.
- A theory is a way of explaining a set of facts.
- A hypothesis is an untested conjecture.
- Research-based theory can be used to justify practices or policies.
- A paradigm is a framework from which to view reality.
- Rigidly adhering to paradigms can stymie growth and lock us into old ways of seeing and doing.
- Educational research helps teachers and school administrators to make good decisions.

QUESTION AND ACTIVITIES

1. What is your favorite branch of scientific inquiry?
2. What scientific inquiry or research influences your teaching?
3. Describe an instance in which you think beliefs are used to determine reality.
4. Describe one thing you believe to be true about teaching and learning; then describe the facts related to this belief.
5. Describe 3 to 10 facts about the act of teaching and about learning how to become a teacher; then describe a belief related to teacher training.
6. Find a topic that interests you. It could be a topic related to education or another topic such as humor, sewing, motorcycles, or football. Using an

Internet search engine or a database at a college library, enter your topic followed by the word *research*. Find and describe a piece of research related to your topic.

7. Pick one of the activities that scientists engage in as described by Gallagher and Gallagher (1994). Describe how this activity is manifested in your classroom or school.

8. Describe a practice in your classroom or school that seems to be based more on tradition than research.

9. Describe your plan for professional development.

10. Ask a question related to student achievement in the area of Civics, Geography, History, Mathematics, Reading, Science, or Writing. Use the NAEP web site at www.nces.ed.gov/nationsreportcard to answer your question.

POSSIBLE RESEARCH QUESTIONS FOR ACTION RESEARCH PROJECTS

1. How do teachers view research in your school?

2. What education theories do teachers feel are important? What educational theories are used to guide practice?

3. What educational theories do principals and administrators feel are important? What educational theories are used to guide their decision making?

4. How do teachers and administrators differ in their perceptions of educational theories and practice?

5. What theoretical foundations seem to shape educational practices in your school or district?

6. How do the schools' standardized test scores in your class, school, or district compare with those of NAEP?

7. What do teachers believe are the most important characteristics of a good teacher? What do principals and administrators believe are the most important characteristics of a good teacher? How do these compare?

8. How has your school's population changed over the past 30 years?

9. How have your school's test scores changed over the past 30 years?

10. How has the focus on standardized tests changed your teaching practice? How has it changed the teaching practices in your school?

11. What types of decisions do you make during the course of the day?

12. Does all-day kindergarten have a lasting effect on student achievement? Do differences show up in fifth and sixth grade?

13. What are the types of professional development activities in which teachers engage in your school or district? What types of professional development activities do teachers think would be most beneficial? What are the topics that teachers would like addressed in professional development activities?

14. How closely do school policy and practices reflect the school mission statement and stated goals?

CHAPTER TWO

RESEARCH PARADIGMS AND THE NATURE OF REALITY

The scientific knowledge that has been gained influences the way we perceive the world.
But the way the world is experienced in a particular culture influences
what kind of science gets developed by that society.
—Willis Harman, 1998, p. 28

This chapter is different from its counterpart in the second edition of this book. For this third edition I have tried to make the ideas related to research paradigms more concrete and also have included some specific examples.

In the previous chapter we learned that a paradigm is a common framework from which to view reality. Paradigms are built on what we believe to be true. As we will see, what we believe to be true can affect (1) how we choose to see (research perspectives), (2) what we see (data), and (3) how we interpret what we see. However, there is a certain cyclic effect here that is not consistent with objectivity and true scientific inquiry. If our paradigms are built on what we believe to be true and at the same time, affect what we believe to be true, we end up believing only what we believed in the first place. Put another way, if we discount all data that do not fit into our preexisting paradigms, we severely limit our capacity to learn and make new discoveries.

For example, my current paradigm discounts the possibility of a talking cow. If I were to walk into my classroom and a large bovine greeted me by saying, "Good morning Dr. Johnson," my first inclination would be to discount the phenomenon (see Figure 2.1). I would most likely think that I was completely insane, that someone was playing a very sophisticated practical joke on me, or that I was on some sort of TV show that tries to catch professors looking foolish. The talking cow in front of me, even though it was clearly perceived, would be immediately discounted.

In the same way, in the mid-1800s the idea that sickness, infection, and disease could be caused by tiny, invisible entities called *germs* was as ridiculous as a talking cow. However, as the germ theory of disease gradually became accepted,

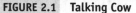

FIGURE 2.1   Talking Cow

there was far less bleeding and purging practiced by doctors and far more steril-
ized surgical instruments and operating rooms, resulting in significantly fewer
deaths. This paradigm-expanding discovery eventually led to a new era of cura-
tive medicines that have saved millions of lives over the past century.

So what do talking cows and the germ theory of disease have to do with
action research in our schools? In education we may be ignoring important data or
discounting creative new ideas simply because they do not match our preexisting
concepts of what we believe to be true or possible. We need to be aware of how our
views related to the nature of reality (ontological perspectives) influence our
research paradigms and how these in turn may affect our educational practices.

ONTOLOGICAL PERSPECTIVES

Willis Harman (1998) described three views of reality, or *ontological* perspectives:
materialistic monism, dualism, and transcendental monism. One's orientation relative to these three perspectives determines the types of questions that get asked
and the types of data that are deemed valid in academic research. Each of these
perspectives is examined here.

Materialistic Monism

The *materialistic monism* perspective is the one with which modern science and
education seems most comfortable (some might even say fixated). According to
this view, the universe consists only of matter and energy. Hence, the only things
said to exist are those that can be weighed and measured. Our human *consciousness*
(that with which we are aware) and our personality arise out of physical matter.

That is, our sense of self is solely an end product of neurological activity, which in turn is an end product of millions of years of evolution. Taken to its logical extreme, humans are merely skin bags full of chemicals sloshing about, guided by neurons zipping back and forth across our brains. A pleasant thought, yes?

This idea represents a purely mechanical understanding of the universe where Newtonian laws of cause and effect govern all events. Every physical effect has a physical cause; every physical cause has a physical effect. If X happens, then Y simply must happen; there are no other alternatives. In this cosmic contraption known as reality humans are said to be able to know, predict, and ultimately have dominion over the universe by breaking bits of it down into their most basic components through the use of controlled variables and objective inquiry. This is a "Yertle the Turtle" view of reality in which science claims to rule all that it sees. *Positivism* is a philosophy consistent with this view (Alkove & McCarty, 1992). In this reality quantitative research methodologies (described in Chapter 1) are the only credible source for coming to know the world we live in.

One of the current problems in education is that we are obsessed with the materialistic monism perspective to the exclusion of the other two. How does this affect education? From this view, learning consists of simply receiving knowledge from outside the individual, which must then be demonstrated outwardly for it to have occurred. The purpose of schools is to supply students with a designated body of knowledge and set of skills in a predetermined order. Teaching is seen as a matter of transmitting objective knowledge from point A (teacher's head) to point B (students' heads) (see Figure 2.2). Academic achievement is perceived as students' ability to demonstrate or retransmit this designated body of knowledge back to the teacher (point A) or some other measuring agency. Teaching and learning exist only in the presence of a norm-referenced, standardized test. Without quantification there is no learning.

FIGURE 2.2   Passively Receiving Knowledge

Dualism

From the *dualistic perspective,* the universe is composed of two distinctly different kinds of stuff: physical and metaphysical. As described above, the physical dimensions consist of matter and energy and are studied using the traditional tools of science. The metaphysical (beyond the physical) dimensions are made up of meta-energy in the form of consciousness. (Stay with me here. This is not as complicated as it sounds.)

There are three separate aspects to consciousness. The first is *ego-consciousness,* or one's awareness and interpretation of the outer physical world. This aspect is studied using the tools of qualitative inquiry such as interviews, journals, ethnographies, and surveys (see Chapter 8). The second is *self-consciousness,* or the awareness and interpretation of the inner world of feelings, memories, intuition, and impressions. The tools of qualitative inquiry are also used here, but we turn them inward and include other things such as gestalt, dream analysis, free association, and art (see Chapter 11). Psychology, educational research, and the other social sciences are adept at examining these first two aspects of consciousness, called *personal consciousness*. The third aspect of consciousness, *universal consciousness* or spirituality, is a bit uncomfortable for those existing in the hyper-rational worlds of science and academia. Universal consciousness refers to dimensions described by our religious and spiritual thinkers and also now being explored by some in quantum physics. This third aspect of consciousness will be described later as part of transcendental monism. Figure 2.3 shows the relationships among the three aspects of consciousness.

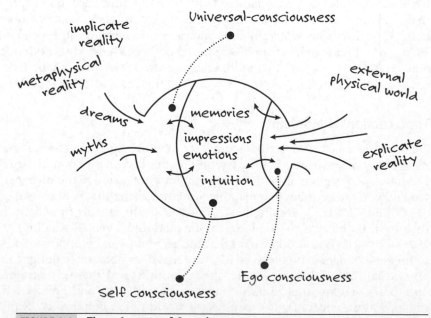

FIGURE 2.3   Three Aspects of Consciousness

The big idea related to dualism is that it acknowledges that reality consists of both physical and metaphysical dimensions; however, they operate independently of each other. Most people are comfortable with this ontological perspective as it recognizes spiritual or metaphysical dimensions while keeping a firm footing in physical dimensions. *Constructivism* is an educational philosophy consistent with this view. In constructivism, knowledge is not passively received; rather, it is actively built up or constructed by students as they connect their prior knowledge and past experiences with new information and skills (Santrock, 2004).

The purpose of schools from this perspective is not simply to slop a designated body of knowledge onto students' plates as they walk through the education line (this is known as the *school-as-cafeteria* model of education). Rather, it is to help students construct knowledge and develop the skills they will need to successfully live in their worlds. Learning is an active process in which students add personally relevant knowledge to their cognitive webs. That is, students use what they know to interpret and understand what they do not know. Teaching is a matter of creating conditions whereby students are able to link new knowledge to acquired knowledge. Academic achievement is seen as students' ability to use their knowledge and skills to solve real-world problems or to create products or performances that are valued in one or more cultural settings. This reflects Howard Gardner's (1983) definition of intelligence. It also complements Robert Sternberg's (1996) concept of intelligence as using creative, analytical, and pragmatic thinking to adapt to or shape the world.

Some think that a constructivist philosophy would prevent there being a required body of knowledge for students to learn, that students would only study what is of interest to them. This is a misunderstanding of this educational philosophy. Constructivism can include having a required body of knowledge and skills for students to learn (performance standards); the difference, however, would be that students would be taught in a way that helped them make personal connections. Constructivists would include choice, active learning, and social interaction as important parts of learning this required body of knowledge. Both quantitative and qualitative research methodologies are used here, but qualitative research using inductive thinking is more reflective of this ontological perspective.

Transcendental Monism

Transcendental monism describes a universe in which the basic essence is consciousness. Here consciousness is primary, and matter and energy materialize from this. From this perspective ultimate reality is found not solely in the physical world as we know it; rather, it lies in a metaphysical dimension that is universal consciousness (Talbot, 1991). Quantum physics describes such a reality in which all things in the physical universe are connected at the quantum level (Al-Khalili, 1999; Talbot, 1991). Physicist David Bohm said that the universe can be understood only if the unbroken wholeness is perceived in a way that does not reduce things to a series of individual entities (Nichol, 2003). At the quantum level, there is no fragmentation, only parts that are interconnected with greater systems and greater wholes. The things that we encounter in our physical world (what Bohm calls "explicate reality") are merely an unfolding of a deeper reality ("implicate reality"), which is beyond our senses in the metaphysical world. It is consciousness, a subtle form of energy (meta-energy), that creates movement from implicate order to the explicate order of our physical world (Bohm, 1980). Thus, consciousness is the cause and physical phenomena are the effect.

A helpful analogy can be found in music and the images created in the heads of listeners as they engage in the act of consciously attending to the music. The music can be thought of as *holomovement,* or implicate reality. As the consciousness of the human listener interacts with the music, various mental images are created. These mental images, which do not exist in the absence of a conscious listener, are analogous to explicate reality. In this sense, physical reality does not exist in the absence of an observer. This reflects the Copenhagen interpretation (Herbert, 1985), which posits that if a tree falls in a forest and nobody is there to hear it, not only does it not make a sound, but the tree does not exist in the first place.

Holism, a thesis consistent with this perspective, states that the universe is made up of integrated wholes that cannot be reduced to the sum of their parts. We can never come to know the whole of reality by isolating variables to examine small parts of it (the staple of quantitative methodology). Instead, the whole is best understood by examining the principles that govern behavior within the system. Both quantitative and qualitative methodologies are used here; however, they must always be combined with a greater perspective in the form of transpersonal research methodology to approach truth. Transpersonal research methodologies are those activities that allow an individual to move beyond personal consciousness (ego consciousness and self-consciousness) to approach universal consciousness (Braud & Anderson 1998). Various forms of transpersonal research methods are in listed in Figure 2.4. Admittedly, these may seem a little strange to some; however, they can all be used as a way of seeing, presenting, and re-presenting reality. From this ontological perspective, all types of research are valued; however, transpersonal research methodology should be used to provide the ultimate context for all data and experience.

Holistic education is a philosophical approach based on theories of holism. It is constructed around the principle of interconnectedness and seeks to integrate multiple levels of meaning and experience (Miller, 1996). Making connections is central to the curriculum process here. These connections occur between concepts, subject areas, communities, cultures, humanity, the arts, the sciences, mythology,

- Meditation
- Systematic contemplation
- Vision questing
- The arts
- Intuitive thinking
- Bottomless reflection
- Active imagination

- Journal writing
- Poetry and creative writing
- Personal narratives
- Stories
- Religious traditions
- Associative thinking
- Inductive synchronistic analysis

- Sacred writing
- Deep silence
- Sensory depravation
- Ritual
- Personal metaphor
- Chanting
- B-cognition

FIGURE 2.4   Transpersonal Research Methodology

religion, ecological systems, and history. True knowledge is seen as ultimately residing within each individual. Thus, teachers strive to create experiences whereby students are able to encounter phenomena, both internal and external, so that this knowledge can be realized. Curriculum is designed to enable all students to find and develop their particular strengths and to discover their passions. To learn, one must transcend one's culture, bias, values, ego, past experience, and sense of self to see things as they really are. Learning is said to have occurred when this view elicits a transformation of consciousness that leads to a greater nurturing of self, others, and the community and environment. From this perspective, a school's fundamental purpose is the creation of better human beings, which occurs through self-actualization and self-transcendence (Maslow, 1971).

Three Perspectives in Perspective

Table 2.1 provides a general overview of how the ontological perspectives project into various areas. It is important to note that there are few people who identify with or exist in only one column.

IMPLICATIONS

I have laid out three perspectives in this chapter to move you toward a broader understanding of research. Again, research is a way of seeing, presenting, and rep-resenting (re-presenting) reality. It runs the gamut from strict, empirical, scientific experiments with controls used to isolate variables to descriptive, qualitative research and even to photography, the arts, poetry and creative writing, journal writing, and various forms of transpersonal methodology. All of these can be used in action research projects to help you systematically observe something related to your teaching practice with the goal of understanding and ultimately enhancing your ability to create effective learning experiences in order to better meet the needs of your students. Related to this are four big ideas:

1. *Research comes in a variety of forms.* Beginning action researchers sometimes make the mistake of thinking that it is not research unless something is proved, tested, or compared. However, many good action research projects are designed simply to understand what is going on. Five examples of these kinds of action research projects follow:

- Mr. Tice was interested in the kinds of social or interpersonal problems his seventh grade students encountered and what strategies they used to solve them. To collect data he gave students a simple open-ended survey and did a series of small-group interviews or focus sessions. He combined the data he found with a short literature review. His research helped him understand his students and the unique social problems and pressures they face. It also became the basis of a unit he designed on social skills and interpersonal prob-lem solving.

TABLE 2.1　Overview of Ontological Perspectives

	MATERIALISTIC MONISM	DUALISM	TRANSCENDENTAL MONISM
1. Worldview	Universe consists of only matter and energy	Universe consists of matter and energy, and mind-consciousness-spirit	The primary stuff of the universe is mind-consciousness-spirit
2. Consciousness	Consciousness arises from matter	Exists separate from matter	Matter arises from consciousness
3. Reality	Objective universe separate from the observer	A personal construction based on the objective and subjective reality	A dream that exists in metaphysical dimensions
4. Knowledge	*Positivist:* exists outside the self	*Constructivist:* constructed by individuals as they interact with the environment	*Holistic:* exists within each individual and has the ability to transform
5. Truth	Objective examination of knowledge	Requires a value judgment and is different for each individual	Requires reflection and examination, an inward journey
6. Learning	Demonstrated outwardly for it to exist	Inner state, constructing cognitive webs	Free one's self from illusion, expand consciousness, transcendence
7. Intelligence	Ability to use linear thinking and deductive reasoning	Ability to solve problems, create products, and shape environment	Ability to perceive wholes and nurture self, others, and environment
8. Educational model	Factory model, cafeteria model	Dewey, social constructivist	Waldorf, Montessori, holistic education
9. Primary psychological perspective	Behaviorism	Cognitive psychology	Transpersonal psychology
10. Primary research perspective	Quantitative methodology	Qualitative methodology	Transpersonal methodology

- Ms. Robinson, a fourth grade teacher, wanted to observe her own math instruction to find areas to improve. She collected data by (1) audiotaping and analyzing lessons over a 3-week period, (2) writing her reflective analysis on the back of each of her math lesson plans, and (3) creating and administrating a simple, open-ended survey that asked students what helped them understand and what made it harder to understand in math class.

- Mr. Moore, a high school principal, was interested in studying the personal and professional journeys of the teachers in his district. He wanted to understand such things as what teaching meant to them, how they perceived their profession, how they came to education, and how they have changed as both teachers and people. Over the course of 2 months, he collected a variety of data. First he asked several teachers to write personal narratives describing their journey as a teacher. He had others create a past, present, and future timeline showing important events in their teaching journeys. In small focus groups teachers looked for personal metaphors to describe both teaching and their growth as teachers. And over a two week period, he also asked a group of teachers to record any movies, song lyrics, TV shows, or commercials that seemed related to their experiences as teachers on a website that he had created for this purpose. Finally, he asked teachers to create visual art to represent their teaching experience. He collected all these data, looked for themes and patterns to arise, and created a video along with an accompanying report to present his findings.

- Ms. Chavous, a second grade teacher, wanted to get a sense of the types of reading instruction that took place in the primary grades in her district. She sent out open-ended surveys asking teachers how they go about reading instruction. She also prepared a menu of research-based practices that she gave to teachers each week over the course of a month. She asked teachers to put tally marks beside the strategies every time they used them. Finally, she asked teachers to audiotape two reading classes. These data provided her with a sense of what, how, and how much reading instruction was taking place.

- Mr. Kleinsasser, a fifth grade teacher, taught in a school that used cluster grouping to meet the needs of students who had been identified as highly creative or intellectually gifted. Cluster grouping places three to eight identified students in one classroom with a teacher who has been taught specific curriculum differentiation strategies. He wanted to get a sense of what was happening with his differentiation strategies. Over the course of 3 weeks he collected data three ways. First, he listed the differentiation strategies used in his weekly planner. At the end of the day he would describe how he used each strategy and what things seemed to work and what things he would like to change. Second, using the Internet he conducted a short literature review focusing on strategies for gifted learners in a general education classroom. He synthesized the major recommendations and compared them to what he was doing. Finally, he conducted a short written survey, asking his gifted students how they best liked to learn and what things they would like to learn about. These data helped him refine his teaching practice.

2. *The type of research used should match the question asked.* One form of research is not inherently better than another. That is, quantitative research is not better than qualitative or even transpersonal research methodologies. However, certain questions are best answered with certain methodologies. In conducting action research projects, everything always starts with the question. Always find and define the

question first, then consider the methodology that might best answer the question. The question should determine the methodology. The methodology should never determine the question.

3. *We need to recognize our own biases and preconceived ideas.* As I have already alluded to, one of the current problems in education is that there is an overreliance on materialistic monism and an overuse of quantitative research methodologies to define academic achievement and describe the quality of our learning experiences. We must recognize how our culture's predominant (some would say parochial) ontological perspectives serve to shape the questions that get asked relative to education and educational practices. Recognizing this, the field of education needs to move toward a more expansive research agenda in terms of questions, methodology, and subject matter.

4. *We should reexamine and redefine the purpose of our schools.* We do not ask the "why" questions often enough. Our educational philosophies and assumptions about the nature of reality and the purpose of education become the basis for our educational practice. I posit, as does Maslow (1971), that the fundamental purpose of education is self-actualization, which is to be fully human and to realize one's full potential. In this sense, our schools should be designed to help students identify and develop their abilities and discover their passions and interests. However, we cannot become fully human if we do not first recognize what makes us so: our emotions, imagination, intuition, ideals, values, and creativity, none of which conveniently lend themselves to measurement.

The function of education is to create human beings who are integrated and therefore intelligent. . . . Intelligence is the capacity to perceive the essential, the what is; and to awaken this capacity, in oneself and in others, is education (Indian philosopher Jiddu Krishnamurti, 1953, p. 14).

SUMMARY

- The three primary ontological perspectives are materialistic monism, dualism, and transcendental monism.
- Our ontological perspectives influence educational research, which in turn affect our teaching practices.
- Materialistic monism suggests a universe that consists of only matter and energy. Knowledge exists outside the individual. Quantitative research methods align most closely with this perspective.
- Dualism suggests a universe that consists of matter and energy, and also mind, consciousness, and spirit. Knowledge is constructed by individuals as they interact with knowledge found in the environment. Qualitative research methods align most closely with this perspective.
- Transcendental monism suggests a universe that consists primarily of consciousness. True knowledge exists within each individual. Transpersonal research methods align most closely with this perspective.
- Research comes in a variety of forms.

QUESTIONS AND ACTIVITIES

1. Which ontological perspectives do you align with most closely? Within that perspective, which things do you disagree with?
2. How does your teaching philosophy align with your ontological perspectives?
3. What do you perceive to be the purpose of our schools?
4. What are some important things relative to school, teaching, and learning that cannot be measured and quantified? How else might these be expressed or represented?
5. If grades or standardized tests could not be used, how else might you describe a student's learning or growth?
6. What metaphors describe you as a person and you as a teacher?
7. Find an interesting place. Use as many numbers as you can to describe that place quantitatively. Then, use words to describe that place qualitatively. Finally, use pictures, metaphors, poetry, or symbols to describe that place. What does the difference in your three descriptions tell you?

POSSIBLE RESEARCH QUESTIONS FOR ACTION RESEARCH PROJECTS

1. What do teachers and parents see as the purpose of schools in our society? That is, why do we educate students? To what end? How does this compare with different philosophical orientations toward education such as those of Plato, John Dewey, Paulo Freire, Rudolph Steiner, Maria Montessori, or Neil Postman?
2. Consider adopting and adapting one of the five examples of action research projects on pages 22–24.
3. To which ontological perspective do the teachers in your school or district ascribe? How are their teaching practices reflective of their perspective?
4. What do teachers consider to be their strengths or special talents as teachers and as human beings?
5. What do students consider to be their strengths or special talents?
6. What do students consider to be their passion? What are they very much interested in? What would they like to know more about?
7. What do teachers consider to be their passion? What are they very much interested in? What would they like to know more about? What would they like to be able to incorporate into their learning curriculum?
8. What does your intuitive self have to say to you about teaching and life? Sit in silence for 10 to 15 minutes a day over a period of 2 weeks. Use a timer to keep track of the time. Take deep breaths, concentrating only on breathing in and breathing out. You may even say, "breathe in . . . breathe out . . ." as a form of chant. The goal is to move around your logical mind. After the silent period immediately write down the thoughts and images without regard to content. That is, do not try to make sense of them, simply associate in a

stream of consciousness mode. Put these in a folder and do not look at them for 2 weeks. After 2 weeks, look for patterns and trends and then metaphors or deeper meaning within the patterns and trends.

9. What do your students value? What physical things do students value or see as important? What traits or personal characteristics do students value? What experiences do students value?

10. What do your colleagues value? What physical things do your colleagues value or see as important? What traits or personal characteristics do your colleagues value? What experiences do your colleagues value?

11. Who are your students' heroes? What traits do these heroes have in common?

12. Who are your colleagues' heroes? What traits do these heroes have in common?

13. Whom do your students identify as villains or adversaries? What traits do these villains have in common?

14. Whom do your colleagues identify as villains or adversaries? What traits do these villains have in common?

15. What do students consider to be the important events in their lives? What does this tell you about your students?

16. What do your colleagues consider to be the important events in their lives? What does this tell you about your colleagues?

17. What dreams do your students have? Where do they see themselves at age 25, 35, and 45?

CHAPTER THREE

INTRODUCTION TO ACTION RESEARCH

Chapter 1 described research and the two major research categories. This chapter defines and describes action research and its various parts and examines the importance of action research in education.

RESEARCH IN ACTION

Action research can be defined as the process of studying a real school or classroom situation to understand and improve the quality of actions or instruction (Hensen, 1996; McTaggart, 1997; Schmuck, 1997). It is a systematic and orderly way for teachers to observe their practice or to explore a problem and a possible course of action (Dinkelman, 1997; McNiff, Lomax, & Whitehead, 1996). Action research is also a type of inquiry that is preplanned, organized, and can be shared with others (Foshy, 1998; Tomlinson, 1995).

A Quick Overview of Action Research

The action research process involves five essential steps or parts. First, ask a question, identify a problem, or define an area of exploration. Determine what it is you want to study. Second, decide what data should be collected, how they should be collected, and how often. Third, collect and analyze data. Fourth, describe how your findings can be used and applied. You create your plan for action based on your findings. And finally, report or share your findings and plan for action with others.

Action research is a recursive process that does not always proceed in a linear fashion (Patterson & Shannon, 1993). You may find yourself repeating some of these steps several times or doing them in a different order (see Figure 3.1). Also, some action research projects incorporate a sixth step, which is to put the findings or the question in a theoretical context called the literature review. This and the other steps are described in detail in the chapters that follow.

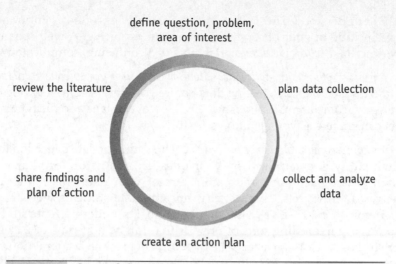

define question, problem,
area of interest

review the literature

plan data collection

share findings and
plan of action

collect and analyze
data

create an action plan

FIGURE 3.1   Steps of the Action Research Process

Descriptors of Action Research

The following ten descriptors may help bring this type of research into clearer focus.

  1. *Action research is systematic.* Although data can be collected, analyzed, and presented with a certain amount of freedom, you must create a systematic way of looking. Action research is not an "anything goes" type of methodology. Nor is it simply a matter of describing what you think about an issue, depicting an interesting project or unit you have created, or explaining a pedagogical method that works well in your classroom. Action research is a planned, methodical observation related to one's teaching.

  2. *You do not start with an answer.* An assumption underlying any research is that you do not know what you are going to find when you start; you are an unbiased observer. After all, if you had the answer, why would you be doing the research? Thus, even though you think Method X is the best way to teach reading, it is not appropriate to do a study describing why Method X is good and why Method Y is bad. Instead, you become an impartial observer (to the greatest degree possible) and study the effects of Method X as it is used in your classroom. The goal is to understand fully Method X and its effect (both positive and negative) on students' reading performance.

  3. *An action research study does not have to be complicated or elaborate to be rigorous or effective.* Many beginning action researchers make the mistake of creating overly thick descriptions of every detail of their study in an attempt to be rigorous. This may often defeat the purpose. If too much material or too many details are included, you may miss what you are looking for, and the report will probably not be read or understood. Thus, what you do not include is often as important as what you do include in your observing and in your reporting. A well-organized, concisely described study is always preferable to a confusing, complicated study.

4. *You must plan your study adequately before you begin to collect data.* Having a plan and a schedule for collecting data before you start is what separates a systematic inquiry from an impressionistic view. However, plans and the type of data you collect can change as you get into your study.

5. *Action research projects vary in length.* The length of data collection in an action research study is determined by your question, the nature of your inquiry, the research environment, and the parameters of your data collection. For smaller action research projects I suggest that my graduate students who are classroom teachers consider 2 weeks as a minimum length. For undergraduate students, there are some very interesting sorts of projects that can be done in 1 or 2 class periods. Major studies, such as a master's thesis or an article for an academic journal, generally have a duration of 2 months to a whole school year. Keep in mind that if your data collection period is too short, you run the risk of presenting an unrealistic view of that educational setting.

6. *Observations should be regular, but they do not necessarily have to be long.* The duration of observations might be anywhere from 1 minute to 1 hour or more. Many of your observations might be a quick note with the date and time recorded, whereas others might be longer and more formal. Although they do not have to be long, observations do have to be made on a consistent, preplanned schedule. Also, observations are only one form of data collection. Other data collection forms and methods are described in Chapter 8.

7. *Action research projects exist on a continuum from simple and informal to detailed and formal.* As stated, some interesting projects are short and simple. I suggest that beginning action researchers practice with these kinds of projects before tackling larger, more complicated ones. Action research can also be used for formal studies. Many of my graduate students who are teachers have done action research projects for their master's theses. A sample guideline for this purpose is described in Chapter 15. Because these projects directly related to what was happening in their classrooms, these teachers were able to link theory to practice in a meaningful way. Graduate students have been far more enthusiastic about investing themselves in these kinds of projects than in the kinds of secondary research often done as part of a master's thesis. And not surprisingly, action research projects always seem to be more interesting and enjoyable to read.

8. *Action research is sometimes grounded in theory.* Relating the questions, results, and conclusions to existing theory provides a context in which to understand your research. Let the reader know how your data relate to what others have said about the same topic. Some action researchers do a short review of the literature before they begin collecting data, to provide a framework for the data collection. Others wait until the data are collected and then compare their conclusions to what others have written. Opinions as to the place and extent of a literature review in action research vary. This topic is discussed further in Chapter 7.

9. *Action research is not a quantitative study.* In talking with beginning action researchers, this point seems to be the most common area of confusion. Thus, although I addressed this in the previous chapter I want to mention it one more time here. Many beginning action researchers have to divest themselves of their previous notions of the nature of research. In an action research project you are not trying to prove anything. You are not comparing one thing to another to determine the best possible thing. Also, there are no experimental or control groups, independent or dependent variables, or hypotheses to be supported. The goal is simply to understand. As an action researcher you are creating a series of snapshots in various forms and in various places to help us understand exactly what is going on.

To illustrate this concept of understanding, consider the following example. One night in a graduate class I asked a group of teachers to describe an event that happened that day. Alison Reynolds wrote of her interaction with a particular student that morning. Although she had described her teaching situation in early classes, it was not until I saw her snapshot of this student and the nature of their interactions that I began to understand some of the dynamics of her teaching situation. Her descriptions went far beyond the numbers and test scores in helping to comprehend the nature of teaching in an alternative high school and provided insight as to what an action research project might be. If she were to continue with this and make it an action project, she would create a plan for describing a number of students and situations in her school.

10. *The results of quantitative action research projects are limited.* Although quantitative methods are sometimes used in action research, caution must be exercised in coming to generalized conclusions or in applying the results to larger populations. Such caution is necessary because of the small sample size of most action research projects and the many variables that are uncontrolled or unaccounted for.

For example, Mr. Miller did an action research project using quantitative methods to compare two approaches to reading instruction in his second grade classroom. His statistical analysis found that the group using Method A scored significantly better than the group using Method B; however, Mr. Miller cannot reasonably conclude that Method A is the superior approach. The only conclusion he can reasonably make in this case is that Method A appears to be more effective than Method B. We do not know if the two groups were equal to begin with, and we do not know if the samples were representative. The action research was conducted in an uncontrolled environment, and there was nothing to address the bias and subjectivity of the researcher. In order to make a stronger conclusion, each of these issues would need to be addressed.

In another example, Ms. Reuter wanted to see whether her new approach to spelling instruction was effective. Using quantitative methods, she found that when using her new approach, students showed a statistically significant gain in their ability to spell words over the period of 3 months. However, like Mr. Miller she has to be careful in the kinds of conclusions she can reasonably make. In this case, we do not know how much of this gain was a result of general learning and maturity. That is, students naturally become better spellers as they write and are exposed to more print. Also, she cannot reasonably compare her class to another class because of the differences in teaching styles and approaches as well as many other unaccounted variables. At best, she might be able to say that her new approach appears to be effective in helping students learn new words.

THE IMPORTANCE OF ACTION RESEARCH

This section describes how action research can be used to fill the gap between theory and practice in education, empower teachers to become agents of change, and enhance the professional growth and development of teachers.

The Gap between Theory and Practice

Among other things, research is used to build theories that in turn help determine the best practices in education. These practices are then used to help teachers create effective learning experiences. However, sometimes a gap exists between researchers conducting and reporting their education research and teachers practicing in the field (Hensen, 1996; Patterson & Shannon, 1993; Tomlinson, 1995). That is, what goes on in public schools often does not reflect the wealth of research related to best practice in teaching and learning.

There are two possible reasons for this gap. First, it may be because research in education is sometimes written in a way that does not respect the demands of teachers' daily schedules, in which time is a precious commodity. Research articles in academic journals can sometimes get overly descriptive, use jargon familiar to few readers, and focus on methodology and hypothetical notions that are not germane to the daily needs of teachers. This leads to the belief held by many teachers

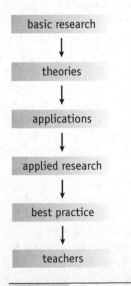

FIGURE 3.2   The Moses Effect

that education research is practically irrelevant (Barone, Berliner, Blanchard, Casanova, & McGown, 1996; Patterson & Shannon, 1993).

Second, the gap between research and practice might also be a result of the Moses Effect. The Moses Effect occurs when researchers hand down research edicts from on high with the expectation that teachers will be passive receivers of these edicts (see Figure 3.2). This creates a one-way flow of information that often does not value teachers' points of view, fails to reflect the complexities of teaching, or does not address the concrete problems and concerns that teachers face in their classrooms on a daily basis (Patterson & Shannon, 1993).

Action research is one solution to use in bridging this gap (Hensen, 1996; Knight, Wiseman, & Cooner, 2000). The Action Research Quadrant (Figure 3.3) illustrates the two-way flow of information in action research. Theories and research related to best practice are used to understand and observe what is happening in a classroom setting. At the same time, this data is used to understand or inform theories and research related to best practice.

Teacher Empowerment

Action research also facilitates teacher empowerment. Teachers are empowered when they are able to collect their own data to use in making decisions about their schools and classrooms (Book, 1996; Erickson, 1986; Hensen, 1996). Empowered teachers are able to bring their talents, experiences, and creative ideas into the classroom. They can implement programs and strategies that best meet the needs of their students. Empowered teachers also are able to use the methodologies that complement their own particular philosophy and teaching style. When teachers are allowed to take risks and make changes related to teaching and learning, student achievement is enhanced (Marks & Louis, 1997; Sweetland & Hoy, 2002) and schools become more effective learning communities (Detert, Louis, & Schroeder, 2001). The top-down approaches that are sometimes used to manage schools and solve classroom problems create an external locus of control that inhibits teacher empowerment and thereby lessens the effectiveness of schools (Book, 1996).

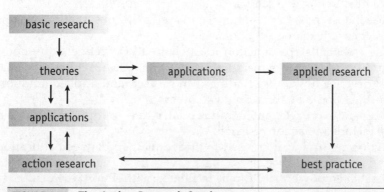

FIGURE 3.3 The Action Research Quadrant

Teacher Inservice and Professional Growth

Action research can also be used to replace teacher inservices as a means of professional growth and development. Traditional teacher inservices are often ineffective (Barone et al., 1996). Teachers are gathered, usually after a long day of teaching or on a busy workshop day, to listen to an expert describe an approach or methodology that often does not relate to their classroom situation or align with their teaching style. These traditional inservices generally do not give teachers sufficient time, activities, or content to increase their knowledge or affect their practice (Birman, Desimone, Porter, & Garet, 2000). To be effective, inservices need to be longer or extended over multiple sessions, contain active learning to allow teachers to manipulate the ideas and enhance their assimilation of the information, and align the concepts presented with the current curriculum, goals, or teaching concerns.

In regard to teachers' professional growth and development, Hensen (1996) describes the following benefits of action research: It (1) helps teachers develop new knowledge directly related to their classrooms, (2) promotes reflective teaching and thinking, (3) expands teachers' pedagogical repertoire, (4) puts teachers in charge of their craft, (5) reinforces the link between practice and student achievement, (6) fosters an openness toward new ideas and learning new things, and (7) gives teachers ownership of effective practices. Thus, providing teachers time and incentive to engage in action research projects and giving them a platform to present their findings and engage in professional dialogue with peers enhances their professional growth and development, which in turn moves the field of education forward. Using action research as a form of teacher development also increases the sense of professionalism in education (Tomlinson, 1995), and it enables teachers to become agents of change (Hensen, 1996). Using action research for professional development is described further in Chapter 5.

SUMMARY

- Action research is the process of studying a real school problem or situation.
- The goal of action research is to improve one's teaching practice or to enhance the functioning of a school.
- Action research is a preplanned and systematic observation of one's teaching practice or teaching situation.
- The essential steps of action research are to (1) define a question or area of study, (2) decide on a method for collecting data, (3) collect and analyze data, (4) describe how those findings can be used and applied, and (5) share the findings and plan for action with others.
- A review of the relevant literature related to your topic or question might also be included in action research.
- Action research can be used to bridge the gap between education research and teaching practice.
- Teacher empowerment can be facilitated with action research.

■ Action research can be used as a replacement for traditional inservices to enhance teachers' professional growth and development.

QUESTIONS AND ACTIVITIES

1. List or describe three to five things that interest you in your classroom or school.
2. What are some problems in your classroom or school that you would like to solve?
3. What are some aspects of your teaching that you would like to improve?
4. Describe some theory or bit of research that seems to have no direct link to your teaching situation.
5. Describe some theory or bit of research that seems to have a direct link to your teaching situation.
6. Describe a situation in which someone else has made a decision regarding your classroom practice. Would you have made the same decision?
7. Describe an instance when you would have made a different decision than what was made regarding your school or classroom. What reasons or evidence do you have to support your idea?
8. Think about the teacher inservices you have attended. What characteristics were effective? What characteristics were less effective?
9. What topic or topics would be of interest to you in a teacher inservice? Where might you go to get information on this topic?
10. Design a method that you think would be effective as a means for teacher growth and development.

POSSIBLE RESEARCH QUESTIONS FOR ACTION RESEARCH PROJECTS

1. What do teachers see as the use or uses of educational research?
2. What major decisions have been made by a school or a district in the last two years? What educational research or theoretical context was used to support these decisions?
3. What subjects or topics would teachers like to see addressed in a teacher workshop or inservice?
4. What do teachers think is the best method for introducing and implementing new teaching strategies?
5. What sorts of professional development activities are used by teachers in a particular school or district? How often and to what extent have they been used?
6. What sorts of professional development activities are used by principals and administrators in a particular school or district? How often and to what extent have they been used?

7. What does the research literature say is the difference between reading readiness and emergent literacy? Which is more effective? What approach is used in the kindergarten and first grade classrooms in a particular school or district?

8. What does the research literature say about the best ways to meet the special needs of gifted learners in a general education classroom? How does this compare with what is currently being done in a particular school or district?

9. What does the research literature say about the best ways to meet the special needs of students with learning disabilities in a general education classroom? How does this compare with what is currently being done in a particular school or district?

10. What does the research literature say about the best ways to meet the special needs of students with emotional or behavioral disorders in a general education classroom? How does this compare with what is currently being done in a particular school or district?

11. What does the research literature say about the best ways to meet the special needs of students who are learning English as a second language in a general education classroom? How does this compare with what is currently being done in a particular school or district?

12. What does the research literature say about the best ways to develop students ability to comprehend expository text? How does this compare with what is currently being done in a particular grade level, school, or district?

13. What types of decisions would the teachers in a particular school or district like to make? What types of decisions are being made by somebody other than teachers?

14. What changes would teachers like to make in a school or district in order to enhance learning?

15. What changes would students like to make in a school or classroom in order to enhance learning?

CHAPTER FOUR

USING ACTION RESEARCH FOR SOLVING PROBLEMS

Teachers are constantly challenged with a variety of problems for which they are required to develop solutions. Teachers who engage in action research projects become more flexible in their thinking, more receptive to new ideas, and thus better able to solve problems as they arise (Dinkelman, 1997). Problem solving consists of three elements: finding the problem, finding a solution, and testing the solution. This chapter examines the use of action research in problem solving.

FINDING THE PROBLEM

Problems cannot be solved unless they are first identified and defined. Identifying the problem occurs when the situation is observed and there is a recognition that things could be done better. Defining the problem involves seeking to understand the nature of the situation and discovering the possible causal factors. You look to see why things are as they are. For example, why are students not learning? Why are behavior problems occurring on the playground? Why does Suzanne have problems getting her work in on time? Why has Steven been acting the way he has? As stated in previous chapters, action research can be used to help see what is happening in a school or classroom or to identify and define problems.

The graphic organizer in Figure 4.1 can be used to help you define a problem. A problem is a difference in the present state and the desired state. To define a problem, start by describing the present state and desired state. Then list any and all objective facts in the first column. Next, list the possible consequences of the present state in the middle column. That is, what could happen or what is happening in regard to the present state? In the last column include any other information or facts you feel are important or relevant. State the problem as simply and succinctly as possible. Finally, restate the problem using different words.

Present state:

Desired state:

Objective Facts	Consequences	Relevant or Related Facts

The problem:

Restate the problem:

FIGURE 4.1   **Problem Definer**

FINDING SOLUTIONS

A variety of strategies can be used to find a solution. Two are described next: creative problem solving and means–end analysis.

Creative Problem Solving

Creative problem solving (CPS) begins by defining the problem and generating ideas for solutions. The key to successful implementation of this strategy is to produce as many ideas as you can. No evaluation of these initial ideas should be made because doing so would prevent the full range of possibilities from being explored. Sometimes when a new idea is put forth at a meeting or in a committee, individuals immediately respond by telling why that idea will not work. This only serves to preserve the status quo and prevent new and creative solutions from being considered. It is most effective to get all the ideas generated and listed, then to engage in an evaluative discussion to choose the one that seems best. Often two or three ideas can be combined for a solution. This would not be possible had you not first generated a number of ideas. The final steps are to refine, implement, and review and evaluate the solution. The CPS steps are listed in Figure 4.2.

Means–End Analysis

Means–end analysis (MEA) begins with a description of the desired outcome or end state. Where would you like to be? What outcome would you like to bring

1. Define the problem.
2. Generate as many solutions as possible.
3. Choose a solution that seems the best.
4. Elaborate and refine.
5. Implement the solution.
6. Review, evaluate, and refine as necessary.

FIGURE 4.2   Thinking Frame for CPS

about? The next step is to define the goals necessary to bring about this end state. Goals are the global objectives, traits, skills, behaviors, or specific conditions that make up your desired outcome. Goals are important in the eventual evaluation of your solution. That is, you can tell whether your solution is successful by ascertaining whether the goals are realized. Once the goals are described, the next step is to assess and describe the current situation. This is followed by an analysis of the means necessary to reach the end state. Finally, a plan is constructed to get from point A (current state) to point B (end state). As with CPS, solutions need to be reviewed, evaluated, and refined after implementation. You may recognize that this problem-solving strategy is similar to the process used in designing new curricula. The MEA steps are listed in Figure 4.3.

Problem-Solving Strategies in the Classroom

We cannot assume that students know how to solve problems effectively unless they first have been taught how to do so. The two problem-solving strategies just described can be taught to students in the form of thinking skills. This will improve their ability to solve problems and also enhance learning (Johnson, 2000). I recommend starting with CPS because this is usually easier for most students. You may want to simplify some of the steps for younger students.

You can teach problem-solving strategies in six steps. First, use the thinking frames in Figures 4.2 and 4.3 to create a poster to display in the classroom as a teaching aid. A thinking frame is a concrete representation of a particular cognitive process broken down into specific steps and used to support the thought process (Johnson, 2000; Perkins, 1987). Second, identify the problem-solving strategy and describe each step. Third, model the problem-solving strategy by thinking out loud

1. Describe the desired outcome.
2. Define the goals necessary to reach the end state.
3. Describe the current state.
4. Analyze the means necessary to get the desired outcome.
5. Construct and implement a plan.
6. Review, evaluate, and refine the plan.

FIGURE 4.3   Thinking Frame for MEA

as you go through the steps to solve a problem. Fourth, use guided practice to solve a problem together. Fifth, create problems for students to solve by themselves or in small groups. And finally, embed problems into all aspects of the curriculum. For example, in reading or literature use problems found in stories for students to solve. These can be interpersonal problems, problems that need the invention of a new product or process, or organizational problems. For social studies, science, and math, use problems that are found in history, society, or real life.

TESTING THE SOLUTION

The final part of problem solving is to implement the solution and test it to see whether it works. Every new plan, program, or solution needs some adjusting during the implementation stage. Action research can be used as formative and summative evaluation. The next section is a description of how I used action research along with the three elements of problem solving to improve my teaching practice.

AN EXAMPLE OF ACTION RESEARCH AND PROBLEM SOLVING

I used to be the gifted education specialist for an elementary school in rural Wisconsin. In my first year in this position I conducted pullout sessions in which I met with small groups of students once a week. (This was several years ago. I would not recommend this as the most effective strategy today.) My students used to love the chance to learn more complex subjects, engage in high-level thinking, and have discussions and debates with like-minded peers. During my third year in the district, my job expanded and I took over the gifted education duties in the middle and high schools. I was excited to resume weekly pullout sessions with a group of middle school students with whom I had not worked since my first year. However, at our first pullout session I found that my formerly eager and excited students were sullen and distant. They sat at the back of the room and rarely spoke or contributed, and when they did, it was with little enthusiasm.

Finding the Problem

A bit of problem finding and defining was needed. Had I tried to address this problem without first trying to understand the situation, I would have missed the whole point and probably made the situation worse. Instead, I gathered data by creating a systematic plan whereby I talked with students individually, talked with their teachers, and observed these students in a variety of classroom situations. I also went back and reread my textbooks on human development. What I discovered was that these young adolescents were reacting negatively to being singled out from their peers. They did not want to be apart from the group or be thought of as somehow different, which was a normal reaction for students at this developmental stage.

Finding a Solution

Having identified and defined the problem, the next step was to find a solution. I used MEA. The desired outcome was to create meaningful and enriching learning experiences whereby these students could reach their full potential. The goals were to engage these students in enriched content, teach high-level skills, and give them choices so that they could pursue topics of interest to them. The current state comprised three elements: (1) these students were engaged in a classroom curriculum that was far below their capabilities, (2) my pullout sessions were unrelated to their regular curriculum, and (3) a certain amount of social stress was being caused by separating these students from their peers.

It was clear that I had to create a structure that allowed these students to solve problems and create plans or products within their regular classroom experience. The gifted education literature describes a strategy called compacting and differentiation, in which students are able to test out of a unit to free up time to do other projects (Renzulli & Reis, 1997). The advantage of this approach is that it can be made available to all students and thus bypass the need for the formal identification of gifted students. It also reflects Howard Gardner's definition of intelligence, which is the ability to solve problems or create products that are valued in one or more cultural settings (1983).

To implement this plan, I worked with classroom teachers to design a structure that allowed students who had met a criterion pretest score to engage in inquiry projects, individually or in small groups, that were related to the curriculum. Contracts were used to define specific goals, steps, and timelines to be met (see Figure 4.4). Instead of conducting weekly pullout sessions, I was in charge of a resource center where students would come to work on their independent projects. Among other things, I worked with students to teach them the skills necessary to complete their projects.

In looking at Figure 4.4, note that the inquiry projects contain the same elements as a teacher action research project. The research process I am describing in this book can be used and adapted to design inquiry activities for students at all grade levels.

Testing the Solution

Once this structure was in place (it took about 2 months to get it up and running), I designed a systematic plan for collecting data to evaluate the effectiveness of this program. I used student and teacher surveys, recorded field notes related to my work in the resource center, and analyzed students' projects. Essentially, I was using action research as a form of program evaluation. This collection and analysis of data helped me to revise and refine this program. Some of my findings included the following:

1. I worked with more students than just those who were formally identified.
2. Many students who were not formally identified as gifted created projects that were just as outstanding as those who were formally identified.
3. Students enjoyed having choice as well as challenge.
4. Teachers enjoyed having a gifted education strategy that augmented the regular curriculum.

Plan to Investigate

Investigator: _____

BEFORE THE INVESTIGATION

1. What is your question? What are you curious about? What do you want to investigate?

2. Important background knowledge? Use at least two sources to get information about your question. You may want to interview experts, read books or magazines, or use the Internet.

3. How will you collect data?

read ___	observe ___	checklist ___
weigh ___	measure ___	survey ___
interview ___	time ___	create and test ___
listen ___	count ___	other ___

4. When will you present your findings to the class?

AFTER THE INVESTIGATION

5. Organize your data. Look for groups or patterns, put data in order, or use tables or graphs.

6. What conclusions can you make or what interesting ideas do you have based on your data?

7. How will you present your data and conclusions or ideas?

lab report ___	video ___	poster ___
photos ___	plan ___	visual art ___
graph ___	story ___	demonstration ___
brochure ___	speech ___	other ___

FIGURE 4.4   Contracts for Inquiry Projects

SUMMARY

- Solving problems is an inherent part of teaching.
- Problem solving consists of three parts: finding the problem, finding a solution, and testing the solution.
- Creative problem solving and means–end analysis are two strategies that can be used to solve problems.
- Problem-solving strategies can be taught to students to improve their ability to solve problems.

- Problem solving can be embedded within a curriculum to enhance learning and reinforce problem-solving strategies.
- Action research can be used to identify and define problems and to evaluate solutions.

QUESTIONS AND ACTIVITIES

1. Find a picture book or a chapter in a trade book that you might use with students. Generate a list of problems associated with each.
2. List 5 to 10 real-life problems related to science or society. Describe where and how these might be integrated into a curriculum.
3. Find a problem related to your daily life in some way. This could be an interpersonal problem or a problem related to school, work, or some product or process. Use CPS to generate ideas and find a solution.
4. Find a problem specifically related to education. Use MEA to design a plan.
5. Find a problem in your classroom or personal life situation and then define it. Why is it occurring?
6. Find a solution to a problem occurring in your classroom or personal life. How might you evaluate that solution?

POSSIBLE RESEARCH QUESTIONS FOR ACTION RESEARCH PROJECTS

1. What do teachers see as the major problems in their classrooms, school, or district?
2. What do students see as the major problems in their classrooms or school?
3. What do principals and administrators see as the major problems in their school or district?
4. What do parents see as the major problems in their school or district?
5. What interpersonal or social problems do students at a particular age or grade level encounter?
6. What kinds of ideas do students have for a specific interpersonal or social problem?
7. Identify a problem in your classroom or an area of teaching that you would like to improve. Use one of the problem solving strategies to address this problem. As your action research, do a summative evaluation.
8. What makes students at a particular age or grade level happy?
9. What types of questions are most often asked by you during a classroom discussion?
10. What topics or kinds of things would students at a particular age or grade level like to learn about? What would the experience be like if you could incorporate this into a curriculum?

CHAPTER FIVE

STRATEGIES FOR PROFESSIONAL GROWTH AND DEVELOPMENT

ACTION RESEARCH AND THE PROFESSIONAL DEVELOPMENT OF TEACHERS

It is not possible, in 2 years of preservice teacher education, to create a finished teaching product. (My undergraduate students are always surprised when I tell them this.) To think otherwise demonstrates a lack of understanding related to the complexities and multiple dimensions of teaching. Master teachers spend years learning, developing, and refining their teaching craft. At best, teacher preparatory institutions can get preservice teachers ready to begin their teaching journey by helping them (1) construct a body of knowledge related to teaching and learning, (2) identify a philosophy and cultivating certain dispositions, and (3) acquire a few pedagogical skills. These are all necessary and important things to get one started in education, but they in no way indicate that a new teacher has reached his or her full potential as a teacher.

Once in the field, professional development is up to each teacher and to the school districts that employ him or her. But is professional development really necessary? Must we always be changing? Yes and yes. As our society and our students change, so too must our educational institutions change to address their varying needs. And as new educational research gives us more insight into teaching and learning, our teaching practices need to continue to evolve to reflect these new findings. Change is the only constant in the universe. To stay the same in the midst of change is to devolve (which is a form of change).

There are a variety of other ways to develop professionally. Following are strategies for professional development. Of course, action research can be a powerful tool to help with each of these.

More Knowledge Please

One of the major differences between experts and novices in any field is their amount of knowledge (Sternberg & Williams, 2002). Experts have more of it; novices have less of it. Thus, one effective form of professional development is to expand one's knowledge base related to teaching and learning or to a particular subject area. This can be done most simply by developing a plan for reading books and educational journals. If you have not taken an educational psychology course in a while, I would recommend starting with a basic text in this area. This will reacquaint you with some of the basic theories. You will most likely find that having been in a classroom for a couple of years, the information found here now seems much more relevant and interesting than when you first encounter these ideas as an undergraduate preservice teacher. After that, the following steps can be used to guide you.

Step 1: Identify a Topic of Interest or Importance.   What is it that you want to know more about? Is there some area of your teaching in which you want to develop expertise? If you are unsure of where to start, it may be helpful to quickly list things that are of interest to you. The process of writing quickly (without thinking or analyzing) allows your unconscious mind to kick in a few ideas. Also, conversation with other teachers is another way to generate possible professional development ideas. Looking to your own professional practice to identify topics creates a much more powerful professional development experience than having somebody else decide what you should learn (like in the typical after-school workshop or teacher inservice).

Example.   Ms. Vinatieri was interested in helping her second grade students enhance their reading fluency. The school district in which she was working had recently bought an expensive new commercial reading program that had tutors working individually with low-ability readers, drilling them in letter sounds and word lists that were read outside of any meaningful context. Although the commercial program cited research that claimed success, this approach did not seem efficient or effective to Ms. Vinatieri. Further, the meaningless drill and practice was dreary and seemed to reinforce the negative attitudes her low-ability readers already had toward reading. She wondered whether the curriculum director and the superintendent had done any research before investing so much time and money into this commercial program. Thus, her topic was reading fluency.

Step 2: Identify a Goal or Goals.   Why is this topic of interest to you? What is the end result? What do you hope to do with this knowledge? Do you want to develop content area knowledge? Are you looking for activities related to a subject or unit of study? Are you looking for new pedagogical strategies? Do you want to align your teaching with best practice? Do you want to make sure your teaching methods reflect the latest research and theories in the field? Identifying a possible goal will enable you to be more focused as you search.

Example.   Ms. Vinatieri had three goals: First, she wanted to see whether there was any objective research that supported the methods used in the new program. She was looking for research conducted by qualified researchers who were not affiliated with the company producing the commercial program and that was published in peer-reviewed journals. Second, she wanted to find a variety of practical, research-based strategies that could be used to help develop reading fluency. She was looking for methods that were effective and aligned with the way students naturally learn. Her third goal may seem a bit subversive, but she wanted to know if those responsible for making these decisions in her district were responsible decision makers. Did they spend a little time up front reviewing the research literature before reaching a conclusion that would affect so many? Did they take a broad, unbiased look? Or did they instead start with the answer and look only for bits of data that supported their preconceived ideas? In a sense, she wanted to hold those in administration accountable.

Step 3: Put Your Topic in the Form of a Question or Questions.   There is a tremendous amount of information published on most topics in education. Having a specific question in mind before reviewing the literature will help you focus only on that information that is of direct relevance to your goals.

Example.   Ms. Vinatieri's specific questions were, What research-based strategies or practices can be used to enhance students' reading fluency? How should these strategies be used?

Step 4: Find Peer-Reviewed Books and Academic Journal Articles.   Just because it is in a book does not mean it is a credible source. What books are credible? First, look to see who publishes it. You can generally put more trust in those that are published by major publishing companies in education such as Allyn and Bacon, Sage Publications, Merrill/Prentice Hall, Heinemann, McGraw-Hill, Association for Supervision and Curriculum Development, Houghton-Mifflin, and Harcourt Brace. These can be considered peer-reviewed publications. To publish with these companies, authors must write a prospectus in which they provide a research-based perspective and justification for their book. Authors must also include an outline describing the content and sample chapters. These prospecti are then sent out for a blind review by various experts in the field who either recommend them for publication or for rejection. Once accepted, publishing companies usually send out each chapter for further peer review. This process allows one to be fairly certain that the information found in these texts has some theoretical context or research-based support. A second way to check the credibility of books is to scan the chapters to see if the authors cite their sources. Avoid books that make broad undocumented claims without citing their sources such as, "Research reports that . . ." or "Scientists say that . . ." or "It has long been documented that . . ." or "It is well known that . . ." Also, if sources are cited, check the reference section at the end of the book to see if they are from peer-reviewed academic journals.

Also look for peer-reviewed academic journals. It is not likely that these would be available at most public libraries. If it is possible, find a college library or look for them on the Internet. Also, many public schools now have access to databases such as ERIC (Educational Resource Information Center) that contain peer-reviewed research and journal articles. You can go directly to the ERIC database at www.eric.ed.gov, although most peer-reviewed journal articles found there are not

Council for Exceptional Children provides access to two journals, *Exceptional Children* and *Teaching Exceptional Children:* http://journals.sped.org

The Allan Review (journal related to adolescent literacy): http://scholar.lib.vt.edu/ejournals/ALAN/alan-review.html

Early Childhood Research and Practice: www.ecrp.uiuc.edu

Electronic Journal of Science Education: www.unr.edu/homepage/jcannon/ejse/ejse.html

International Journal of Special Education: www.internationaljournalofspecialeducation.com

Issues in Educational Research: www.education.curtin.edu.au/iier/iier.html

The Journal of Educational Enquiry: www.literacy.unisa.edu.au/jee

The Reading Matrix: An International Online Journal: www.readingmatrix.com/journal.html

Academic Journal Exchange (many peer-reviewed academic journals can be found here): www.rapidintellect.com/AEQweb

---

FIGURE 5.1   Free Online Peer-Reviewed Journals

---

available without paying a subscription fee. There are, however, many websites that provide free access to peer-reviewed journals. Doing a quick Internet search brought me to the websites in Figure 5.1. And there are many more to be found.

Magazine articles should not be used when looking for credible information in education for two reasons: First, magazines, as well as newspaper articles, are written by reporters who have little expertise in the field; therefore they are not likely to be able to put information in any sort of meaningful context. Also, reporters tend not to be familiar with relevant research and related theory; thus, they are not able to distinguish between conjecture and theory-based ideas. And second, magazines and newspapers do not have peer review. They are instead reviewed by an editor or editors who have little expertise in the field of education.

The Internet provides a tremendous amount of knowledge literally at our fingertips. Internet websites can be invaluable tools for getting information very quickly; however, they should never be the sole authority on anything. Although they can contain a great deal of useful information, the vast majority of websites cannot be considered credible sources. Anybody can put things up on a website. (Even I have a website: www.teachergrowth.com.) Thus, things found on Internet websites should be taken with a grain of salt (or perhaps the whole salt shaker). (Note that websites are different from peer-reviewed journals and journal articles that can be found online. These can be used with a fair amount of confidence.) The best way to use Internet websites is to look for information or ideas after you have done some initial reading from academic books and journals.

Example.   Ms. Vinatieri first did a search for peer-reviewed articles on her school's ERIC database. Using the advanced search engine, she put in the key words *reading, fluency,* and *research.* For the types of publications, she narrowed her search to journal articles and research reports. Her search came up with 456 publications.

Ferrara, S. L. (2005). Reading fluency and self-efficacy: A case study. *International Journal of Disability Development and Education, 52,* 215–231.

Hudson, R. F., Lane, H. B., & Pullen, P. C. (2005). Reading fluency assessment and instruction: What, why, and how? *Reading Teacher, 58,* 702–714.

Kubina, R. M. (2005). Developing reading fluency through a systematic practice procedure. *Reading and Writing Quarterly, 21,* 185–192.

Kuhn, M. R. (2005). Comparative Study of Small Group Fluency Instruction. *Reading Psychology, 2,* 127–146.

Martin-Change, S. L., & Levy, B. A. (2005). Fluency transfer: Differential gains in reading speed and accuracy following isolated word and context training. *Reading and Writing, 18,* 343–376.

Mastropieri, M. A., Leinart, A., & Scruggs, T. E. (1999). Strategies to increase reading fluency. *Intervention in School and Clinic, 34,* 278–283, 292.

Richards, M. (2000). Be a good detective: Solve the case of oral reading fluency. *The Reading Teacher, 53,* 534–539.

Stahl, S. A. (2000). Fluency-oriented reading instruction. Atlanta, GA: Center for the Improvement of Early Reading Achievement.

FIGURE 5.2   Journal Articles Related to Reading Fluency

She skimmed titles and abstracts and selected the eight in Figure 5.2 to examine more thoroughly.

She also found a couple of books related to literacy instruction in her school's professional development library. In each she located the sections that described fluency and strategies to promote fluency (Figure 5.3.)

Step 5: Read, Take Notes, and Look for Applications.   As you skim your articles and chapters, record only information that is directly related to your question.

Example.   Having her questions identified made it easier for Ms. Vinatieri to quickly read and comprehend her articles and chapters. She skimmed until she found the specific information was looking for. Then she recorded only the necessary information in her notes.

Step 6: Look for Internet Ideas and Applications That Are Supported by Research-Based Theory.   Because of the abundance of information found there, an Internet search is most effectively done with some degree of relevant background knowledge. This knowledge enables you to quickly evaluate websites.

Allington, R. L. (2005). *What really matters for struggling readers: Designing research-based programs* (2nd ed.). Boston: Allyn & Bacon.

Gipe, J. P. (2006). *Multiple paths to literacy: Assessment and differentiated instruction for diverse learners, K–12* (6th ed.). Upper Saddle River, NJ: Merrill Prentice Hall.

FIGURE 5.3   Books Related to Literacy Instruction

www.auburn.edu/~murraba/fluency.html

www.readingserver.edb.utexas.edu/downloads/primary/guides/Fluency_
Presentation.PDF

www.jimwrightonline.com/pdfdocs/prtutor/prtutor_lesson3.pdf

www.balancedreading.com/fluency.html

www.ncpublicschools.org/schoolimprovement/effective/briefs/developing

---

FIGURE 5.4   Websites Related to Reading Fluency

Example.   Ms. Vinatieri first gained background knowledge by reading journal articles and books. She then used this knowledge-based context to search the Internet and look for additional fluency strategies that could be supported by research-based theory (Figure 5.4).

Step 7: Apply and Take Action.   Examine your notes carefully. What trends or patterns do you notice? What do they suggest? The last step is to create an application and plan of action based on the information you find.

Example.   Ms. Vinatieri found nine fairly simple research-based strategies that could be used to help students develop their reading fluency. She realized that many of the strategies she found were superior to the ones described in the expensive commercial program. Also, her students seemed to be more inclined to want to do her activities. She wrote the steps to each of the strategies she found (Figures 5.5 and 5.6) and gave a quick after-school inservice to the teachers in her building.

Process and Empowerment

The steps described in the previous section are similar to those used to conduct an action research project (described in the next chapter). In fact, this sort of literature review is a form of action research as the same basic process is used: Ask a question and then look for data to answer that question. The only difference here is that the data are found in academic books and peer-reviewed journals instead of in your classroom or school. Again, I stress the importance of not starting any sort of research project with an answer. This bias limits what you might see and makes the process much harder. In research, as in life, let the data speak.

Understanding this process enables you to construct knowledge and become an expert in any area. This can be empowering. One of the big ideas that I hope you will take from this book is that knowledge is power. Having a body of research-based and theory-based knowledge related to teaching and learning allows you to take control of your profession. You no longer need to rely on or believe the top-down recommendations that are given to you by school districts or government agencies. Neither do you have to depend on administrators, publishers, or college professors to tell you what "the research" says about a particular subject or what the appropriate method or approach is. Instead, a body of knowledge related to teaching and learning enables you to offer research-based alternatives, and with a highly informed teaching population we can all begin to say "no" in a loud and

PPPP (Preview, Pause, Prompt, Praise)

1. Preview: Tutor engages students in brief preview of the story/section: title, pictures, headings, predictions ("what do you think this story is about?").
2. Tutor/student read aloud together until the student wishes to read alone.
3. Pause: If student stumbles, tutor will pause.
   a. Provides opportunity to self correct.
   b. Student uses context clues, words parts, reread sentence.
4. Prompt: At the end of the sentence, if the student has not figured out the word, the tutor will prompt, "Let's read that again."
   a. Give semantic clues ("What makes sense here?")
   b. Give pronunciation if needed.
5. Praise: Praise for self-correction.
6. Continue reading with the student, then drop out.
7. At the end: "What was your favorite part?" There are no wrong answers.

Reread to Meet Standard

1. Find a piece of reading at a particular grade level.
2. Count off 100 words.
3. Set a goal for time.
4. Students reread until they meet the WPM standard.
5. Use zone of proximal development (get a little outside and a little ahead of the student).

Tape, Check, Chart

1. Distribute photocopy of reading selection.
2. Using audiotape, have students read selection out loud.
3. Replay tape and check mispronounced words (put a check on copy for mispronounced words).
   a. Listening gives them a sense of what makes sense.
4. Reread and audiotape again.
5. Replay and draw an X through mispronounced words.
6. Reread and audiotape.
7. Replay and circle mispronounced words.
8. Record the number of errors each time: Students see the number of errors go down.
   a. Record in portfolio— 8—3—1

Older Peer Tutor

1. Pair older students with younger ones to help "tutor."
2. The tutoring is designed to help older students read easier text and develop fluency.

Time Chart

1. Read passage out loud.
2. Time with stop watch and record.
3. Repeat twice more.
4. Record times in portfolio.

FIGURE 5.5   One-on-One Tutorial Approaches for Fluency Development

united voice when a principal, superintendent, college dean, or government agency asks us to do something that is not in the best interest of our students. Knowledge is power.

Other Professional Development Opportunities

A more generalized approach to wide reading also serves to enhance your ability to plan, teach, and make sound decisions. A subscription to a peer-reviewed academic

Choral Reading for Fluency
1. Have students read together.
2. Find short stories, picture books, segments of longer books, poems, or even song lyrics.
3. Read together, picking individuals and small groups to read parts.

Reader's Theater
1. Students work in groups.
2. Create a play out of a story or create their own.
3. Use narrators and characters.
4. Can use sound effects and music.

Echo Reading
1. Teacher reads a sentence in book or board.
2. Students read it back.

Repeated Reading
(large group or small group)
1. Find a piece of text.
2. Divide students into pairs.
3. One student reads as fast as s/he can for one minute. Buddy checks to make sure no words were skipped.
4. Stop and record number of words read (have prenumbered pieces of text).
5. Repeat the process with the same buddy. Record the number of words read in one minute.
6. Put scores on a graph in a portfolio and switch (other buddy reads).

FIGURE 5.6   Small-Group and Whole-Class Activities to Develop Fluency

journal will keep you up to date on the latest developments in a particular field. Figure 5.7 contains a list of some of the major journals and national organizations in various educational disciplines. Some books that may be of interest and serve to enhance your professional development are listed in Figure 5.8. Other professional development strategies include conferences and workshops, college courses, professional discussions with colleagues, experimentation with reflection in regards to trying new strategies in your classroom, and of course, deep reflection.

OBSERVING YOUR OWN PRACTICE

Observation, reflection, and analysis of one's own teaching practice are simple yet effective ways to approach one's professional development. Action research, a systematic observation of your own teaching practice, can become a vehicle to help with this. Following are described some simple ways to enhance your own teaching practice through this process. As is the case throughout this book, the stress should be on the concept of *simplicity*. Rigor and effectiveness are much different from complexity. The best and most useful action research projects are usually the simplest ones.

Best Practice

In their book *Best Practice: New Standards for Teaching and Learning in America's Schools*, Zemelman, Daniels, and Hyde (2006) describe was has come to be known as *best practice*. These are the teaching strategies and educational practices that a

Gifted Education

Gifted Child Today, Journal for the Education of the Gifted, and *Journal of Secondary Gifted Education,* published by Prufrock Press. Website: www.prufrock.com.

Roeper Review. Website: www.roeperreview.org.

National Association for Gifted Children is the most recognized national organization. They do not have a journal that I can recommend for teachers. Website: www.nagc.org.

Literacy

The Reading Teacher and *Journal of Adolescent and Adult Literacy,* published by the International Reading Association. Website: www.reading.org.

Language Arts, Voices from the Middle, and *English Journal,* published by National Council of Teachers of English. Website: www.ncte.org.

Social Studies

Social Education and *Social Studies and the Young Learner,* published by the National Council for the Social Studies. Website: www.ncss.org.

Mathematics

Teaching Children Mathematics, Mathematics Teaching in the Middle School, Mathematics Teacher, and *Online Journal for School Mathematics,* published by the National Council of Teachers of Mathematics. Website: www.nctm.org.

Science

Science and Children, Science Scope, and *The Science Teacher,* published by National Science Teachers Association. Website: www.nsta.org.

Holistic Education or Progressive Education

Encounter: Education for Meaning and Social Justice, published by Great Ideas in Education. Website: www.great-ideas.org.

Young Children

Young Children, published by National Association for the Education of Young Children. Website: www.naeyc.org.

Special Education

Exceptional Children and *Teaching Exceptional Children,* published by the Council for Exceptional Children. Website: www.cec.sped.org.

Journal of Whole Schooling, a free online journal published by the Whole School Consortium. Website: www.wholeschooling.net.

FIGURE 5.7   Academic Journals

---

body of research has shown to be effective in keeping all students engaged in appropriate learning activities and enhancing learning. Figure 5.9 contains a chart that summarizes some general best practice recommendations that go across all curriculum areas. A simple way to use Zemelman, Daniels, and Hyde's chart for professional development is to record instances of each best practice recommendation in a weekly planner. At the end of each day use a red tally mark to indicate when something from the Provide Less list occurred in your classroom and black

Allington, R. (2006). *What really matters for struggling readers: Designing research-based programs.* Boston: Allyn & Bacon.

Cunningham, P. M., & Allington, R. L. (2003). *Classrooms that work: They can all read and write* (3rd ed.). Boston: Allyn & Bacon.

Harman, W., & Rheingold, H. (1984). *Higher creativity: Liberating the unconscious for break-through insights.* Los Angeles: Tarcher.

Johnson, A. (2000). *Up and out: Using creative and critical thinking skills to enhance learning.* Boston: Allyn & Bacon.

Johnson, A. (2006). *Making connections in elementary and middle school social studies.* Thousand Oaks, CA: Sage.

Kessler, R. (2000). *The soul of education: Helping students find connection, compassion, and character at school.* Alexandria, VA: ASCD.

Marzano, R. J. (2003). *What works in schoools: Translating research into action.* Alexandria, VA: ASCD.

Marzano, R. J., Pickering, D. J., & Pollock, J. E. (2001). *Classroom instruction that works: Research-based strategies for increasing student achievement.* Alexandria, VA: ASCD.

Popham, W. J. (2001). *The truth about testing: An educator's call to action.* Alexandria, VA: ASCD.

Sternberg, R. (1996). *Successful intelligence: How practical and creative intelligence determine success in life.* New York: Plume.

Tomlinson, C. A. (2001). *How to differentiate instruction in a mixed-ability classroom* (2nd ed.). Alexandria, VA: ASCD.

Zemelman, S., Daniels, H., & Hyde, A. (2006). *Best practice: Today's standards for teaching and learning in America's schools* (3rd ed.). Portsmouth, NH: Heinemann.

FIGURE 5.8   Recommended Books for Professional Development

marks to indicate when something from the Provide More list occurred. At the end of each week, count the number of red and black tally marks and record these on a graph or chart. This sort of tallying helps you become aware of your own teaching practice as it relates to best practice. As the year goes on, you should see an increase in black tally marks and a decrease in red tally marks. To get more specific, you can number the items in each list so that you have a sense of the types of the specific practices that occur in your classroom each week.

I highly recommend Zemelman, Daniels, and Hyde's book for every school's professional library. It could become the basis of a weekly book club for teachers. There are chapters related to best practice in each of the subject areas: reading, writing, mathematics, science, social studies, and the arts. And at the end of every chapter, charts like those in Figure 5.9 are included that list things to increase and decrease for effective learning. If you are an elementary or middle school teacher who teaches more than one subject area, one subject area could be the focus for a month with the same sort of tally system used as previously described. This book also includes a chapter devoted to the seven structures of

PROVIDE LESS

- Whole-class, teacher-directed instruction (e.g., lecturing); student passivity (sitting, listening, receiving, and absorbing information)
- Presentational, one-way transmission of information from teacher to student
- Prizing and rewarding of silence in the classroom
- Classroom time devoted to fill-in-the-blank worksheets, dittos, workbooks, and other seatwork
- Student time spent reading textbooks and basal readers
- Rote memorization of facts and details
- Emphasis on competition and grades in school
- Use of pull-out special programs
- Use of and reliance on standardized tests

PROVIDE MORE

- Experiential, inductive, hands-on learning
- Active learning in the classroom, with students doing, talking, and collaborating
- Diverse roles for teachers, including coaching, demonstrating, and modeling
- Emphasis on higher-order thinking; learning a field's key concepts and principles
- Reading of real tests, whole books, primary sources, and nonfiction materials
- Responsibility transferred to students for their work (goal setting, record keeping, monitoring, sharing, exhibiting, and evaluating)
- Choice for students (e.g., choosing their own books, writing topics, team partners, and research perfects)
- Enacting and modeling of the principles of democracy in school
- Attention to affective needs and the varying cognitive styles of individual students
- Cooperative, collaborative activity, developing the classroom as an interdependent community
- Heterogeneously grouped classrooms where individual needs are met through inherently individualized activities, not segregation of bodies
- Delivery of special help to students in regular classrooms
- Reliance on teachers' descriptive evaluation of student growth, including observational/anecdotal records, conference notes, and performance assessment rubrics

---

FIGURE 5.9   Best Practices for Enhancing Learning

---

best teaching practice: small-group activities, reading as thinking, representing to learn, classroom workshop, authentic experiences, reflective assessment, and integrative units.

Audiotaping Lessons

For teachers involved in the complex act of teaching, observation, reflection, and analysis during a teaching episode is not always possible or pragmatic. However, audiotape can be effectively used to record teaching episodes for later analysis. I prefer audiotape over videotape because it is much easier and far less

Open-ended question	
Closed-ended question	

FIGURE 5.10   Types of Questions

intrusive to use. It is easy to turn on a tape recorder, set it on the front table, and begin teaching. It is much more difficult to set up a camera, adjust the view, and get students acclimated to it. Except for student movement and certain nonverbal behaviors, I find that almost as much information is collected with audiotape as with videotape.

1. *Types of questions.* Use tally marks to indicate the number of times a particular type of question is asked (see Figure 5.10).

2. *Level of questions and activities.* Use tally marks and Bloom's Taxonomy to determine the level and frequency of your questions or activities (Figure 5.11).

3. *Students responding.* Do you call on the same students during discussions? Are all students involved? Record the students called on to answer questions during a lesson. Use a table or graph to show this information.

4. *Wait time.* Do you pause to allow students to fully process the question before calling on them? Use a stopwatch to determine the length of time between when you ask a question and when you call on a student. Record these time intervals. Use a bar graph to show the number of times at each interval level, or use a line graph to show how the average time interval changes over time.

5. *Management statements.* Are you proactive in preventing management issues? Or do you react to a problem situation that has already happened? Figure 5.12 can be used to record the types of statements made related to classroom management.

6. *T-chart for observation and analysis.* Many times researchers do not know exactly what they are looking for until they see it. The T-chart in Figure 5.13 can be used to record interesting or important parts of your lesson and your analysis of those parts. This is an open-ended inquiry. Record your objective observations or what you noticed in the left column and your subjective thoughts, applications, or analysis of the idea in the right column. On the bottom, jot down any big ideas or conclusions made based on this observation and analysis. Focus on a class or subject area that seems to be more troublesome for you than others. Also, the T-chart is useful for trying a new strategy, methodology, or activity where you simply want to find out how it is working. Doing a series of T-chart observations over time will provide you valuable information you would not have otherwise noticed.

7. *Analysis of time.* We can increase learning in our classroom by making better use of our time. There are four concepts of time; see Figure 5.14.

Level or Type of Thinking	Times Used
1. Knowledge. Recalls facts or remembers previously learned material *Knowledge level operations:* define, describe, identify, list, match, name, tell, describe, show, label, collect, examine, tabulate, quote, duplicate, memorize, recognize, relate, recall, repeat, reproduce, or state	
2. Comprehension. Grasps the meaning of material *Comprehension level operations:* interpret, explain, summarize, convert, defend, distinguish, estimate, generalize, rewrite, contrast, predict, associate, differentiate, discuss, extend, classify, express, indicate, locate, recognize, report, restate, review, select, or translate	
3. Application. Uses learned material in a new situation *Application level operations:* apply, change, compute, demonstrate, operate, show, use, solve, calculate, complete, illustrate, examine, modify, relate, change, classify, experiment, dramatize, employ, interpret, operate, practice, schedule, sketch, or write	
4. Analysis. Breaks things down into parts in order to understand, organize, or clarify *Analysis level operations:* identify parts, distinguish, diagram, outline, relate or associate, break down, discriminate, subdivide, analyze, separate, order, explain, connect, classify, arrange, divide, select, infer, appraise, calculate, categorize, compare, contrast, criticize, differentiate, examine, experiment, question, or test	
5. Synthesis. Puts parts together to form a new whole *Synthesis level operations:* combine, compose, create, design, rearrange, integrate, modify, substitute, plan, invent, formulate, prepare, generalize, or rewrite	
6. Evaluation. Uses a given criterion to determine the value of a thing or quality of a product or performance *Evaluation level operations:* appraise, criticize, compare and contrast, support, conclude, discriminate, find main points, explain, infer, deduce, assess, decide, rank, grade, test, measure, recommend, convince, select, judge, argue, choose, compare, defend, estimate, judge, predict, rate, select, value, or evaluate	

FIGURE 5.11   Bloom's Taxonomy

| Proactive management statements: | |
| Reactive management statements: | |

FIGURE 5.12   **Management Statements**

1. Allotted time is the time allotted to teach a specific subject. If math class lasts from 1:00 to 2:05, the allotted time is 65 minutes.
2. Instructional time is the time you are actually engaged in instruction. This is the allotted time minus the transition time and time getting settled and organized to teach.
3. The time on task (TOT) is the time students are actively engaged in relevant learning tasks. Rather than sitting passively, students are doing something. They are actively engaged in discussion, small-group activities, practice, note taking or something else. However, students may be struggling with tasks that are too difficult for them or too easy.
4. Academic learning time (ALT) is the time students are successfully engaged in tasks that are relevant to the purpose of the lesson. Academic learning time is different for each student.

It may be hard to get this information on an audiotape; instead, record the time when differentiated strategies are used, such as tiered activities, agendas, literature circles, group investigations, cooperative learning activities, or learning contracts (Tomlinson, 1995). By the way, a simple, effective, and inexpensive way to increase learning is to increase TOT and ALT.

Descriptive, Not Prescriptive

A word of caution in regard to research on effective teaching: Educational research was never meant to prescribe a standard teaching experience; rather, when used appropriately it describes effective practices that can be used to enhance learning. Not understanding this important concept, some have chosen selectively from the vast array of educational research in an attempt to break the complex act of teaching into a series of mechanical behaviors. Choosing only research studies that

Things Noted	My Analysis

Ideas or conclusions:

FIGURE 5.13   **T-Chart for Observation and Analysis**

Class period or lesson:
Date: *Time:*

Allotted time:	
Instructional time:	
Time-on-task:	
Academic learning time:	

Ideas or conclusions:

FIGURE 5.14   Data Retrieval Chart for Analyzing Time

measure isolated teaching behaviors as they affect standardized scores, some have created and prescribed standardized lists of teaching behaviors. The implication here is that such lists represent what effective teachers must do. Such is the case with Danielson's *Framework for Teaching* (1996), and Hunter's *Mastery Teaching* (1982). Both of these texts reduce teaching to simply performing a standardized series of subskills (Johnson, 2000). Teaching becomes a contrived, lifeless act. And having this concrete list of "research-based" practices, administrators and university student teaching supervisors (who should know better) have used these as evaluative devices, insisting that all teachers must have these prescribed elements in all lessons. This view demonstrates a severe misunderstanding of educational research and a limited exposure to research and theories related to teaching and learning.

Research-based teaching practice and other theory-based strategies are meant to describe general principles and practices that are to be adopted and adapted to fit the particular teaching and learning situation. This is the case with Zemelman, Daniels, and Hyde's (2006) description of best teaching practices in Figure 5.8 (p. 53). These do not prescribe what must be; rather, they describe what might be—general principles and practices that can be used to enhance learning.

FINAL WORD

Action research is perhaps the most efficient and effective way to address the professional development of teachers. As stated at the beginning of this book, action research allows teachers to connect education theory and research to their classroom practice and helps them to become more reflective and analytical in their teaching practice. Action research is also economical in terms of the time and money invested and the returns garnered in the form of increased learning by students and improved practice by teachers.

SUMMARY

- A knowledge base related to subject areas, learning theory, classroom management, and pedagogical methods is important in teaching and learning to teach.
- Action research is an efficient and effective method of attending to the professional development of teachers.
- Experts in any field have a body of knowledge from which to draw to help in solving problems.
- You can develop a knowledge base and become an expert in any area by following these seven steps: (1) identify a topic of interest or importance; (2) identify a goal or goals; (3) put your topic in the form of a question or questions; (4) find peer-reviewed books and academic journal articles; (5) read, take notes, and look for applications; (6) look for Internet ideas and applications that are supported by research-based theory; and (7) apply and take action.
- A literature review is a form of action research as you ask a question and answer it with data.
- Understanding how to acquire knowledge and become an expert empowers teachers and makes them less dependent.
- Having a body of knowledge related to teaching and learning enables you to effectively evaluate new programs and offer research-based alternatives when necessary.
- Other professional development opportunities include wide reading, conferences, workshops, college courses, professional discussions, and experimentation with reflection.
- Systematically observing your own teaching practice is one form of professional development.
- Zemelman, Daniels, and Hyde's (2006) recommendations for best teaching practices can be used to help you chart and increase instances of best practice occurring in your classroom.
- Individual lessons can be audiotaped for later analysis to examine (1) types of questions asked, (2) level of questions and activities, (3) student responses to questions and classroom discussions, (4) wait time, (5) management statements, (6) general observation and analysis, and (7) time-on-task and academic learning time.
- Education research describes effective teaching practices; it should never be used to prescribe the experience.

QUESTIONS AND ACTIVITIES

1. Describe the knowledge you think is important for teaching. What do teachers need to know?
2. What skills are important for teaching? What do teachers need to be able to do?

3. Describe your philosophy of learning. How do students learn?
4. Practice using one of the techniques for observing your own practice described in this chapter. Share your results and any insights you have about the process.
5. What do you think is the best way for classroom teachers to continue their professional growth and development?
6. What are some topics or areas of interest you would like to investigate as part of a professional development project? Put your inquiry in the form of a question or questions.
7. Visit one or more of the free online journals. Look for three to five interesting or important articles.
8. Knowledge is a form of empowerment. What is an area in your classroom, school, or district that you would like to change? Find and list the titles of three articles or book chapters that might provide you with credible information related to this area.
9. List five professional development activities in which you would be mostly likely to engage. Put them in order from most useful to least useful in terms of your professional growth.
10. Examine Zemelman, Daniels, and Hyde's list of best practice recommendations. Describe five areas you want to focus on for your own classroom.
11. Examine the recommended journals. If you do not already subscribe to one, which journal seems to be of most interest to you? Visit the websites to get more information.

POSSIBLE RESEARCH QUESTIONS FOR ACTION RESEARCH PROJECTS

1. Find three to five inspiring teachers. Ask them to describe a beautiful teaching experience that they've had. Look for commonalities among their descriptions.
2. What is your philosophy of teaching? What traits and practices do you value? Keep track of which practices, strategies, and reactions reflect what you believe to be true about teaching and learning.
3. Find an area or situation that interests you. How might you look at it from many angles?
4. What instances of best practice occur in your classroom each week?
5. How much time do your students spend each day engaged in authentic reading experiences (reading silently for pleasure or to get information that is of interest to them)?
6. What types and levels of questions do you usually ask in a whole-class teaching situation? How do your questions compare to research related to teacher effectiveness?
7. What taxonomical level do most of your activities and assignments represent? What would happen if you gave your students choices, providing a low-level and a high-level activity for an assignment (a tiered activity)?
8. What type of management statements do you use? How does this compare to research related to teacher effectiveness?

9. Pick a class or subject area. Examine this class for two or more weeks using an audiotape recorder. What is the average TOT and ALT? What are strategies that can be used to increase these?

10. How do you differentiate the curriculum to meet the varied needs of learners? What different strategies do teachers in your school or district use to differentiate the curriculum?

11. Read Tomlinson's book, *How to Differentiate Instruction in a Mixed-Ability Classroom* (2001). Pick one or two strategies to try. Use a T-chart or field notes to record what happens.

12. Use one of the reading fluency strategies described in this chapter. Use timed reading to record students' progress in reading fluency. Are there differences among students? Do you notice an effect?

CHAPTER SIX

THE BEGINNING

"But how do I start for Emerald City?" Dorothy asked. Glinda replied, "It's always best to start at the beginning. And all you do is follow the Yellow Brick Road."
—The Wizard of Oz, 1939

AN OVERVIEW OF THE ACTION RESEARCH PROCESS

I want to reiterate an important point once again: *Action research does not mean that you have to prove something. It is not an experiment* (although it could be). It is often conducted simply to find out what's going on. The goal is to understand, evaluate, or even to find new ideas and see how they work. Chapter 3 described five essential parts of action research. In this chapter, these five parts are broken down further into ten steps. You will notice that these are similar to those described in the previous chapter. These steps are meant to be a guideline to be adapted to your particular research topic or situation. Also, as stated previously, there is no universal order to these steps. You might find yourself skipping steps, rearranging their order, or repeating some steps.

Action Research Steps

1. *Identify a problem or research topic.* The first step is to decide what to study. What are you curious about? Ask a question, identify a problem, or define an area of interest for exploration. Find something that intrigues you, something you would really like to examine in depth.

2. *Set the problem or research topic in a theoretical context.* This means doing a review of the literature (described in detail in Chapter 7 and Chapter 16). Look in professional journals, books, and web sources to see what others have found out or have to say about your research topic. Relating your research topic to current theories gives you more credibility and provides a theoretical context for your findings. It also

enables you to link theory and practice by connecting what you find in the literature to what is happening in your classroom. You might take one of three approaches in doing a literature review. The first approach is to do the review of the literature before you begin collecting data. Besides setting your study in a theoretical context, the literature review might also be used to help formulate your question, refine a pedagogical method to be studied, or give you ideas for collecting data. The second approach is to review the literature as you report the data and make your conclusions. The literature is related to each of your concluding points. The third approach is not to do a review of the literature at all. Many short action research projects do not include this element. As you can see, you have a certain amount of freedom in organizing your action research project. The onus is on you, however, to create a credible and coherent report. Linking your study to theories and previous research is one way to do this.

3. *Make a plan for data collection.* In traditional research this is known as methodology. What data are you going to study? How are you going to collect the data? How often will you collect data? Action research is not impressionistic, nor is it a brochure supporting a particular teaching methodology. Rather, action research is a systematic observation; therefore, data collection must be focused and the elements of data collection must be determined before the research begins.

4. *Begin to collect and analyze data.* After you have identified at least two kinds of data, you begin the data collection process. As you collect your data, analyze them by looking for themes, categories, or patterns that emerge. This analysis will influence further data collection by helping you to know what to look for.

5. *If necessary, allow the question or problem to change as you collect data.* Action research is a dynamic, ever-changing process. As a human you cannot help but be influenced by the data you collect. It is common, therefore, to change a particular teaching strategy, the sources of data, or even the focus of the study as you are collecting data. This is acceptable as long as you let the reader know what you did and why you did it. That is, in writing your report take the reader along with you in all phases of your action research.

6. *Analyze and organize the data.* Hopefully you have been analyzing and organizing the data as you have been collecting them, thus, this should be the final step of an ongoing process. In analyzing your data, you need to establish how many total things were recorded, how many categories or kinds of things there are, and how many things are in each category. This is a quick view of analytic induction, which is described in Chapter 9.

7. *Report the data.* Present the facts or findings. This presentation includes an overview with detailed descriptions and illustrative samples of important events, activities, and responses. Also reported are the number and types of themes, categories, or patterns present in the data. In this section of your report you take the role of a journalist or anthropologist by describing what you saw and providing examples that demonstrate your perceptions.

8. *Make your conclusions and recommendations.* The next step is to interpret the data or tell the reader what they mean. Based on the data, what can you conclude?

What do you recommend, based on your conclusions? You then answer your research question, provide answers for a problem, or make suggestions based on your new understanding. Also, as stated in step 2, some action researchers do a review of the literature at this point to set their conclusions in a theoretical context.

9. *Create a plan of action.* This is when you put the action in action research. Based on your conclusions and recommendations, what will you do? You create a plan of action. And as you implement your plan of action, you assess what is happening or how effective it is; thus, the action research cycle continues.

10. *Put your plan into action and evaluate.* Does it work? What needs to be changed or tweaked? Few plans work perfectly. Evaluating your plan could become the basis of another action research project, and thus, the circle of action research life continues.

FINDING YOUR RESEARCH TOPIC

To begin, you must first determine an area to research. Three common research possibilities are (1) study or evaluate a teaching strategy, (2) identify and investigate a problem, or (3) examine an area of interest.

A Teaching Strategy

Would you like to try a new teaching strategy or technique? Maybe you want to see how a writing workshop works. Perhaps you are interested in finding out what happens if you let students choose their own writing topics. What new method or teaching idea might you be willing to experiment with in your classroom?

Chris Reed, a primary grade teacher, was intrigued by the idea of using an embedded approach to spelling. Instead of the prescribed list of spelling words and traditional approaches to spelling instruction, she used words found in students' literature and science units and created her own activities. Some weeks she also experimented with allowing students to choose their own words to study. She wanted to see whether this approach was effective in improving students' ability to spell under real writing conditions. As she started her action research project, she also became interested in seeing whether this approach was more enjoyable for her students, what effects it might have on students' writing, what kind of words students chose to study, and how those words related to the lives of students.

Mary Kaymeyer, a fifth grade teacher, had always loved teaching her poetry unit in language arts, but because of a crowded curriculum, she felt she never had enough time to really enjoy and explore this form as much as she would like. She decided to try embedding poetry across her fifth grade curriculum. Mary redesigned her curriculum so that poetry was included in social studies, math, science, health, and reading as well as in language arts classes. Poetry was used to reinforce important concepts and to create alternatives to tests and written reports in helping students organize and demonstrate their knowledge. After her first year of using this approach, she decided to use action research to see how it was going and to provide support for either continuing or abandoning this idea.

Identify a Problem

Problems can be turned into action research projects. Is there a subject or an area in your teaching that does not flow as well as others? Is there a particular problem in your school or classroom that is disrupting the learning process? Action research is a tool that can be used to systematically study a problem area. It can help to understand what is happening and the possible causes of the problem. It can also be used to explore various solutions. In addition, a review of the literature will help you connect the literature to the problem and to find solutions that others may have tried. The prompts in Figure 6.1 can be used to identify possible problems for your action research project.

Al Norton, a high school social studies teacher, noticed that the students in his senior-level classes seemed to be bored and disinterested. They appeared to be going through the motions on weekly assignments and often were talking or zoning out during class. He conducted a series of short written surveys and class discussions to find out what students were interested in, what they wanted to learn, how they best liked to learn, and what was useful in helping them understand new ideas. This allowed Al to connect his social studies curriculum to

---

The following prompts might be of help in finding problems
for action research projects:

- My class would be better if . . .
- This is a problem on the playground . . .
- This is a problem in the cafeteria . . .
- This is a problem in my classroom . . .
- Our school would be better if . . .
- Learning would improve if . . .
- Classroom management would improve if . . .
- I would like . . .
- I would like to improve . . .
- I wish that I could . . .
- I am interested in finding an answer to . . .
- If only . . .
- I would like to increase . . .
- I would like to decrease . . .
- I am looking for a better way to . . .
- I would like to help students . . .
- I would like to make _____ better.
- I wish that I did _____ better.

FIGURE 6.1   **Problem Prompts for Action Research Projects**

issues that were relevant to students. A review of the literature gave him ideas for using different teaching strategies and activities. Al also shared his findings with his students and, in so doing, modeled a method of inquiry used by social scientists.

Examine an Area of Interest

Are you interested in a particular topic? Are you curious about something? Action research can be used to explore your interests. For example, Jim Soderholm, a middle school English teacher, has always been interested in comedy and humor. He wanted to discover what middle school students found funny and how they used humor in their socialization process. He began his study by recording instances of students' humor that he observed in classes, in the halls, or in other situations. From this, he created a form that allowed him quickly to note the instance of humor, the name and gender of the humorist, the recipient of the humor, and the type of humor (see Figure 6.2).

This project improved Jim's teaching in three ways. First, it helped him further his understanding of his students and the nature of their social interactions and emotional status. Second, he found humor to be a hot topic for these middle school students. This led him to incorporate humor into his English curriculum by teaching students to write and perform their own stand-up routines and comedy sketches. Third, Jim shared the findings of his action research with his students. They were fascinated by what he discovered and the process he used. This led to his teaching students how to do their own inquiry projects. Jim was able to use their accompanying reports as vehicles for teaching technical writing skills, oral speaking, and presentation techniques.

Date: Time: Place/setting:

Name of humorist: Gender:

Humor recipient:

Type of humor:

Key for humor recipient: 1 = student to student; 2 = student to teacher; 3 = student to anybody else

Key for type of humor: P = physical; SC = sarcastic; A = absurd or silly; W = word play; S = sexual

FIGURE 6.2   Form for Recording Students' Humor

STILL HAVING TROUBLE STARTING?

It may be possible that you are still having trouble getting started—not to panic. The key is to first find something of interest for your topic and then create a question related to this topic. The question helps to narrow and define your action research project. Following are some additional ideas that might help you get started.

  1. *Brainstorm and list.* Draw a line down the middle of a blank sheet of paper. On the left side begin listing topics of interest. Do not think about or evaluate your ideas yet as this will only stymie the flow. Then begin conversing with other faculty, asking what they are interested in or would like to know more about in regard to their classroom or teaching and learning. You will see that as the ideas appear, they lead you to other ideas. When you have exhausted your possible topics, on the right side of your paper, list specific questions for each topic. Each topic can have one or many questions related to it.

  For example, Mr. Fife, a sixth grade teacher, knew that he wanted to spend some time looking at his science class (Figure 6.3). He was never satisfied with the way he was teaching it. He hoped his action research project might give him some ideas.

Possible Topics

Science

Possible Action Research Questions

1. What's going on in my science class?
2. What things make learning interesting for my students in science?
3. What best practice ideas might I incorporate into my science class? How will these work?
4. What are some new strategies or teaching ideas that I might use in my science class to make it more interesting? How will these work?
5. What topics are of interest to my students?
6. How might I go about incorporating current events into my science class? How will this work?
7. How do the school mission statement, goals, and philosophy apply to my science class? What elements are reflected? How?
8. What topics are generally covered in a science class?
9. What interesting projects or ideas are other teachers using in their science classes?
10. Am I helping students make personal connections with the content? If not, what happens if I do?
11. How do students perceive science?
12. How does my science curriculum compare to thematic standards as proposed by the National Science Teachers Association (NSTA)?
13. What important skills and concepts should students learn in my science class?

FIGURE 6.3   Possible Questions for a Science Action Research Project

For his action research project Mr. Fife simply wanted to find some ways to improve his science class. His research question was, How can I make my science class better (enhance learning, increase interest and motivation, and make it more active and student centered)? For his action project, Mr. Fife audiotaped some of his science classes to get a sense of what was happening. He used field notes to jot down what he noticed as he listened. He also reviewed his science lesson plans. Next he used surveys and interviews to find interesting or creative strategies that the teachers in his school and district were using. He was looking for ideas here that he could adopt and adapt. Finally, he did a quick review of the literature to look for new teaching strategies. He examined his data (field notes, surveys and interviews, notes from his review of the literature) and looked for groups or patterns. From this he created his action plan for improving his science class.

This led to a second, follow-up action research project, which was to evaluate his new approach. His research question here was, How is my new approach to science working? For this he used student surveys, analyzed audiotapes, and had a colleague come in and observe several of his classes during a 2-week period.

2. *Evaluate programs, policies, pedagogy, or plans.* Evaluation examines the effectiveness of an endeavor. Every program, policy, pedagogical strategy, and plan should have some sort of formal as well as informal evaluation. You want to see if the plan is working. To do this, first identify its original purpose. Is that purpose being served? Next examine the criteria. What would it look like if the program, plan, teaching strategy, or policy were successful? Then compare the current program, plan, or policy to the criteria.

Teachers at Greenwood Elementary School wanted to improve students' writing. After reviewing the literature they found two things that might improve students' writing: (1) teaching writing as a process and (2) allowing students to choose their writing topics. They developed a plan that included these two elements along with monthly teacher inservices and updates. After the first year, Ms. Furley, the principal, decided to evaluate the new plan.

The purpose of the new plan originally had been to improve students writing ability by using a process approach to writing instruction and allowing choice of writing topics. Her evaluation consisted of three parts. The first part was designed to find out whether writing processes were being taught (see Figure 6.4) and to see whether students were indeed being allowed to choose their own writing topics. She did this by surveying students and teachers and by making observations. For the second part Ms. Furley looked at students' writing. Greenwood Elementary had been doing a holistic writing test every year in which students were given a prompt and a piece of scratch paper for prewriting and thinking. Students were then asked to compose a writing sample within a 50-minute time period. Writing samples were then sent off to be rated by the testing company. Although it is not a valid indicator of students' ability to write by itself, Ms. Furley also looked at the language arts/writing portion of yearly achievement tests to get a sense of how students were scoring in regard to grammar and punctuation. For the third part of her evaluation, she wanted to know students' perceptions of

1. Prewriting strategies: lists, brainstorming, conversations, semantic webs
2. Drafting: using the first draft to capture ideas without regard to quality (allowing the first draft to look truly terrible)
3. Multiple revisions with feedback from others
4. Edit for grammar, spelling, and punctuation only after revision process is complete
5. Publish: to get a sense of audience, create books and collections of writing, public posters, author's chair, radio drama, and other methods to get students reading and listening to each other's work

The mechanics of writing (grammar, spelling, and punctuation) are taught in short minilessons using the context of students' own writing.

FIGURE 6.4   Five-Step Writing Process

---

the process approach to writing. Did they see it as helpful? What parts were seen as helpful? Did they enjoy writing? Ms. Furley used a Likert scale (see Chapter 8) in which students were asked to rate various statements related to writing and the writing process. She planned to continue this type of evaluation every year. To do this, she kept her measures and evaluation processes simple. Remember, rigor is different from complexity.

3. *Examine perceptions and attitudes.* Would you like to know what somebody thinks about something? You might examine the perceptions or attitudes of students, teachers, or parents on a variety of issues: How do students perceive something? What do they find valuable? What helps them learn? What makes learning more difficult? What are their preferences? What kinds of books would they like to read? How do they like to learn? How do they like to demonstrate their learning? What do they think about current events? How much time do they spend reading each day? What types of things do they do at home? Home much time do they spend on homework each day? What do parents think about the homework policy? What do parents know about whole-language approaches? What do parents value?

Note again that action research projects do not have to be long, complicated, or filled with many subjects to provide useful information (although they could be). Becky Yuzna of Crystal, Minnesota, conducted the action research survey in Figure 6.5 with only the 15 students from a reading class. Her goal was to get some ideas about how to make the class more interesting and student centered, while enhancing students' ability to read.

4. *Check for learning.* Are students learning in your classroom? How do you know? What are they learning? What are some ways, other than using scores on standardized tests, that you could demonstrate what students learn? What types of measures might you use? What products or performances would indicate learning? What kinds of checklists or other data sources might be used (see Chapter 8)? What big lessons are students taking from your classroom?

5. *Make a case for your effectiveness as a teacher.* What evidence can you collect to demonstrate that you are an effective teacher? Can you collect lesson plans that demonstrate your effective use of one or more new teaching strategies?

I surveyed 15 sixth and seventh grade students using open-ended questions to get information about their attitudes toward and interests in reading. In this survey, students were asked to finish nine open-ended sentences.

1. When I have to read . . .
2. I like to read when . . .
3. I read more if . . .
4. Reading is . . .
5. I cannot read . . .
6. My favorite type of reading material is . . .
7. School is . . .
8. When I read new words . . .
9. In reading class I wish we would do more . . .

Their attitudes varied quite a bit. Some students indicated that they like to read, others that they read only when they have to, and still others indicated that they do not like to read at all. When asked to name their favorite type of reading material, 10 students answered with a specific genre such as comedy, mysteries, comics, sports, scary stories, and "anything that's not fantasy." Many students also said that they liked reading alone or in a quiet place.

Given this information, it seems apparent that students like reading more when they are reading something they like or are interested in. A course of action I will take is to allow students to have input on the reading selections they will be accountable for. They can make choices about the type of material or the topic they read for reading class. I will probably need to establish some parameters on this. I will also make sure there is quiet time and space available during the day to read. I feel that if students are given the opportunity to get hooked on a book during school, they will be much more likely to take it home and enjoy it merely for the sake of reading and not because they had to.

Another interesting response was that several students wanted to do more "fun things" in reading class. Others indicated that they would like to draw or do activities. Given this information, I will try to do more fun activities designed to engage kids in reading. Drawing can easily be incorporated into reading class. Students can draw characters, book covers, maps, etc. I also think I will incorporate book talks for those kids who like to get up in front of people. Students like to share things that they are interested in. Fun is often underrated in an academic setting. It is much easier to engage students in the learning process when they enjoy it. I understand that there are times for traditional academics; however, getting kids to enjoy reading and learning makes traditional academic subjects much more meaningful and interesting.

FIGURE 6.5   Reading Survey Conducted by Becky Yuzna of Crystal, Minnesota

Can you provide a list of books and articles that you have read to demonstrate your continued growth? Have you written articles or designed units, curriculum, or other programs and policy? Can you show that you are engaged in teaching as an intellectual endeavor? Can you provide evidence of your continued involvement with and service to the school, students, families, or community?

6. *Evaluate practice as compared to the school mission statement.* Although I suspect many mission statements are ignored and unused, a school's mission statement should be the starting point from which effective schools or school districts begin

all endeavors. It is like the objective on a lesson plan that sets the purpose and course for everything a school does. Like a lesson plan objective, all activities and endeavors thereafter should support the mission statement. Many action research projects can be based on one or more of the elements in a school's mission statements (see Figures 6.6 and 6.7). Ask yourself whether this element of the mission statement is occurring. If so, to what extent does it occur? These projects can be undertaken for schoolwide improvement (see Chapter 11), but also at the classroom level.

7. *Observe students.* If you are still having trouble wondering where to begin, simply start observing students. During free time when students are working independently or on the playground, become an anthropologist and begin recording what you see. Using a form for field notes similar to that in Figure 6.8, record your observations on the left and interesting insights or questions on the right. Start these sorts of observations with no intent in mind. Research questions will arise out of your observations. That is, you will find something you would like to know more about or explore in depth as you begin to observe.

Bass Lake High School Mission

The mission of Bass Lake High School's faculty, staff, students, parents, and community is to provide a safe learning environment that enables all students to develop their full potential through a variety of rich educational experiences.

The Belief Statements of Bass Lake High School

A Caring Environment
- Learning is enhanced by a community of learners that supports the growth, exploration, and self-actualization.
- An emotionally and physically safe environment promotes student learning.
- A student's education is enhanced by positive relationships, extracurricular activities, and a system of intellectual and emotional support.

Focus on Learning
- Students' intellectual growth should be the primary focus of all decisions impacting the work of the school.
- Students learn in different ways and should be provided with a variety of instructional approaches, including the use of technology, to support their learning.
- Students need to be given the opportunity to participate in extracurricular activities to fully develop all skills and potential.

Commitment to Quality
- The commitment to continuous growth and evolution is imperative if our school is to enable students to reach their full potential and enhance local and global communities.
- Students need to define personal goals and demonstrate their ability to work toward and achieve their goals.
- Student learning will be demonstrated using a wide variety of methods and criteria, including authentic assessment, student products and performance, performance-based standards, and standardized tests.

FIGURE 6.6   Mission Statement for Bass Lake High School

Mission Statement for Elmwood Elementary School

Our mission is to create a community of independent, lifelong learners equipped to

- Think critically, creatively, and compassionately
- Make decisions that nurture the self, society, and the environment
- Make effective use of their multiple intelligences
- Interact with others cooperatively
- Read, write, and use mathematics
- Effectively use the various forms of inquiry for personal and intellectual growth

To actualize this mission, Elmwood uses a constructivist, experiential approach to teaching and learning. We believe that children must become independent thinkers and learners. Further, we believe the most effective way to achieve this is to offer them a number of experiences to solve meaningful problems with connections to theory. Constructivism or experiential teaching provides children with the opportunity to connect new learning to prior experiences to create new understandings of the world in which they live. The experiential approach to teaching and learning offers students opportunities to apply the various disciplines in meaningful ways or learning with connectedness.

Elmwood's foundation supports these principles:
- Children are our most precious resource.
- We devote the necessary energy and resources to actualize our "ideal" elementary school.
- We remain committed to performance-based learning, in which learning has an experiential connection and makes sense to the learner.
- We continue to deliver an educational program in which students are encouraged to be closely observant—in which they exhibit skeptical and open minds.
- We ensure that all our children master the essential elements for continued learning.

FIGURE 6.7 Mission Statement for Elmwood Elementary School

Objective Observations	*Thoughts, Analysis, Questions*

FIGURE 6.8 Form for Field Notes

SUMMARY

- The five parts of action research described in Chapter 3 can be broken down further into 10 steps: (1) identify a problem or research topic, (2) set the problem or research topic in a theoretical context, (3) make a plan for data collection, (4) begin to collect and analyze data, (5) allow the question or problem to change as you collect data, (6) analyze and organize the data, (7) report the data, (8) make your conclusions and recommendations, (9) create a plan of action, and (10) put your plan into action and evaluate.

- The order and nature of these ten steps should be adapted to suit the demands of one's research topic and teaching situation.
- Finding a topic or an area of interest is one of the beginning steps of an action research project.
- Three research possibilities are to examine a teaching method, a problem, or an area of interest.
- In starting an action research project you must first find a topic and then create a question related to this topic.
- Additional ideas for getting started include the following: (1) brainstorm and list; (2) evaluate programs, policies, pedagogy, or plans; (3) examine perceptions and attitudes; (4) check for learning; (5) make a case for your effectiveness as a teacher; (6) evaluate practice as it compares to the school mission statement; and (7) observe students.

QUESTION AND ACTIVITIES

1. Describe the new teaching methods or ideas you would like to try.
2. Generate a list of problems or areas that might be improved in your school or classroom.
3. Describe your interests related to teaching, learning, or human interaction.
4. Find your school's mission statement. Which elements might become the basis for an action research project?
5. Find four colleagues or classmates. Brainstorm and list a minimum of 15 possible action research projects.
6. Using the form for field notes in Figure 6.8, observe a group of students interacting on the playground or during a class. Look for two or three possible research questions.
7. Give the reading survey in Figure 6.5 to your students. Are your results similar to Becky Yunza's? What was interesting or surprising in what you found?
8. What things might you include to make a case for your effectiveness as a teacher?

POSSIBLE RESEARCH QUESTIONS FOR ACTION RESEARCH PROJECTS

1. Are students in your class learning? How are students doing in your math class? How are students doing in your science class? What things are they learning? What skills have they mastered? How does their mastery of skills compare to those skills identified by a national organization in a particular field?
2. What things help students learn? What things get in the way of students' learning?

3. Do students have and use study skills? What skills do they use? What comprehension skills do students use to read expository text? What do students do to prepare for a test?

4. Find one or more elements of your school's mission statement that you feel need examination. How does this element compare to practice in your classroom? How does it compare to practice in the school? Use any discrepancies to make a case for change.

5. What do students like to read? What types of books or genre does your class prefer? How do they prefer to read?

6. What would your students like to write about? What would make a writing or language arts class more interesting? How would they like to write?

7. What type of social interactions do you see occurring on the playground? What kinds of games do students play? Are there any rules? What characteristics of students do you see in a playground setting that you do not see in the classroom?

8. What subjects or things are students interested in? What questions do they have? What would they like to know more about? How might these be incorporated into one of your curriculum areas?

9. Who are students' heroes? Who do they look up to? What characteristics do these heroes share? How might you use these characteristics to teach about values or citizenship education? How might students identify these characteristics within themselves?

10. Based on your observation of students and their conversations, what social skills would be of value to teach? According to a review of literature, how should these be taught?

CHAPTER SEVEN

A THEORETICAL CONTEXT

This chapter contains a brief description of a literature review and how it might be used in an action research project. More specific instructions on how to create a literature review are described in Chapter 16.

REVIEWING THE LITERATURE

A literature review is an examination of journal articles, ERIC documents, books, and other sources related to your action research topic. The purpose of the review is to set your topic in a theoretical context and to make a connection between theory and your classroom practice. A literature review also helps tie your action research project to what others have said and done before you. That is, you do not have to reinvent the wheel; instead, you can use the insights of others to make your research more efficient and effective. A review of the literature may also provide you with examples of classroom applications, research questions, data collection methods, or data analysis techniques.

Finally, a thorough review of the literature enables you to become an expert in the area you are studying and a more knowledgeable teaching practitioner. This will guide you in all phases of your action research and enhance your ability to teach.

SOURCES FOR THE LITERATURE REVIEW

This section describes the kinds and number of sources that might be used in a review of the literature for an action research project.

Academic Journals

Academic journals are usually the best source for literature reviews. They contain articles written by specialists in the field (usually college professors) who describe their research, secondary research, novel applications of existing theories, or interesting new ideas set in a theoretical context. Hundreds of different academic journals are published in all areas, from medicine to psychology, cosmetology, farming, and education.

An academic journal is not the same as a magazine. Magazines are designed to attract a wide audience and generate profit. They are usually written by a staff of writers or reporters who often have little expertise in the subjects about which they are reporting. To report accurately about a subject of which you have little knowledge is difficult; thus, accuracy is often compromised. Also, magazines depend on advertising revenue, which does in some way affect what is published.

Academic journals, on the other hand, are designed to inform the field. Journal articles are written by scientists, researchers, and other academicians who send in their work to be considered for publication. Each article is then peer reviewed, which means it is critiqued by a jury of three to six experts in the field to check for accuracy and validity. Each reviewer makes a recommendation about whether to accept the article for publication. Often many revisions are made before an article is finally accepted for publication. Also, most academic journals contain little or no advertising, and authors are required to cite and list all their sources.

The Internet

As noted in Chapter 5, the Internet is a good place to find a great deal of information quickly; however, this information is not always credible. Whereas journal articles are peer reviewed before being published, the only criteria for putting information on the Internet is that one has a website and the technical knowledge to post it. Therefore, the Internet should always be used with caution because the information is not always credible.

The U.S. Department of Education maintains the ERIC (Educational Resources Information Center) website at www.eric.ed.gov, which is designed specifically for educators. This site contains thousands of journal articles, research reports, curricula, conference papers, and teaching guides. Again, one must discriminate when selecting documents because the review process is minimal; thus, documents vary widely in their validity and credibility.

Books

Books are fairly credible sources. Keep in mind, however, that just because information is printed in a book does not mean it is true. Authors who cite their sources and books that are published by major publishing houses are generally those that can be trusted to provide credible information. When using books, learn to skim and read only the chapters or parts that pertain to your research topic.

Nonprint Sources

Several nonprint sources can be used to provide background information for your action research project. You might want to find out what other teachers have done or experienced related to your topic and include their insights in your report. If you are looking at curriculum issues, curriculum coordinators usually are aware of the latest trends. Parents can provide insight related to the emotional issues of their children and tell you how their children are responding to or talking about school issues. With a little searching you can often find community members or university-based researchers and teachers who have specialized knowledge related to your topic. For this last group, I have found that a short e-mail with a specific question is generally the most effective way to solicit insights.

How Many Sources?

Exactly how many sources or pieces of literature do you need for your literature review? Again, this is dictated solely by your research topic, the purpose of your research, and the type of research you are conducting. A master's thesis generally calls for 25 or more sources, and a doctoral dissertation, 50 or more sources. Smaller action research projects designed to be published in an academic journal, presented at a conference, shared with your peers, or conducted to fulfill a graduate course requirement might use from 2 to 15 sources. Moreover, many action research projects conducted for professional development or for evaluative or problem-solving purposes do not include a review of the literature and so do not use any sources.

SAMPLE LITERATURE REVIEWS

As stated in Chapter 3, a literature review varies widely with regard to its form and placement in your report. Following are two examples of literature reviews: one inserted at the beginning of an action research report and one at the end.

A Literature Review at the Beginning

I was interested in designing a new method to be used in identifying students for inclusion in gifted education programs in elementary schools. What follows is a sample of part of the literature review that was included at the beginning of my action research report. This review gave me some ideas to use in designing my new identification method; it also lent credibility to my eventual design by putting it in a theoretical context. Nine sources are used here. The author and the year of publication of each of my sources are in parentheses. Specific information related to citations, quotes, and the reference page can be found in *A Short Guide to Academic Writing* (Johnson, 2003a).

IDENTIFYING STUDENTS FOR GIFTED EDUCATION PROGRAMS

The methods many schools use to identify students for gifted education services are not based on what is known about intelligence and creativity.

Intelligence

Howard Gardner (1996) defines intelligence as the ability to solve problems and create products that are valued within a cultural setting. Robert Sternberg (1996) describes it as knowing when and how to use analytic, creative, and practical abilities to reach a goal. Few in the fields of psychology and gifted education would define intelligence solely in terms of scores on standardized measures; yet IQ and achievement test scores are the predominant criteria for entrance into gifted education programs (Aamidor & Spicker, 1995; De Lieon, Argus-Calvo, & Medina, 1997; Hunsaker, Abeel, & Callahan, 1991; Richert, 1997). Identifying prospective students based solely on standardized quantitative measures does not reflect the latest theories related to intelligence, creativity, and productivity, yet schools continue to use such measures because their use is clean, efficient, and quantifiable. These methods are outdated and should not be used as the exclusive means for identification or acceptance into gifted education programs.

Creativity

Creativity is a cognitive process that leads to new or improved products, performances, or paradigms. It is a quality of thought that allows an individual to generate many ideas, invent new ideas, or recombine existing ideas in a novel fashion (Gallagher & Gallagher, 1994). Creativity is the ability to go beyond the given to generate novel and interesting ideas (Sternberg, 1996) or to produce something apart from the ordinary: something remarkable and something new (Feldman, Csikszentmihalyi, & Gardner, 1994). This is an important trait for achievement in all fields; however, the creative process is a trait that does not easily lend itself to measurement. Although standardized creativity tests may be useful in identifying students with creative capabilities such as the ability to generate many ideas or many different kinds of ideas, such measures cannot predict an individual's eventual creative achievement (Davis, 1997). The best predictor of future achievement, especially creative achievement, is past achievement (Davis, 1997; Sternberg, 1996). Therefore, it is reasonable to suggest that past performance be included in identification processes.

A Literature Review at the End

I could also wait until my data are collected and then compare my findings or recommendations to what others have written. The sample literature review that follows uses the same topic as the previous review—identification methods in a gifted education program; however, this literature review appears at the end of the action research report.

RECOMMENDATIONS

In reviewing my data, three recommendations are made for identifying students for our gifted education program.

1. *Make methods of identification consistent with your school's definition of giftedness.* A common definition of giftedness must precede any

discussions related to methods of identification so that we are clear about what exactly we are trying to identify. Our district uses the U.S. Department of Education's (1993) definition in which a variety of talents is described, including the visual and performing arts, creativity, specific academic areas, leadership, as well as intelligence. If we are not going to address all these areas with equal emphasis, we need to revise our definition.

2. *Use the threshold model to identify gifted students.* The threshold model describes a more inclusive method of defining and identifying gifted students (Davis, 1997; Piirto, 1994). Instead of using high criterion scores on intelligence tests for inclusion into gifted education programs (140 or above), students break a lower threshold (score of 115 to 120), as well as meeting other types of criteria. This allows for a conception of giftedness that includes a variety of talents. The threshold model also complements Renzulli and Reis's (1997) schoolwide enrichment model. Anywhere from 10% to 20% of the population are eligible to go to an enrichment center for special instruction.

3. *Use products and performances as one type of identifying criterion.* Identification for any type of special programming requires more than one type of measure or multiple criteria (Davis & Rimm, 1998; Richert, 1997). Students, teachers, or parents are allowed to make a case for inclusion by gathering a variety of evidence to support the need for special programming opportunities.

SUMMARY

- A review of the literature contains an examination and description of journal articles, Internet information, books, and other nonprint sources related to a particular topic.
- The literature review sets your topic in a theoretical context.
- A review of the literature enables you to connect education theory directly to your classroom practice.
- The number of sources used in a literature review is determined by your research topic and the type of research you are conducting.
- Some action research projects do not require a literature review.
- A review of the literature can be included at the beginning or the end of the action research report.

QUESTIONS AND ACTIVITIES

1. Find a topic you are interested in as a possible action research project. Find one journal article that contains a review of relevant literature at the beginning. What do you notice about the style of writing?

2. Using a topic that interests you, find and list one of each kind of the following sources: journal article, Internet website, book, and a nonprint source.
3. Find an example of an article in an academic journal that has a well-written literature review. Describe at least three things the author does well.
4. Use ERIC to find articles related to an area of interest.
5. Find an example of an article in a magazine and one related to a similar topic in an academic journal. What differences do you notice in the writing styles?

POSSIBLE RESEARCH QUESTIONS FOR ACTION RESEARCH PROJECTS

1. How does your school identify students for gifted education programs? How does this compare with most current definitions of intelligence? How does this compare with most definitions of giftedness?
2. How does your students' writing change throughout the year? Are there changes in structure, themes, organization, topics, or mechanics? To what might these changes be attributed?
3. How do students perceive themselves as learners?
4. How do students identify themselves? To which group or groups do they seem to relate?
5. What are the demographics of your students in terms of gender, ethnicity, culture, SES, religion, ability, and family size? Why is this important? How do these data appear in your classroom?
6. How do students solve problems? When given a task, what steps or processes are used?
7. What types of thinking are used in open-ended class discussions? What types of thinking are used in small group discussions?
8. What management issues are of concern to most teachers in your school or district? What strategies do successful teacher employ in maintaining an effective learning environment?
9. How does competition appear in your classroom and in your school? What seem to be the positive and negative effects?
10. How does cooperation appear in your classroom and in your school? What seem to be the positive and negative effects?
11. What decisions are made by the school board over the course of a year? What values seem to be used in making these decisions?
12. What educational decisions are made by you or your colleagues? What values seem to be used in making these decisions?
13. What issues are parents most concerned about?
14. What issues are students most concerned about?

CHAPTER EIGHT

METHODS OF COLLECTING DATA

This chapter contains practical suggestions related to data collection techniques. Many of these techniques are also forms of authentic assessment that can be used as part of your classroom teaching practice.

DATA COLLECTION

The goal of action research is to understand some element of your classroom by collecting data. Data (plural) are any form of information, observations, or facts that are collected or recorded. Collecting data is what separates the action research project from a newspaper editorial. As stated previously, action research is not simply writing about what you think to be true; rather, it is collecting data and making conclusions based on that data.

Systematic

In reviewing the literature related to action research, the one descriptor that is used in almost every book and article is the word *systematic*. Action research is systematic. This means that before the research begins a plan is in place that describes what data you will collect and when, how, and how often you will collect them. However, action research is a dynamic process; thus, it is common to abandon certain forms of data collection and adopt others as you are conducting the study.

One way to ensure that you are collecting data on a regular basis is to use a calendar or a checklist. Figure 8.1 shows a simple checklist that can be used to record which data were collected and when. This ensures that data are collected systematically and that all types of data are equally represented.

Data Collection and Soil Samples

Collecting data in an action research project is not a snapshot of a single incident like a test score. Nor should data collection rely on a single type of data, for

Type of Data	Dates Collected						
Individual quiz scores	8/18	8/25	9/2	9/9	9/16		
Audiotapes	8/13	8/19	8/26	9/2	9/17		
Student writing samples	8/17	9/9	10/1				
Homework	8/17	8/18	8/23	8/27	9/2	9/10	9/16
Student journals	8/27	9/17					
Small-group conference/focus group	8/20	8/27	9/3	9/10	9/17		

FIGURE 8.1   Checklist for Collecting Data

example, collecting only survey data or only homework scores. Rather, action research is a series of quick looks taken at different times and in a variety of ways. In this sense, data collection in action research is much like collecting soil samples: You collect little bits of soil in different places over time.

A Television Sports Analyst

In your action research project you are the lens through which a bit of classroom reality is described. It is a given that this reality will be filtered through your own experiences and perceptions; however, you have the responsibility to present an accurate portrayal and to be as unbiased as possible. Any biases you are aware of should be stated up front so that readers of your report are able to take this into account. You are not creating a brochure for the Chamber of Commerce, nor are you advocating a particular methodology or approach; rather, you are examining what is happening in your classroom and letting us read your thoughts as you analyze what you are perceiving and experiencing. In this sense, you act as a television sports analyst for a football game as you describe what is happening and break it down so that others can understand it.

TYPES OF DATA COLLECTION IN ACTION RESEARCH

A wide variety of data to collect and methods used to collect them exist. This section describes 13 data collection methods. I would encourage you to select only two to four types of data to collect to keep your research focused. Nothing is more confusing than trying to read research that seems to go off in all sorts of directions.

Keep your action research simple and focused. Trying to collect too many kinds of data is a good way to make your life miserable. Often, my graduate students find a lot of interesting ideas as they start their projects and want to go off chasing all of them. Those who do this usually end up making a mess of their research projects.

Finally, you may notice that some overlap or commonality exists between the methods described in the following sections. The goal is not to have categories and labels with precise edges; rather, it is to generate some ideas with fuzzy borders. In all cases in this chapter, and as I have continued to emphasize throughout this book, find or adapt the methods that best suit your research question or your teaching situation and that seem to make the most sense to you.

Log or Research Journal

A research journal is a notebook used to record thoughts and observations related to all parts of your research. Use this to describe each step of your research process. It is an important source of information to use when trying to piece together the chronology of your research project. You may choose to include a variety of data, such as observations, analyses, diagrams, sketches, quotes, student comments, scores, thoughts, or even feelings and impressions.

How you use your research journal and the form it takes is a matter of personal preference. Some choose to use their research journals to collect field notes and other forms of data, whereas others keep their field notes separate and use the research journal to record their impressions and ideas related to the research process. I sometimes use a computer file as my research journal. The advantage of this is that it is quick and easy to organize and read, and I can print copies or share disks with colleagues. The disadvantage is that I can usually see only 30 lines of print at any one time, I have to scroll up and down in linear fashion, I cannot draw or sketch, and it is less spontaneous. I suggest you choose the method that you will most likely continue using.

Field Notes—Your Observations

Field notes are the written observations of what you see taking place in your classroom. Beginning action researchers are often unsure of what they should record. My advice is to stop thinking and just write what you see. Once you start recording, you begin to see things that are interesting or important. In this way field notes help you notice details you might not otherwise have noticed. And as you make many observations over time, patterns begin to emerge from the data. Also, as stated in the previous chapter, a review of the literature may give you clues as to what kinds of things you might attend to in your field notes. Field notes can be of either of three types: thick descriptions during, quick notes during, and notes and reflections after.

Thick Descriptions During.   The first type of field notes involves taking notes while teaching is taking place. However, few teachers are able to check out during their teaching to become an objective observer recording thick descriptions of ongoing classroom events. Most need to be fully engaged in the teaching process and thus are not able to enter an effective researcher/recorder mode during teaching. Also, by becoming a researcher during your teaching, you run the risk of becoming a nonteacher and thus becoming a foreign entity in your research environment. That is, by transforming yourself from a teacher who regularly responds to students' immediate concerns into an impartial researcher who observes and takes careful notes, you introduce something into the classroom environment that does not reflect what is normally there.

You can, however, observe another teacher's classroom or observe your own when somebody else is teaching. I have spent considerable time observing classrooms and taking field notes as both a researcher and a supervisor of preservice teachers in their field experiences. In this process I have learned much by watching master teachers at work. Providing training in some basic action research techniques and creating opportunities for teachers to do this each year is a very economical and effective form of teacher development. Here are five tips for observing a classroom and taking field notes:

1. *Enter the classroom as quickly and quietly as possible.* Move quickly to a spot in the classroom that offers the least distraction and sit down. Usually this is in the back or to the side.

2. *If students ask you who you are, answer them.* "I'm Mr. Johnson. I'm here to look at interesting things happening in your classroom." Students will attend to you for a short time, but you will quickly begin to fade from their consciousness.

3. *Begin taking notes without looking directly at students.* A person writing with his or her head down is much less distracting or imposing than a person staring and recording. Also, it is not always important that you see to know what is going on. It is possible to observe by listening and still get a good sense of a classroom setup, feelings, general impressions, and emotional tone. You can also record interesting or important dialogue by the teacher or students simply by listening.

4. *Smile.* A person smiling is much less threatening.

5. *Do not think—write.* Start by recording the time in the margin of your notes and then simply describe what you see happening. Whenever a new event or circumstance appears, record the time to provide a sense of chronology. Then write quickly without thinking. Working memory has a limited capacity, and it is difficult to perceive, record, process, and analyze information simultaneously. Writing quickly without thinking or analyzing frees up space in working memory and enables you to perceive more things.

Quick Notes During.   Whereas it is difficult to record thick descriptions while you are teaching, it is possible to make quick notes to hold your ideas. Three tips for you to use are described:

1. *Keep a file in your desk drawer for every student with his or her name on it.* If something interesting occurs related to a particular student, make a quick note on the nearest scrap of paper, record the date, and put it in that student's file. Along with observations and field notes, these files can be used to collect representative samples of students' work, checklists, and test scores. The student file is a good data-collecting technique for action research, and at the same time it helps you become a more knowledgeable teacher when assessing growth, planning instruction, or speaking with parents about their children's progress.

2. *Keep a file related to the research project.* Whenever an idea, observation, or insight occurs to you during the day related to your research, make a quick note to yourself, record the date, and put it in your research file.

3. *Take notes on the margins or back of your lesson plans.* Often I am hit with a unique insight in the middle of a lesson. I find it most effective to make little notes to myself in the margin of my lesson plan. I use just enough words to hold the idea, then revisit it after class or after school when I am ready to record and write more fully. The more you do this, the better you will become at finding your original thoughts with single-word clues.

Notes and Reflections After.   Like many teachers, I prefer to record my observations after the lesson or at the end of the day. I am more relaxed, I am not rushed for time, and I find that I am able to think and remember much more clearly. There are three ways you might do this:

1. *After each lesson, make a quick note to yourself in your research journal.*   In my college classroom, I go back to my office after a class, shut the door, and scribble a few quick notes in my journal. When I have more time, I use these jottings to make more extensive field notes.

2. *Record your insights and observations at the end of the day.*   It requires a certain amount of discipline to ensure that you do this on a regular basis. Set aside 10 minutes every day and make that time sacred.

3. *Reflect on the back of your lesson plans.*   This becomes a good source of data telling you what was taught, when you taught it, how it was taught, how it went, and insights for change.

Checklists

Checklists come in many forms. A checklist is a list that specifies certain attributes, such as behaviors, traits, assignments, or skills. When that attribute is seen, some method is used to either check it off or indicate the number of times it was present.

Student Checklists.   Student checklists are created by the teacher and filled in by the students. Ping Hew was using action research to study writing workshops in her fifth grade class. As part of this, all students had portfolios they were required to maintain that included, among other things, the weekly checklist in Figure 8.2. Each day of the workshop, students used tally marks to indicate the activities they participated in that day. The bottom three boxes are open ended, allowing for a variety of responses related to topics, skills, and questions. As the quarter progressed, these checklists gave Ping a good sense of where her students were spending the majority of their time, of their writing topics, of the skills learned, and of the skills that needed to be taught.

Teacher Checklists.   Checklists can also be designed for use by teachers to indicate exactly what skills have been introduced or mastered and when. Checklists like these are also helpful in guiding instruction and providing evidence that skills have been covered. Figure 8.3 contains a teacher checklist for writing skills. One checklist for each student is kept in a three-ring binder. The skills necessary for successful second and third grade writers are listed in

Weekly Checklist for September 2006

At the end of each class, put a tally mark beside any activities done in that session.

Generating/prewriting	
Drafting	
Revising	
Editing	
Conferencing/talking	
Reading	
Other	

Writing topics:

Special skills learned or used:

Things I have questions about:

FIGURE 8.2   Student Checklist for Skills and Activities

the first column. During writing time or in individual writing conferences, it is a simple matter to take out this checklist and make a quick assessment.

An important note when using a teacher checklist: Do not try to cover all attributes during a single session; rather, look for a few attributes during each observation. One observation tells you little; however, many short observations over time tell you much. Plan on using one checklist each quarter.

Open-Ended Checklists.   An open-ended checklist contains a list of skills with enough space for students to describe their ability, understanding, or usage of each skill (see Figure 8.4). This provides you with an accurate indicator of students' levels of understanding and also enables you to plan instruction to meet specific needs.

Conferences and Interviews

There is an important difference between conferences and interviews. In a conference one or more students talk about their work or some aspect of classroom

Writing Checklist for Second- and Third-Grade Students

Student: _____

Describe the student's progress using the following key: 3 = very much, 2 = some, 1 = very little, 0 = not at all.

Attributes	Dates					
1. Uses invented spelling to hold ideas						
2. Can spell most words on the 100 MFW list						
3. Uses capital letters for beginning of sentences						
4. Uses periods and question marks						
5. Displays a willing attitude toward writing activities						
6. Is able to write attentively for about 15–20 minutes						
7. Is able to brainstorm ideas for writing						
8. Knows what nouns, verbs, and adjectives are						
9. Has ideas to share						
10. Is able to organize ideas						
11. Is able to talk about his or her writing						
12. Is able to write an acceptable rough (first) draft						
13. Is able to edit or revise the rough draft effectively						
14. Uses complete sentences						

Words per fifty (WPF) spelling scores:

Observations or comments:

FIGURE 8.3   Teacher Checklist for Writing

functioning. Prompts may be used to get students talking about a particular topic; however, lists of planned questions are not used. Conferences can be conducted individually or in small groups (focus groups). In an interview students respond to planned questions, which are best conducted on an individual basis.

Individual Student Conferences. Students should always do the majority of talking and lead the conversation in a conference. The exchange is open ended, and teacher questions are used simply as prompts to get students talking. Conferences can last anywhere from 2 to 15 minutes. Figure 8.5 contains a list of possible conference questions that can be used as prompts.

When conferencing with a student, take notes but do not try to get a verbatim transcript of the conference. Instead, record only the items you think are important, such as strengths, weaknesses, general impressions, skills learned, progress,

Writing Skills

Skill	Explanation of How You Use Each Skill
Capitalization of names	
There versus their	
Adjectives	
Writing dialogue	
Paragraphs	
Commas	

FIGURE 8.4   Open-Ended Checklist

insights, or what the student is currently working on. You may want to design some kind of a checklist to use for taking notes during conferences. Again, this is a matter of personal preference. It is normal to feel a little unsure of this process at first; however, after you have done it a few times you will get a good sense of what to record and how to best record it.

As a teaching tool, individual conferences are also an effective way to touch base with each student in a personal way. For example, in Jason Hinkle's ninth grade biology class, his students are assigned conference times to talk about their projects, which include a series of experiments and lab reports. Knowing they are going to meet with him, students are able to prepare and make sure they have something to say. In these short conferences, Jason listens, takes notes, asks questions, gives responses, encourages, and makes one or two suggestions for improving their experiments or lab reports. He schedules no more than three to five conferences in any day because conferences can be wearing. This allows him to see each student every 2 weeks.

A checklist can be used to keep track of students and conference times (see Figure 8.6). Conferences such as these can be used across the curriculum as you

How's it going?
What are you working on?
Tell me about that.
What is something that you seem to do well?
What might be something that gives you problems? (Tell me about that.)
Read part of your story.
Do a long division problem, and talk out loud as you are doing it.
Tell me what you do when you work in a cooperative group.
What skills have you learned?
What part of science is most interesting to you?
What is something interesting or important that you have learned in our social studies class?

FIGURE 8.5   Questions and Prompts for Student Conferences

Checklist for Individual Student Conference Dates

Billy A.	8/23	9/13	10/4				
Sally B.	8/23	9/13	10/4				
Amy C.	8/23	9/13	10/4				
Molly D.	8/24	9/14	10/11				
Michael E.	8/24	9/14	10/11				
Thomas F.	8/24	9/14	10/11				

FIGURE 8.6   Checklist of Individual Conferences

work on teaching specific skills. They can also be used as a means of checking in and staying in touch with your students. Finally, conferences might also be used to address social issues or interpersonal issues within your classroom. You are limited only by your imagination.

Small-Group Conferences.   In a small-group conference (sometimes known as focus groups) you meet with three to eight students at one time. This is an effective data-collecting method that allows you to see a number of students fairly quickly and watch them interacting with each other. It is also a valuable teaching tool because students are able to hear and respond to the thoughts of other students. As in the individual conference, the teacher should talk as little as possible.

Small-group conferences can be adapted for use in a variety of situations. For example, it may be used to discuss subjects such as good books, current or historical events, research projects, writing projects, moral dilemmas, math skills, problem-solving skills, textbook reading assignments, homework problems, and personal issues. You cannot, however, assume that students instinctively know how to function in small groups. Thus, structure must be provided so that they know how to speak and respond to each other (see Figure 8.7). It is common to spend a few class sessions teaching students how to interact in small groups and to use students to help model the process. Each group can use a checklist to report its progress. This helps the group focus on the key elements of successful group behavior and provides you with another form of data (see Figure 8.8).

Before
1. Be prepared.
2. Bring all materials with you.

Speaking
1. Only one person talks at a time.
2. Say what you have to say, then let others respond.
3. Do not dominate the conversation.
4. Listen.

Responding
1. Ask a question.
2. Find something you like.
3. Ask for clarification.
4. Find something it reminds you of.
5. Offer suggestions or ways to do it differently.
6. Do not make put-downs or personal remarks.

FIGURE 8.7   Rules for Small-Group Conferences

Group:_____   Date:_____

	yes	no	some
1. The group stayed on task.			
2. Everyone responded or asked a question.			
3. The group used time wisely.			
4. Everyone was prepared for the conference.			

Interesting or Important Ideas
1.
2.
3.

FIGURE 8.8   Checklist for Small-Group Conferences

Interviews.   An interview differs from a conference in that an interview consists of a specific set of questions prepared in advance and is teacher directed. The questions should be asked in the same order each time to maintain consistency. Figure 8.9 demonstrates a hierarchy of questions, going from lower-order closed-response questions to higher-order open-ended questions. Make sure to include both types in your interview.

A common mistake most beginning interviewers make is having too many questions. Keep your interviews short (you can always ask follow-up questions). End each interview with an open-ended question, such as, Is there anything else that you want to say about . . . ? Finally, do not try to take detailed field notes during the interview; rather, write down only a few interesting ideas or impressions. Keep your focus on the responses and follow-up questions. Use an audiotape to record the interview (videotape is too obtrusive), then go back and take detailed notes.

Video- and Audiotapes

Videotapes provide you with information related to students' nonverbal behaviors, their location or movement throughout a lesson, and a general overview of your performance or pedagogical techniques. However, as stated in an earlier chapter, a video camera is an obtrusive instrument, and thus it creates a nonreal

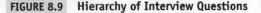

1. Which would you rather read? (a) fiction, (b) science fiction,   closed-response
   (c) nonfiction, (d) historical fiction, or (e) mysteries
2. What is your favorite reading genre?
3. Name a very good book or your favorite book.
4. Tell me what you like to read.
5. Tell me about your reading.   open-ended

FIGURE 8.9   Hierarchy of Interview Questions

Allow others into the conversation.	
Affirm and encourage others.	
Find areas of agreement and disagreement.	
Ask questions.	
Seek clarification.	

FIGURE 8.10   DRC for Analyzing Positive Discussion Elements

teaching environment. One way to diminish this effect is by videotaping a great deal so that students get used to the camera. Another way is to use audiotapes. Audiotapes are quicker, easier, less intrusive, more natural, and easy to listen to in a car or with a small handheld unit. Although you might miss nonverbal behaviors and movement, you will find that you get just as much important information with an audiotape.

Data Retrieval Charts

Data retrieval charts (DRCs) are visual organizers that are used to help you (or your students) collect and organize information. These come in a variety of forms. Bob Larson was teaching his sixth grade students the positive discussion elements (PDEs) as part of his social studies class (Johnson, 2006). He gave students a question related to an important current event topic and then put them in groups of five to discuss this topic. Each day he chose one group to observe during that day's discussion. The DRC in Figure 8.10 was used to record the number and types of PDEs that occurred. This DRC provided data that could then be quantified and compared across grade level or over time. Gender differences can easily be compared by including an extra column (Figure 8.11).

	Male	Female
Allow others into the conversation.		
Affirm and encourage others.		
Find areas of agreement and disagreement.		
Ask questions.		
Seek clarification.		

FIGURE 8.11   DRC for Analyzing Positive Discussion Elements Sorted by Gender

Science Skills

Key: 4 = outstanding, 3 = very good, 2 = average, 1 = low

STUDENT	SKILL	TEACHER
	Observe and describe	
	Create a graph	
	Weighing	
	Predicting	
	Organize data—create groups	
	Conclude	
	Use a lab report	

Student: _____

Teacher: _____

Grade: _____

Comments:

FIGURE 8.12   Rating Checklist for Science Skills

Rating Checklist

A rating checklist specifies traits you are looking for in a product or performance and allows the observer to assign levels of performance to each trait. This is similar to a rubric; however, whereas a rubric uses a sentence or more to provide a description of each level, a rating checklist uses one-word indicators (see Figure 8.12). I find rating checklists to be a more pragmatic method to use for collecting data for action research and for use in classroom assessment. The rating checklist in Figure 8.12 was used at the end of a science unit. Students evaluated their own level of performance on one side, and the teacher evaluated their performance on the other.

Students' Products or Performances

Samples of students' work can be used as data sources. Remember that you do not need to collect every bit of students' work; rather, take only representative samples at different time periods to give you a feel for students' performances and their changes over time. It is often helpful to create a flexible schedule to determine when you will collect students' work before you begin.

Product and Performance.   Figure 8.13 shows a product and performance assessment form (PPAF). This rating checklist can be used to analyze and evaluate any type of product or performance, such as science projects, inventions, dramas,

Product and Performance Assessment Form

Student:_____   Age:_____

Grade:_____   Type of Product or Performance: _____

Key: 5 = very high, 4 = high, 3 = average, 2 = low, 1 = very low

When compared to other students of a similar age, rate the product or performance on the following criteria:

1. Creativity _____

2. Integration of ideas _____

3. Technical merit _____

4. Sophistication and level of detail _____

5. Aesthetics: artistic expression, emotion, feeling _____

6. Overall effect _____

Comments:

FIGURE 8.13   Product and Performance Assessment Form

dances, or experiments. Incidentally, all forms described in this chapter can be used by both students and teachers. Just like teachers (Watts & Johnson, 1995), students who analyze and assess their own work become more critical and skillful practitioners.

Writing Samples.   Figure 8.14 contains a rating checklist that can be used to analyze and evaluate any type of writing. This is also a good teaching tool in that it forces you to define exactly what is expected and it puts the onus on you to teach

Writing Assessment Form

Writing prompt:

Key: 5 = very high, 4 = high, 3 = average, 2 = low, 1 = very low

content, ideas _____	mechanics: spelling, grammar, punctuation _____	met deadlines; fulfilled assignment requirements _____
organization, structure _____	fluency, communication _____	appearance _____

Ideas or insights:

Skills to work on:

FIGURE 8.14   Writing Assessment Form

Checklist for Independent Research Projects

Key: 3 = trait is present to a high degree, 2 = trait is present,
1 = trait is present to a low degree, 0 = trait is not present

___ A question was asked, a problem was identified, or an area of exploration was defined.

___ Data collection was systematic.

___ Data was analyzed in a way that made it credible and trustworthy.

___ The results were described clearly and accurately.

___ Recommendations or conclusions were made based on the results.

___ The research project was linked to a theoretical context.

___ The research was communicated in a way that was understandable.

___ Met all deadlines and requirements.

Focus of the action research:

Major results and conclusions:

FIGURE 8.15   Checklist for Independent Research

each skill associated with those expectations. Students appreciate knowing the requirements and getting the precise feedback that this form provides.

Independent Research Projects.   Figure 8.15 shows a rating checklist used for students' independent research projects. Notice that all the elements of action research are found on this checklist. Understanding action research will enable you to incorporate more effectively methods of science, inquiry, and research into your own teaching, and also provide you with a variety of ideas to use in getting students to create their own independent research projects.

Scores and Other Quantifiable Data.   Students' scores on tests, homework, quizzes, grades, and standardized assessment measures can also be used as a data source. However, they should never be used as the only source of data.

Surveys

Surveys allow you to get a variety of information quickly. They can be designed using both closed-response or open-ended questions.

Closed-Response Questions.   A closed-response question provides a number of choices for respondents to select. An example follows:

What is your favorite reading genre? (a) history (b) comedy (c) science fiction (d) mystery

The advantage of this type of question is that you can ask a number of questions and get quantifiable data on many types of issues. For example, after surveying a group of students with the previous question, one could safely report that 84.4% of students surveyed preferred comedy as a reading genre. The problem with these kinds of questions is that they can be inaccurate, misleading, or controlling. What if the first reading choice of a respondent was not even listed in the question? Or what if a respondent liked to read three or four different kinds of books equally well?

Open-Ended Questions.   An open-ended question allows respondents unlimited choices. An example follows:

> What kinds of books do you like to read?

These questions provide a more accurate sense of what respondents are actually thinking. Some respondents may report four or five different kinds of books, whereas others may report only one. The researcher would then create categories out of all the books listed and report the number of books in each category (see inductive analysis in Chapter 9). This data might be reported as in the following:

> Forty-five students provided 152 responses to the survey question. The greatest number of responses (49%) indicated realistic fiction as the preferred genre.

Problems with open-ended survey questions are that they are somewhat messy in terms of analysis, and you can generally ask fewer of them.

Tips for Preparing Surveys.   The following tips will help you in preparing surveys:

   1. *Do not use too many questions or questions that are not necessary.* I have found that using four to eight questions is most effective. Too many questions frustrate respondents. A frustrated respondent will not complete the survey or will not give you accurate information. Err on the side of using too few rather than too many questions.

   2. *Make your questions short, concise, and reader friendly.* If a reader has to work to figure out exactly what you are asking, chances are that the question will not be read, or if it is, it will be misunderstood.

   3. *Proofread your questions several times.* Make sure the questions say exactly what you intend.

   4. *Be very clear with your questions.* Always assume the reader knows nothing.

   5. *Do not use leading questions.* A good survey is completely objective. Respondents should not know your position on any of the issues asked about.

   6. *Always include at least one open-ended question.* If you are using closed-response questions, provide an opportunity for respondents to make comments at the end.

   7. *Create a neat, professional-looking document.* The presentation should be attractive, well organized, and easy to read.

Attitude and Rating Scales

Attitude and rating scales provide respondents with a question or statement for which they are asked to select one of several answers that determine the strength of their response.

Attitude Scales.   Students' attitudes are assessed by asking them to respond to a series of statements in a way that indicates their level of agreement or disagreement. Attitude scales like this can quickly provide you with information about students' attitudes and yield quantitative data that can be used to make comparisons. A 5-point rating scale is usually most effective for students in grades 3 and above.

> **Key:** SA = strongly agree, A = agree, NO = no opinion,
>   D = disagree, SD = strongly disagree
>
> **1.** Reading is fun. SA . . . A . . . NO . . . D . . . SD

These responses can also be numbered to provide you with quantitative data.

> **Key:** 5 = strongly agree, 4 = agree, 3 = no opinion,
>   2 = disagree, 1 = strongly disagree
>
> **1.** Reading is fun.   5 . . . 4 . . . 3 . . . 2 . . . 1
> **2.** I know how to use science skills. 5 . . . 4 . . . 3 . . . 2 . . . 1

With younger students, provide fewer choices and use graphics.

> **1.** I like to read: very much ☺,   some 😐,   little ☹

Rating Scales.   A rating scale is used to determine the strength of a response. These are often used to determine how much, how often, or how many times something occurs.

> **Key:** 4 = often, 3 = some, 2 = little, 1 = not at all
> **1.** I read at home each day.   4 . . . 3 . . . 2 . . . 1
> **2.** I watch TV at home each day.   4 . . . 3 . . . 2 . . . 1
> **3.** I complete my homework at school.   4 . . . 3 . . . 2 . . . 1
> **4.** I use some sort of prewriting strategy. 4 . . . 3 . . . 2 . . . 1

The Arts

The arts are another way of seeing the world and can be used to bring a different level of understanding to your action research. Elliot Eisner (1998) suggests that literature and poetry be used as a research device to capture and illuminate some portion of reality. Artists and researchers are very much alike in that the work of both are like lenses through which reality is interpreted and translated.

Certain kinds of art lend themselves naturally to action research. These are (1) two-dimensional visual art, such as sketches, collage, paintings, drawings, and photography and (2) the language arts, such as poetry, creative writing, short story, drama, and written dialogue. You might also include students' use of these media along with your analysis. I would encourage you to experiment with the arts as one of your data sources. Your credibility will not be diminished if you collect multiple forms of data and if you include an analysis of your artistic data.

Archival Data

Archival data include past grades, test scores, cumulative folders, health records, parental occupation, or attendance records. Make sure you follow your school procedures for obtaining access to this data, and that they are used and reported in an ethical manner.

Websites, Class Journals, or E-Mail

Websites.   Websites can be used to create a living, dynamic classroom entity. Students can log on to a specific site and read and respond to what others have said on a given topic. The transaction can be printed for use as a data source. I often use our university website to create discussion groups of four students. The comments in these groups becomes a good data source.

Class Journals.   The class journal is a nontechnical version of the website. Simply provide a blank notebook that is passed around the class or put in a learning center for several weeks. Students then enter their thoughts, ideas, impressions, or any other forms of response such as pictures or diagrams. You may need to provide some guidelines and check in quite often so that this does not turn into a form of graffiti that might be highly offensive to some. The website and class journal are effective methods to use in getting to the underbelly of classroom discourse.

E-Mail.   E-mail is a quick, easy, and private form of communication between a student and teacher. In my courses, I usually assign students a certain number of e-mail messages to write to me during the semester. These messages allow me access to students' thinking and provide valuable insight in the planning of my classes. In action research, students could e-mail you on a variety of topics.

SUMMARY

- Data are any form of information, observations, or facts that are collected or recorded.
- A flexible plan for collecting data should be in place before you begin collecting them.
- The data collected in action research should be varied and collected in different ways over time.
- There are a wide variety of data that could be collected; however, selecting only two to four kinds will keep your action research focused.

QUESTIONS AND ACTIVITIES

1. Go to an interesting place. Practice taking field notes by recording what you see. Plan on spending at least 30 minutes at this place on two or more occasions.
2. Pick an assignment or project that you have your students do or that you plan to do with them. Create a checklist that has the specific skills or attributes necessary to complete the assignment.
3. Create a short open-ended checklist for students and experiment by using it with one class or subject area.
4. Think of an area or topic you are interested in. Create an interview with four to eight questions. Interview one or more students or adults using follow-up questions you feel are appropriate. Tape-record your interview.
5. Use an audiotape to record one of your classes. What did you discover? Based on this tape, create a DRC to indicate the number and type of some observation. For example, the level of questions, the gender of those who were asked or who responded to the questions, the number of times you said the word *um*, or the number of positive statements.
6. What are five characteristics or qualities of a good movie? Use these to create a ratings checklist. Evaluate two to four recent movies. You may want to do this in small groups. This can be extended to TV shows, dramas, or any other performance.
7. Create a rating checklist for a student product or performance that you plan to have your students do.
8. Create a survey related to any topic that interests you. Experiment with different types of questions and have at least five people respond to it. If you are reading this book as part of a class, you may want to bring your survey to class and practice with your classmates by responding to each other's surveys.
9. Go to an interesting place. Describe that place using visual art or a form of language art.

POSSIBLE RESEARCH QUESTIONS FOR ACTION RESEARCH PROJECTS

1. How are your lessons going? What things seem to be working? What things could be done more effectively?
2. As a teacher, what things do you need to focus on or pay more attention to?
3. As a human being, what things do you need to focus on or pay more attention to?
4. What takes place during small-group discussions?
5. What social skills do students in your room seem to lack?
6. What are the social expectations of children in your classroom? How are children coping? What are the common traits among those who seem to be having trouble in this area?

7. What does it feel like to have a learning disability? What things make learning more difficult? What things help learning with this group? What do students with learning disabilities wish teachers would understand?
8. What makes school difficult for students with emotional/behavioral disorders?
9. How do students in your classroom define themselves?
10. What types of misconduct occurs most often on the playground? In the cafeteria? In the hallway? In your classroom?
11. What common traits do you see among the highly creative students in your classroom? What would make school more interesting for this group? What would they like included in their learning experience? What types of projects or performances would they like to engage in?
12. How do students' concepts of themselves change across grade levels or across ability levels?
13. Whom do you see as the unpopular children? Why do they seem to be having trouble with peer relationships?
14. Given moral dilemmas or problems involving values, how do students in your class tend to solve them? How do they decide what is right and wrong?
15. What do students perceive as the qualities of an effective teacher? What do teachers believe to be the qualities of effective teachers? What do administrators believe to be qualities of effective teachers? What do parents believe to be qualities of effective teachers?
16. What life issues are of most concern to students in your classroom? What school issues are of most concern to students in your classroom?
17. What type of school experiences do the parents in your school desire?

CHAPTER NINE

METHODS OF ANALYZING DATA

This chapter describes data analysis. Analysis means to break something down into its component parts so that it can be understood. In action research, data are analyzed and organized into categories so that others might come to understand the reality you are trying to represent. Three elements related to data analysis are presented in this chapter: (1) accuracy and credibility; (2) validity, reliability, and triangulation; and (3) inductive analysis.

ACCURACY AND CREDIBILITY: THIS IS WHAT IS

The ultimate goal of action research is to use your findings to make effective changes or choices. To this end, the collection and analysis of data must be accurate and credible. Accuracy in action research means that the data you are collecting create a fairly true picture of the bit of reality you are observing. This helps you make decisions that are best for your particular situation. Credibility in action research means trustworthy or capable of being believed. This enables you and others to use your data with confidence. The following seven tips will help you establish more accuracy and credibility as you collect and analyze your data.

1. *Record your observations carefully and precisely.* Always double-check to make sure you are recording exactly what you are seeing.

2. *Describe all phases of data collection and analysis.* In your recording, recount all the steps used in collecting and analyzing the data. In your eventual reporting you want to create a level of clarity whereby another person could duplicate your steps.

3. *Make sure you record and report everything that is of importance.* Record and report fully; do not omit data that may be counter to what you believe. The goal is to understand fully all aspects of what you are observing.

4. *Be as objective as possible in describing and interpreting what you see.* Pronounced biases and hidden agendas are fairly easy to spot and prevent you from seeing all

aspects of what you are trying to study. They also make your action research less accurate and credible.

5. *Use enough data sources.* (See discussion of triangulation in the next section.) Your observations and analysis will be much more accurate and credible if you are able to find similar patterns using two or more forms of data. For a short observation (2 to 4 weeks), I usually ask my students to use a minimum of two sources. For longer action research projects, the number of sources is dictated by the question and the kinds of data you are trying to collect.

6. *Use the right kinds of data sources.* (See the discussion of validity in the next section.) The type of data you choose to collect should provide as accurate an understanding of your research topic as possible. For example, if I were interested in understanding how middle school students use humor, I might interview classroom teachers. Although this could provide some interesting information, the data would be a poor reflection of the reality I was trying to observe. A much more accurate and credible view would be obtained by using audiotapes of actual conversations, by observing middle school students and taking descriptive field notes, and by creating a survey form in which students self-report to indicate the kinds of humor used and the instances in which it was used.

7. *Look long enough and deep enough.* A 3-week observation might provide some interesting data; however, a 3-month observation would make your data even more accurate and credible. Longer observations provide more chances to see and confirm patterns than do shorter observations. Again, the length of your observation and data collection is dictated solely by your question. The final criterion should always be the degree to which you have created an accurate picture of what was studied.

VALIDITY, RELIABILITY, AND TRIANGULATION

Three essential parts of establishing accuracy and credibility in any research project are validity, reliability, and triangulation. In action research, they take on a different form than they do in traditional experimental research.

Validity

How do we know your data actually assess and describe what they say they do? Validity is the degree to which a thing measures what it reports to measure. For example, in trying to assess the writing ability of elementary students, I could give them a standardized test of grammar and punctuation in which they would read a series of questions and choose one of four responses. This would produce some fairly accurate results that could be quantified and used to make comparisons; however, this type of measure does not look at writing in an authentic context, and thus it is not a very valid measure of students' ability to organize

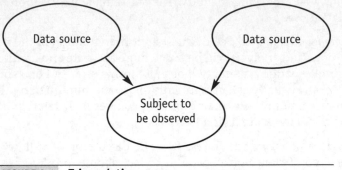

FIGURE 9.1   Triangulation

and communicate their ideas using writing. A more valid assessment would be to look at students' actual writing samples and use the writing assessment form described in Chapter 8 to rate specific elements.

Triangulation

Triangulation means looking at something from more than one perspective. Think of a triangle with the subject to be observed as one point and the various data sources as the other two points (see Figure 9.1). Triangulation ensures that you are seeing all sides of a situation. It also provides greater depth and dimension, thereby enhancing your accuracy and credibility. In action research, triangulation is achieved by collecting different types of data, using different data sources, collecting data at different times, and by having other people review your data to check for accuracy and adjust your findings.

Reliability

Reliability is the degree to which a study or experiment can be repeated with similar results. Unlike action research, traditional experimental research strives to create a hermetically sealed world with all the variables controlled so that X can be said to cause Y beyond all doubt. If the experiment is reliable, X should cause Y each time it is repeated. If this is indeed the case, the experiment is deemed reliable, the results are generalized to similar situations, and the researcher is granted tenure at a major university.

Action researchers, however, observe messy, real-world events in which humans are mucking about. These humans are inherently and wondrously unpredictable and not at all inclined to exist in hermetically sealed worlds. Thus, each time we search and research we expect to see different things. The closest we come to repetition is in noticing recurring items, themes, or patterns that emerge from our data. (See the discussion of inductive analysis that follows.) Therefore, action research findings are not generalized broadly; instead, they are used to help understand particular situations as well as inform similar situations.

INDUCTIVE ANALYSIS

Inductive analysis means to look at a field or group of data and try to induce or create order by organizing what is observed into groups. This should occur as you begin to collect data. Look for recurring items, themes, or patterns to emerge. Similar things should be coded and moved into initial categories. These categories, however, should be very flexible as later data may change their nature and composition. It is helpful to begin this process while you are collecting data because the categories that form initially inform further data collection.

Larry, Moe, and Curly Help with Inductive Analysis

Let me use the Three Stooges to illustrate inductive analysis. I watched a Three Stooges video to understand the Stooges and their humor. My initial questions were, What kind of humor is found? What do these episodes comprise? Who are the Stooges? Note how these questions help inform and provide focus for my search.

I watched a 15-minute episode on videotape called *Grips, Grunts, and Groans* (Columbia Pictures, 1937) and began to look for instances of humor. The events in a Three Stooges episode happen much faster than in real life; thus, I used the pause button often to suspend video reality to make notes. As I watched, I used field notes to record those funny things I saw. *Funny things* (humor), in this instance, was defined as those elements inserted into the movie for the express purpose of creating a comedic effect. As I watched, my notes began to look like the following:

> Bump, stumble, kick, punch, slap, poke, twist ear, word play silly, absurd silly, word play silly, absurd silly, etc.

After the first time through the video, I saw that the types of humor recorded in my notes could be put into four categories.

Thing-to-Head Violence.   This violence represents instances in which a nonhuman thing hit or was dropped on somebody's head. For example, Larry hits Moe on the head with a board, or an anvil falls on Curly's head.

Human-to-Human Violence.   A part of somebody's body was struck, twisted, or otherwise violently engaged by a part of somebody else's physical being. This violence included instances of eye poking, ear twisting, kicks, chokes, punches, pushes, slaps, or general violence such as twisting one's foot.

Self-Mishap.   These are instances in which characters cause their own mishap, including stumbles, bumps, and falling episodes.

Silly Stuff.   Silly stuff represents items, events, phrases, or actions that are incongruous, apart from what is normally expected, or an exaggeration of normality. An example of situational silliness would be the Stooges accidentally pulling off the pants of a drunk wrestler while trying to drag him, revealing funny, long

SILLY STUFF		HUMAN-TO-HUMAN VIOLENCE		THING-TO-HEAD VIOLENCE		SELF-MISHAP	
Situational silliness	26	General hurt	5	Things dropped on head	12	Bump or stumble	9
Verbal silliness	7	Slap	5	Things hit on head	11		
		Kick	4				
		Twist ear	2				
		Poke eye	2				
		Punch	2				
		Choke	1				
		Push	1				
Total	33	Total	22	Total	23	Total	9

FIGURE 9.2   Three Stooges Humor

underwear with garters. An example of verbal silliness would be what is said after a man throws water on the Stooges, who were just knocked unconscious by blows to the head. Curly yells out, "Man the lifeboats." Moe says, "Women and children first." The implication is that the Stooges acted as if they were on a boat that was sinking.

Each category contained different types of humor. Once I had my initial categories and subcategories, I created a version of an open-ended checklist (see Figure 9.2). I then viewed the episode a second time and put a tally mark next to each type of humor every time I observed it. I was thus able to break down the humor into its component parts and get a good sense of what the total episode comprised. It looks as if, more than anything, the Three Stooges material was violent. Forty-three instances of humor were violence inflicted on another person (human-to-human and thing-to-head violence); however, silliness was the largest single category of humor. In this episode, the Stooges were sillier than I had imagined they would be; however, the amount of violence stands out to the viewer watching in the twenty-first century. To add credibility to my observation and analysis, I viewed this particular video several times. I also had somebody else view it to see whether they came up with similar categories and numbers.

This inductive analysis gave me a good understanding of this single episode of the Stooges and their humor. To extend this study, I would need to observe several Stooges episodes and use the same categories to collect and organize data. These data would then be put in the form of a bar graph for easy consumption by the reader. This would also allow me to compare various

Stooges episodes or to compare the Stooges to other comedians of that era or today. I might also choose to investigate further to see whether early Stooges and late Stooges differ. I might want to pursue other questions: Did the type of humor change over time? Did the Stooges get more violent over time? Did they get sillier over time? Do HPM (humor-per-minute) ratios of the Stooges differ in various eras? Do males react differently than females to Stooges humor? You may notice that a good study usually creates as many questions as answers.

Case Studies or Representative Samples

In my report I will use representative samples to bring further understanding to the Stooges reality that I observed. I will include a few examples of the funny things in each category so that the reader fully understands what that category entails. Including representative samples also allows the reader to go beyond the numbers, to make the research come alive.

Verbal Silliness

The scene opens with two railway security guards walking, clubs in hand, by a train car marked *horses*. One foreman taps on the door and says, "Anybody in there?" Curly's high, whining voice is heard, "Nobody here but us horses." The two guards, having gotten an answer to their question, begin walking away. After two steps, they realize the incongruity, stop, do a double take, and wait for the door to open.

Verbal Silliness

A gangster has made a big bet on Gustov, a professional wrestler. The Stooges have been paid by the gangster to keep him from getting drunk for that evening's match. Gustov is about to drink a large container of something when Moe says, "Listen, Gustov, you can't drink that. That's alcohol." Gustov snorts and says, "That's not alcohol. That's just a little tequila, vodka, and cognac." Curly says, "Oh, that's different. Go ahead." Gustov pours the jug down his throat. The bit of incongruity is that although tequila, vodka, and cognac are not referred to as alcohol, they all contain it.

Situational Silliness

Curly goes mad every time he smells wild hyacinth. In a restaurant, a woman accidentally pours some on him. Curly begins making high-pitched "woo, woo, woo" sounds. He slaps his forehead repeatedly, barks, and makes wild twisting, dancing motions with his legs. He goes crazy, trips over a table, and starts breaking a chair, then yells, "Moe, Larry, tickle my foot!" Larry and Moe tackle him, twist his legs, yank off his shoes, and begin tickling his feet. There is much flopping around and manic laughing by Curly and he eventually comes to his senses.

Self-Mishap

Running from the two railway guards, the Stooges round a corner. Two women are standing next to a baby carriage. In unison, the Stooges trip over the baby carriage and fall face first on the sidewalk.

Human-to-Human Violence

Moe tells Curly to put up his hands. He then hits him in the stomach. When Curly makes a sound in protest, Moe uses his fist to pound him on top of the head, twists and slaps his nose, and slaps his forehead. Curly yells in a loud, high voice, "Ow, ow, ow . . . ohhhh!"

Thing-to-Head Violence

In the locker room before the big wrestling match, Larry, Moe, and Curly have finally succeeded in getting Gustov, the drunk professional wrestler, ready to go out and wrestle. They then accidentally knock him into a set of lockers. Five dumbbells that are on top of the lockers fall, one at a time, on Gustov's head.

Vision Quest

As another example of inductive analysis, I was interested in examining the idealized visions of the undergraduate students in my literacy methods course. That is, how did they see themselves teaching literacy when they got their own classroom teaching position? During student teaching I have often noticed a certain amount of stress when the idealized teaching visions of student teachers do not match their current teaching reality. For this action research project I was interested in seeing what the initial idealized vision was and how it changed throughout the semester as a result of my instruction and their field experiences.

Twenty-five students were in my undergraduate literacy methods course, 22 females and 3 males. Most of the students were in their early twenties; however, two females and one male were in their late thirties or early forties. To get at their idealized visions, I gave them the following writing prompt: "Imagine yourselves 5 years from now. You are in a regular classroom teaching some aspect of literacy. What do you see? What's going on? What does it look like?"

Students wrote one to two paragraphs on a sheet of paper. I collected them and analyzed these data, looking for patterns. This was repeated at 1-month intervals four times during the semester. I called this Vision Quest. The following are some examples of students' responses:

8/31/99

I see myself stressing meaning and feeling within the message and words of books. I will probably assign or suggest books with these characteristics—books that share good family ties, struggle, success, hard work, etc. [female]

In 5 years I see my students participating in short skits or role plays to share what a book was about or an individual chapter. The plays will be written and directed by the students themselves (with help as needed). [female]

In 5 years I see myself modeling quiet reading time for my students. I also see myself incorporating reading into other subject areas. I do not see myself doing comprehension sheets or book reports. [female]

I see myself teaching second grade. The students are seated on the floor next to me while I introduce our book. They listen to me read while they follow along in their book. Then they have the opportunity to explain the story in their own words, with a storyboard, or acting it out. Later, they will be able to write about the story, perhaps including themselves. They will be able to draw pictures. These will be displayed. [female]

As I read through students' descriptions, I looked for patterns, themes, or similar kinds of things. For instance, many students described aspects of creating a warm, inviting classroom environment. In my notes I jotted down *warm-fuzzy, environment, atmosphere* as an initial category. Every time I found something related to creating a warm, comfortable environment, I put a tally mark by this descriptor. I read all the selections and made adjustments to my initial categories. Figure 9.3 shows which categories and subcategories I used. I then went through the data a second time and once again put a tally mark every time an instance of an activity fell within that category. This twice-through approach allowed for more accuracy.

I. Warm Environment		**6**
II. Holistic/Nontraditional Activities		**16**
A. Reading choices	4	
B. Creative projects	3	
C. Student-centered activities	4	
D. Class library/books	2	
E. Independent reading	3	
III. Skills-Oriented/Traditional Activities		**23**
A. Vocabulary instruction	4	
B. Basals and worksheets	8	
C. Teacher-led discussion	3	
D. Round-robin reading	8	
IV. Teacher Reading to Class		**8**
V. Specific Pedagogical Methods		**2**

FIGURE 9.3   Vision Quest, First Month

Defining and Describing Categories

One cannot expect the reader to have complete understanding of my categories, so, as with the Three Stooges, I must define and describe each category. To demonstrate, I have included the following examples:

HOLISTIC OR NONTRADITIONAL

This category represents activities that might fit within a whole-language classroom, specifically, activities that would not reflect a basal or skills-based approach. The subcategories include the following:

Reading Choices

Students would be able to make choices about the kinds of books they want to read.

Creative Projects

Activities would include drama, role play, art, games, and puppets.

Student-Centered Activities

Students would be in charge of a process or a final product or performance. For example, students would write and direct their own plays, or students would be able to retell a story in their own words using a storyboard.

Class Library/Books

A prescribed place in the classroom with lots of books would be set aside as a reading area.

Independent Reading

Time would be scheduled for students to read books of their choice independently.

Following is an example of how I might put the data into categories:

I see myself sitting in a cozy chair with my students sitting on a large soft rug in front of me [*Warm Environment*]. In my hands I hold a brand-new book. I introduce the book to the children and I begin to read aloud [*Teacher Reading to Class*]. When I have finished reading, we discuss the book [*Teacher-Led Discussion*]. [female]

I see myself in 5 years with a large selection of books that I have read and am comfortable with [*Class Library/Books*]. Students choose their own books [*Reading Choices*]. I will allow ample class reading time [*Independent Reading*]. [female]

I see myself helping students learn new words by using overheads. As a class we would read the words together, then use them in sentences

[*Vocabulary Instruction*]. I just think it will be exciting to have them learn new words. [female]

I see myself reading to students every day [*Teacher Reading to Class*]. Students in my classroom will have free time to read every day [*Independent Reading*]. Perhaps there will be a special reading corner [*Warm Environment*]. I plan to use trade books in reading class and across the curriculum. I really like that idea. I would like to have a large library in my classroom [*Class Library/Books*]. [female]

I see myself setting up a small library in my classroom where children are able to read when they are done with their work [*Class Library/ Books*]. I would make my library full of color, pictures of books, and many comfortable chairs to create an inviting reading environment that would make children look forward to reading [*Warm Environment*]. [female]

The Next Month

The next month, the same categories were used. As you might expect, the change reflects my instruction, the literacy philosophy I was proposing, and students' interaction with these ideas (see Figure 9.4). In Chapter 18 you can see how this data was reported in graph form. One final thought: Methods used for inductive analysis vary and are a matter of personal preference. Although it might seem messy at first, you will get more comfortable with this process by doing it.

I. Warm Environment		**11**
II. Holistic/Nontraditional Activities		**64**
A. Reading choices	24	
B. Creative projects	12	
C. Student-centered activities	5	
D. Class library/books	5	
E. Independent reading	18	
III. Skills-Oriented/Traditional Activities		**9**
A. Vocabulary instruction	1	
B. Basals and worksheets	3	
C. Teacher-led discussion	5	
D. Round-robin reading	0	
IV. Teacher Reading to Class		**15**
V. Specific Pedagogical Methods		**17**

FIGURE 9.4   Vision Quest, Second Month

SUMMARY

- Analysis means to break down something into its component parts so that it can be understood.
- The collection and analysis of data must be accurate and credible to be of use in making effective changes or choices.
- Validity is the degree to which a thing measures what it reports to measure.
- Triangulation means collecting more than one form of data or looking at something from more than one perspective.
- Reliability is the degree to which a study or experiment can be repeated with similar results.
- Action researchers recognize that the universe they are observing is a messy, unreliable entity, and thus they look for repeating patterns and themes to help them understand it.
- Inductive analysis means to observe a field and create order by organizing items into groups or categories.
- In using inductive analysis, initial categories should be flexible as later data may change their nature and composition.

QUESTIONS AND ACTIVITIES

1. Cut out a newspaper article, a description of research, or a research article that you think lacks credibility. Tell why.
2. Find an interesting person or student to observe for a short time. Use two of the data sources described in Chapter 8 to create understanding.
3. Cut out an ad in a newspaper or magazine that you think lacks validity. Tell why.
4. Practice inductive analysis by randomly generating a list of 25 nouns. Then, in a small group or individually, put order to this field by moving them into groups or categories. Describe your field in terms of categories and numbers in each category.
5. Go to a place that is interesting and unique where you can observe people. Use field notes to record the behaviors you see. Then use inductive analysis to put order to your data. Report your data in terms of categories and numbers in each category.
6. Extend the previous activity by creating a checklist or data retrieval chart that uses the categories described. Go back to your interesting place at a different time of day. Use tally marks to record the instances of behaviors you observe. Add new categories if you need to. Create a graph to compare and report your observations and conclusions.
7. To extend the previous activity further, use the same checklist or data retrieval chart to observe a different but similar place. Create a bar graph to compare and report your observations and conclusions.

POSSIBLE RESEARCH QUESTIONS FOR ACTION RESEARCH PROJECTS

1. There are three types of learning: individualistic, competitive, or cooperative. How much of each occurs in your classroom in an average week? How could you create more cooperative learning tasks? How might this affect learning?
2. How do students view themselves? Ask students to provide written descriptions of themselves. Examine the adjectives used. Use inductive analysis to look for groups and quantify the numbers in each group. Look for differences between male and female, across ability levels, and across cultural and ethnic groups.
3. In what areas are students currently given choice and responsibility in your classroom? To what degree are these given? How would the learning environment differ if you provided more opportunities for choice and responsibility?
4. What would students like to learn about as part of a social studies curriculum? How would they like to learn?
5. What would students like to learn about as part of a science curriculum? How would they like to learn?
6. How can social studies be connected to students' lives outside of school? Does this affect the perception of social studies? Does it affect learning in any way?
7. What forums are presently available in your class for students to discuss or debate the issues of the day? To what degree are students allowed to come to their own conclusions? To what degree are they told what they must conclude?
8. How do students use the Internet?
9. Where do your students get their news about the world? To what degree to they read magazines, newspapers, watch television news, or get their news from the Internet?

CHAPTER TEN

QUANTITATIVE DESIGN IN ACTION RESEARCH

Quantitative research is based on the collection and analysis of numerical data. Earlier it was said that action research falls clearly in the realm of qualitative research because it does not manipulate the environment in order to isolate variables and prove cause-and-effect relationships. This chapter will backtrack a bit. There are three quantitative research designs that can fit within the action research paradigm: correlational research, causal–comparative research, and quasi-experimental research. This chapter discusses all three designs.

CORRELATIONAL RESEARCH

Correlational research seeks to determine whether and to what degree a statistical relationship exists between two or more variables (Gay & Airasian, 2003). It is used primarily to describe an existing condition or something that has happened in the past. This means that it examines a group of people and two or more things (variables) that have already happened to them in order to determine whether there is a relationship between these two things. For example, correlational research found a strong relationship between the amount of independent reading students do outside of school and their scores on standardized achievement tests (Allington, 2001). Those students who did a great deal of reading seemed to have high scores on standardized achievement tests. Thus, there was a fairly high co-relation, or *correlation*, between these two variables. When one score went up, the other also went up and when one score went down, the other also went down.

To determine this correlation, researchers examined the achievement test scores of a large number of students and then looked at the amount of time spent reading at home. Both of these variables (reading time and test scores) were things that had already occurred. There was no need to manipulate an environment to produce these.

Correlation Coefficient

The degree or strength of a particular correlation is measured by a *correlation coefficient*. A positive correlation means that when one variable increases, the other one also increases. A negative correlation means that when one variable increases, the other one decreases. A correlation coefficient of 1.00 would indicate a perfect one-to-one positive correlation. This rarely happens. A correlation coefficient of .0 means that there is absolutely no correlation between two variables. A correlation coefficient of −1.00 would indicate a perfect negative correlation. This also rarely happens.

Misusing Correlational Research

A word of warning here: Correlation does not indicate causation. Just because two variables are related, we cannot say that one causes the other. There may be other variables that have not been accounted for. In the previous example, we cannot say that lots of reading causes test scores to increase, although we may suspect as much. Likewise, we cannot say that standardized achievement tests cause an increase in reading. We can say, however, that the two seem to appear together. A true experiment would then be used to isolate variables with controlled populations. However, in this case a true experiment would be unethical because you cannot deny one group of students the pleasure and benefits of reading while encouraging another.

You can find many examples in the popular media of people (usually with a political agenda) who misuse correlational research by trying to attribute cause and effect. To illustrate this misuse, note that when the water temperature goes down, far fewer people drown. An increase in water temperature correlates fairly strongly with an increase in drowning. It would be spurious to try to say that water temperature causes drowning. A variable not accounted for here, but associated to both, is that when the water temperature gets cold, people are much less likely to be swimming. Also, when the water really gets cold, it turns to ice. It is very hard to drown on an ice-covered lake. (Another misuse of correlational research is described in the section on whole language in California.)

Negative Correlation

Sometimes an increase in one variable causes a decrease in another. This is an example of a negative correlation. An example of a negative correlation would be television watching and GPAs. As the amount of television watching goes up, students' GPAs go down. There is a negative correlation in that an increase in one seems to be related to a decrease in the other. Again, we cannot say that one causes the other; however, we can make predictions based on the strength of the correlation coefficient.

Making Predictions

Correlation coefficient is identified by the symbol r. When $r = 0$ to .35, the relationship between the two variables is nonexistent or low, and it is useless in making predictions. When $r = .35$ to .65, there is a slight relationship. This level is useful for limited predictions, usually with larger groups. When $r = .65$ to .85, there is a strong relationship. This would be useful for making predictions for large groups.

We could say with some certainty that an increase or decrease in one variable is related to an increase or decrease in the other. In the television example, if $r = -.75$, we could reasonably predict that an increase in television would lead to a decrease in GPA. If $r = -.40$, we would be less confident of a prediction. A correlation coefficient of $r = .86$ and above shows evidence of a very strong relationship. Again, keep in mind that correlational coefficient describes the strength and direction of a relationship, not cause and effect.

CAUSAL–COMPARATIVE RESEARCH

Causal–comparative research is used to find the reason for existing differences between two or more groups (Creswell, 2002). It is used when the random assignment of participants for groups necessary for the true experiment cannot be met, which is certainly the case in most classrooms. Like correlational research, it is used to describe an existing situation. That is, it looks at conditions that have already occurred and collects data to investigate why one group is different from the other (Leedy & Ormrod, 2001). It is called *causal–comparative research* because it compares groups to find a cause for differences in measures or scores.

Like correlational research, causal–comparative research uses statistical analysis to describe conditions that already exist. However, whereas correlational research examines one group of participants using two or more variables, causal–comparative research examines two or more groups that differ on one or more variables. For example, if a principal was interested in looking at the effectiveness of a new math program, she could use causal–comparative research to make an informed decision. The math scores of several schools, some of which used the new program and some of which did not, would be compared and analyzed. The independent variable would be the type of math program. The dependent variable would be the average math scores on similar standardized tests from each school. If the schools using the new math program demonstrated higher test scores, and the differences in scores were statistically significant, it would be reasonable to assume that the new math program was more effective.

Whole Language in California

In California in 1996, some critics claimed that whole language approaches to reading instruction were causing reading scores to go down (McQuillan, 1998). These critics wanted all California schools to abandon whole language practices and instead adopt phonics-only reading instruction. The fallacious logic used was that whole language approaches were being used in California schools and reading scores on standardized tests were decreasing (although this was not the case); therefore, whole language approaches must have caused the decrease in scores. Remember again that correlation does not imply causation. In this case there was a whole host of unidentified variables that may have attributed to the decrease in standardized scores, such as an increase in class size, a decrease in funding available for school libraries, an increase in immigrant populations, and others.

TABLE 10.1   Approaches to Reading Instruction

APPROACH TO READING INSTRUCTION	PERCENTAGE OF TEACHERS REPORTING	AVERAGE NAEP READING SCORE
Literature based	49%	221
Whole language	40%	220
Phonics	11%	208

Causal–comparative research was used in this situation to parse out three different groups and make comparisons. The groups consisted of fourth grade students' scores in reading whose classroom teacher identified the primary mode of reading instruction as whole language, literature based, or phonics. The independent variable was the type of reading instruction. The dependent variable was the average score on the NAEP standardized reading tests. The results of this research are shown in Table 10.1.

The results show there was a difference in the groups favoring both teachers who identified their approach to reading instruction as literature based and whole language over those teachers who identified their approach to reading instruction as phonics. Statistical analysis found that this difference was statistically significant. However, again we must be careful in how we interpret these results. This was not a true experiment in that randomized selection of participants into groups was not used. Also, there are many variables, called *confounding variables*, that could have accounted for the difference in scores. For example, we have no way of knowing whether the initial scores of students in each group were equal, or whether the sample of classroom teachers was representative of the entire population. Also, the difference in scores could be a result of teachers instead of approaches. That is, it may be that more effective teachers tend to use newer approaches such as whole language, whereas less effective teachers tend to use more traditional approaches. And finally, only fourth grade teachers were surveyed here. The results may have been different if primary teachers were included.

As you can see, when reading research reports you always have to go beyond the report to look for confounding variables. This report concludes that there was no evidence to support the notion that whole language causes reading test scores to decrease; however, there may be a link between literature-based and whole language instruction and positive performance on standardized reading tests.

QUASI-EXPERIMENTAL RESEARCH

The third type of research design that can be used is the quasi-experimental research design. This is the closest to the true experiment; however, in a quasi-experimental design there is no random assignment of subjects to groups. Random selection ensures that the groups being compared are relatively similar, that you are not comparing apples and oranges. As stated above, in most schools and classrooms, random selection is not possible; therefore, other ways must be used to ensure that the comparison groups are relatively similar. The two most common methods are pretests and matching.

In using pretests to compare groups before an investigation, simply give a test to comparison groups on the variable you are looking to examine. If they are relatively similar, you can continue with the research. If there is a significant difference between groups, there are three options: (1) find another group to compare, (2) reconfigure your existing groups so that they match, or (3) take the dissimilarity of groups into account when describing findings and conclusions.

Matching is used to create relatively similar groups. Here again a pretest is given to the entire population on the variable you are looking to examine. Based on the test results, students are matched with others who have relatively similar scores. Groups are then created by putting each person in the match in a separate group. For example, one would go in the experimental group, and the other would go in the control group.

Quasi-Action Research

As you can see from the previous descriptions, quasi-experimental research involves the manipulation of the environment. Thus, it has to be used with caution in an action research setting. With this type of research you are not observing an authentic classroom environment, but rather one that has been manipulated to examine a particular variable. In this sense, quasi-experimental research is also quasi-action research.

This is a good place for a reminder of what action research is: Action research is a systematic observation of one's own teaching practice. The goal is to understand what is happening in a particular classroom or school. Some types of quantitative research methodologies can be of use to this end. However, action research is not designed to prove or disprove a hypothesis, nor is it meant to provide data that can be generalized to a larger population. Quantitative methodologies in an action research project should be used simply to provide a picture of what is happening in a particular situation.

The following sections describe five different quasi-experimental designs. Figures are used to provide a clear view of the structure of each design. In these figures, Exp = experimental group, Cnt = control group, O = observation or measure, and T = treatment.

Pretest–Posttest Design

The pretest–posttest design is the most primitive quasi-experimental design. Here one group is given a pretest, a treatment, and a posttest (see Figure 10.1). Pretest and posttest scores are compared. This is often done before and after a particular unit. The variable that cannot be accounted for here is maturation. That is, simply

Group	Time →		
Exp	O	T	O

FIGURE 10.1   Pretest–Posttest Design

Group	Time →		
Exp	0	T	0
Cnt	0	—	0

FIGURE 10.2 Pretest–Posttest Control Group Design

by cognitive maturation and exposure, most students make some academic gains regardless of the technique or methodology.

Pretest–Posttest Control Group Design

This is the same as the design above except that a control group is used (see Figure 10.2). This allows the researcher to control for the variable of time and maturation. Groups can be compared based on both final scores and gain scores from pretest to posttest. There are many variables that cannot be controlled, the most significant of which is the administration of the treatment. If different teachers are teaching in the experimental and control group, it is hard to account for teaching style.

Time Series Design

Time series design examines one group over time, both before and after the treatment (see Figure 10.3). This is essentially an elaborate one-group pretest–posttest design except that here the researcher collects an extensive amount a data in order to look for patterns over time. An example of this would be a teacher who gave a spelling test each week for several weeks using traditional methods of spelling instruction. In the middle of the semester a new method was instituted and observations continued. Here the teacher looked for dramatic increases or decreases in spelling test scores over time.

Time Series Control Group Design

Time series control group design is the same as the time series design except that it allows you to conduct a parallel series of observations on experimental and control groups (see Figure 10.4).

Group	Time →								
Exp	0	0	0	0	T	0	0	0	0

Group	Time →								
Exp	T1	0	0	0	0	T2	0	0	0	0

FIGURE 10.3 Time Series Design

Group	Time →								
Exp	0	0	0	0	T	0	0	0	0
Cnt	0	0	0	0	—	0	0	0	0

Group	Time →									
Exp	T1	0	0	0	0	T2	0	0	0	0
Cnt	T1	0	0	0	0	T1	0	0	0	0

FIGURE 10.4   Time Series Control Group Design

Equivalent Time-Sample Design

Using equivalent time-sample design, the treatment is sometimes present and sometimes not (see Figure 10.5). It is presented at irregular intervals; however, the measures or observations are made at regular intervals. This allows the researcher to account for and control outside influences.

THE FUNCTION OF STATISTICS

Statistical analysis can serve two functions: to describe and to infer. It is beyond the scope of this text to describe the specifics of statistical analysis; however, if you understand the concepts and limitations behind these two approaches, software programs can be used to help you with the statistical analysis. I also recommend the following books: *Educational Research: Competencies for Analysis and Applications* (Gay & Airasian, 2003) and *Educational Research: Planning, Conducting, and Evaluating Quantitative and Qualitative Research* (Creswell, 2002).

Descriptive Statistics

Descriptive statistics are statistical analyses used to describe an existing set of data. There are three major types of descriptive statistics: (1) measure of central tendency, (2) frequency distribution, and (3) measures of variability.

Group	Time →							
Exp	T	0	—	0	T	0	—	0

FIGURE 10.5   Equivalent Time-Sample Design

50, 54, 54, 55, 56, 57, 59, 59, 65, 65, 65, 67, 67, 68, 68, 68, 68, 68, 69, 69, 69, 69, 75, 75, 75, 75, 78, 78, 78, 78, 78, 78, 79, 79, 79, 79, 79, **80, 80, 80, 80, 80, 80, 80, 80, 80, 80, 80, 80,** 83, 83, 83, 83, 83, 83, 84, 84, 84, 84, 85, 85, 90, 92, 92, 97, 99.

FIGURE 10.6   Scores from Mr. Smith's Eighth Grade Math Test

Measures of Central Tendency.   Measures of central tendency are a way of describing a set of data with a single number. The three measures of central tendency are the mode, the median, and the mean.

The *mode* is the score that is attained most frequently. For example, Mr. Smith gave the same 100-point math test to the 66 students in eighth grade at his school (see Figure 10.6). On this 100-point test the scores ranged from 50 points to 99 points; however, 12 students had a score of 80 out of 100. Even though the statistical average is higher than this, the mode is 80.

The *median* is the observation where 50% of the scores are above and 50% are below. There were 66 total scores on Mr. Smith's test. The median is 79. Approximately half the scores are above this and half the scores are below this.

The *mean*, the most common measure of central tendency, is the arithmetic average. In this case it is 75.7, or 76 points.

Frequency Distribution.   Frequency distribution is not so much a statistical procedure as it is a way of organizing information. It tells you all the scores that were attained and how many people attained each score. Frequency distribution provides a visual sense of your data and is fairly easy to do. First create a two-column table. Then list all the scores in the left column from highest to lowest (see Table 10.2). Finally, list the number of students represented by each score in the right column.

If there are a large number of scores, put them in groups of 5 or 10 for easier comparison. For example, when Mr. Smith gave the same math test to all the eighth grade students in his school district, he used the frequency distribution for these scores in Table 10.3.

To make this information more visual and to put it in a form that is more amenable to comparison, a frequency polygon can be created (Figure 10.7). This is a frequency distribution represented in a line graph.

Measures of Variability.   Measures of variability tell us about the spread of scores or how close the scores cluster around the mean. There are three measures of variability: range, variance, and standard deviation.

Range is simply the difference between the highest and lowest score. For example, Mr. Smith's eighth grade students had scores from 50 to 99. This range for these scores is 49.

Variance is the amount of spread among the test scores. If the variance is small, the scores are bunched together. Figure 10.8 shows scores with a small variance. If the variance is large, the scores are spread out. Figure 10.9 shows scores with a large variance.

Variance can be described with a number. For example, five children went out trick-or-treating for Halloween. They got the following numbers of candy bars: 25, 35, 40, 45, and 55. The variance can be calculated using the following steps:

TABLE 10.2   Frequency Distribution

Scores	Number of Students
99	1
97	1
92	2
90	1
85	2
84	4
83	6
80	12
79	5
78	6
75	4
69	4
68	5
67	2
65	3
59	2
57	1
56	1
55	1
54	2
50	1

TABLE 10.3   Frequency Distribution for a Large Number of Scores

Scores	Number of Students
95–100	6
90–94	10
85–89	25
80–84	35
75–79	15
70–74	10
65–69	9
60–64	7
55–59	4
50–54	2
45–49	1
40–44	1

1. Find the mean for all scores (second column in Table 10.4).
2. Find the difference between the raw score and the mean for each score (third column).
3. Square this difference value for each score (fourth column).
4. Add the squared scores to find the total (500).
5. Divide by the total number of scores (500 divided by 5 total scores = 10). This indicates that on average, the difference or variation between the numbers of candy bars is 10. (*Note:* This is different from the average spread between numbers, which in this case is 5.)

The variance score is of little value by itself; however, it can be used to calculate the standard deviation. *Standard deviation* is the square root of the variance. It is the most frequently used index to describe variability or the dispersion of scores. Whereas variance tells you how tightly the scores are clustered, standard deviation tells you how tightly the scores are clustered around the mean in a set of data.

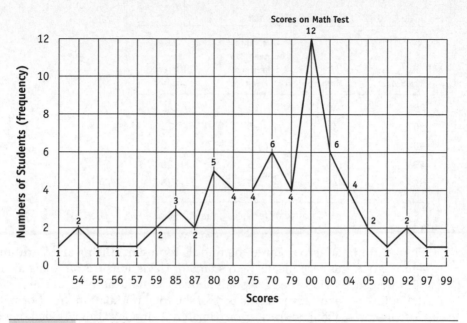

FIGURE 10.7   Graph for Frequency Distribution

			XX	XX	XXXX	XXXX	XXX	XXX			
				XX		XX	X				
				XX							

FIGURE 10.8   Scores with a Small Variance

| X | X | X | X | X | X | X | X | X | X | X | X | X | XX | XX | X | X | X | X | X | X | X | X | X | X |

FIGURE 10.9   Scores with a Large Variance

Figure 10.10 shows what a normal distribution of scores would look like if these were plotted on a graph. This is the bell-shaped curve with which you are most likely familiar. The highest part of the bell is the mean. In a given sample, if the scores are normally distributed and that data were put on a graph, it would look like this. The majority of scores would fall in the middle. This is the large part of the bell, known as the average. Fewer scores fall on the top and bottom. These are the smaller parts of the bell on each side, known as above average and below average.

When scores are tightly clustered around mean as in Figure 10.11, the standard deviation is small. When scores are spread out as in Figure 10.12 the standard deviation is large.

If the mean and standard deviation of a normal distribution are known, it is possible to compute the percentile rank of any given score. On the graph in

TABLE 10.4   Calculating Variance

Raw Scores	Mean	Difference between Raw Scores and Mean	Difference Squared
25	40	−15	225
35	40	−5	25
40	40	0	0
45	40	5	25
55	40	15	225

Total of differences squared: 500

Figure 10.13, the zero point in the middle represents the mean or arithmetic average. Zero in this case means zero standard deviations from the mean. This is the 50th percentile. Half the scores fall above and half fall below. The first standard deviation, (−1 and 1) represents 68% of the total population. In a normal distribution of scores, about 34% are approximately 1 standard deviation above the mean, and about 34% are below the mean. This means that if you gave a 100-point math test to all Americans, 50% of the total population would score 50 points or above and 50% would score 50 points or below. About 34% would score between 50 and 84 points, and about 34% would score between 16 points and 50 points. 68% of the population would score between 16 and 84 points. Both 16 points and 84 points represent one standard deviation from the mean.

Two standard deviations away from the mean (about 13.6% above the first standard deviation) represent 95% of the population. This means that about 95% scored between 3 and 97 points on this mythical math test. About 47% of the population scored between 3 and 50 points; about 47% of the population scores between 50 and 97 points.

Three standard deviations away from the mean (about 2.1% above the second standard deviation) represent about 99% of the population. This means that about

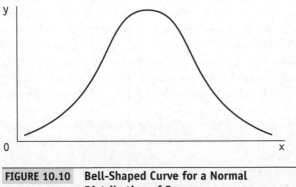

FIGURE 10.10   Bell-Shaped Curve for a Normal Distribution of Scores

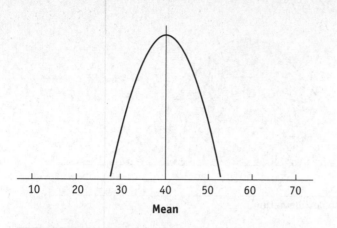

FIGURE 10.11   Small Standard Deviation: Closely Distributed Scores

99% of the population would score between 1 and 99 points on this test. About 2% would score between 1 and 3 points; about 2% of the population would score between 97 and 99 points.

Inferential Statistics

Inferential statistics are statistical analyses used to determine how likely a given outcome is for an entire population based on a sample size. These analyses allow the researcher to make inferences to larger populations by collecting data on a small sample size. The most common inferential statistical analyses are the *t*-test, analysis of variance (ANOVA), and chi square.

The *t*-test is used to determine whether the difference between two different means is statistically significant. Statistical significance tells us that it is very unlikely that difference in mean was caused by chance or sampling error. If the

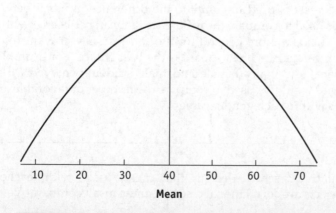

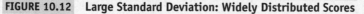

FIGURE 10.12   Large Standard Deviation: Widely Distributed Scores

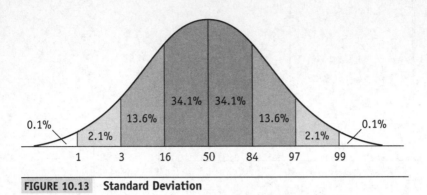

FIGURE 10.13   Standard Deviation

difference between two means is not statistically significant, it tells us that the differences between them are so small, we cannot say for certain whether it was due to chance or an error in selecting the initial sample populations. It must be pointed out also that there is a difference between statistical significance and practical significance. A difference in scores may be statistically significant; however, if this difference does not mean anything or have any practical effect, it is not practically significant. For example, there may be a statistically significant difference between two test scores, but if they both fell within the B range, there would be no practical significance between the two.

In educational research, two different levels of significance or probability are generally used: $p = .05$ and $p = .01$. A level of $p = .05$ means that we can be reasonably certain that only 5% of the differences might be due to chance or sampling error. A level of $p = .01$ means that we can be reasonably certain that only 1% of the differences might be due to chance or sampling error. Smaller sample sizes make it harder to find statistical differences and larger ones easier. For example, it is much easier to find a statistically significant difference in two groups of 3,000 than it is between two groups of 30. The t-test automatically adjusts for sample size.

Whereas the t-test is used to compare the difference in mean between two groups, ANOVA is used to compare the difference in mean between or within three or more groups. This is a more general form of a t-test. If you want to compare frequencies within categories, a chi square is the best choice. For example, if you wanted to compare how many female and male students enjoyed a particular activity, a chi square would be used to compare the number of favorable and unfavorable responses within each gender category.

SUMMARY

- Two quantitative research designs that can be used with teacher action research projects are correlational research and causal–comparative research.

- Correlational research looks at one group to find a relationship between variables.
- Correlation coefficient describes the strength of the relationship between two variables.
- Correlation does not indicate causation.
- Predictions can be made based on the strength of the correlation coefficient.
- Causal–comparative research looks at two or more groups to compare the differences in one variable.
- Correlational research and causal–comparative research are not true experimental research designs because they do not manipulate variables or use random populations for sample groups.
- Both correlational research and causal–comparative research are used to examine existing conditions.
- Quasi-experimental design is a true experiment without random selection of participants.
- Pretests and matching are two ways to ensure groups are relatively similar before a quasi-experimental research project.
- Because quasi-experimental design manipulates an environment, it should be considered quasi-action research.
- Quasi-experimental design in action research should be used to understand a particular situation; it should not be used to prove or disprove a hypothesis or to make generalizations to a larger population.
- Descriptive statistics are used to describe an existing set of data.
- The four major types of descriptive statistics are frequency distribution, measure of central tendency, measures of variability, and measure of relationship or correlation.
- Frequency distribution tells you the scores that were attained and how many attained each score.
- Measures of central tendency (mode, median, and mean) use a single number to describe a set of data.
- Measures of variability (range, variance, and standard deviation) describe how spread out a set scores is.
- Inferential statistics are used to make predictions for a general population based on a small sample size.

QUESTIONS AND ACTIVITIES

1. Find and evaluate an example of correlational research found in the popular media.
2. What are some examples of common correlations that seem to have become fact?
3. Describe three correlations that you would like to examine in a school or classroom.
4. Find an example of causal–comparative research. Identify three or more possible confounding variables.

5. Find and describe examples of quasi-experimental research. Identify three or more possible confounding variables.

POSSIBLE RESEARCH QUESTIONS FOR ACTION RESEARCH PROJECTS

1. Use one of the quasi-experimental designs described in this chapter to examine the effectiveness of a new approach or methodology. For example, instead of reading the stories from a basal reader, encourage a group of students to select the books they want to read during reading class. Are there differences in reading scores, fluency, or perception of reading? Alternatively, encourage students to work on math problems together; one person does the problem and thinks out loud while another watches, listens, and guides. Is there any difference in students' abilities to solve problems? Is there any difference in students' perceptions of math or math class?

2. Is spelling instruction effective in moving words into students' productive, writing vocabulary? Analyze students' writing. Look for instances of words from weekly spelling lists. Are they spelled correctly? Are there any differences among any of the following groups: gender, ability, SES, age?

3. Is spelling instruction more effective than allowing students to choose their own words for their weekly spelling? Find two relatively similar classrooms. Before the study collect samples of students' writing. Randomly pick 100-word passages from each sample and record how many words per hundred (WPH) were spelled correctly. This would be their WPH score. For a month, allow one group to choose their own words to study during spelling instruction while the other class receives the traditional spelling instruction. At the end of a month, are there differences in the WPH scores of the two groups?

4. How much time do students spend reading for pleasure during the school day? How much time do they spend at home? Are there any differences among any of the following groups: gender, ability, SES, age?

5. What types of books, genre, or topics do children like to read? Are there any differences among any of the following groups: gender, ability, SES, age?

6. What strategies are used to teach children how to comprehend expository text in your school? How often or to what extent are these strategies used?

7. What opportunities does your school or district provide for professional development? How does this compare to other schools? Are there recommendations related to professional development from the U.S. Department of Education or other national organizations?

8. Approximately how many hours a night do your students spend doing homework? Are there any differences among any of the following groups: gender, ability, SES, age? How do these hours compare with homework recommendations or guidelines outlined by the U.S. Department of Education or other research-based national organizations?

9. What homework policies are used by your school your district? How do these compare with other schools or districts? (*Note:* The Internet has a lot of good information here.)

10. What do teachers perceive to be the purpose of homework?

11. What types of extracurricular activities do students participate in each week? How many hours a week are spent doing extracurricular activities? To what degree are these activities school related and non–school related? Are there any differences among any of the following groups: gender, ability, SES, age?

12. How many students are working? How many hours a week do students spend working? What types of jobs do they have? When do they work? How might this affect their school performance? Are there any differences among any of the following groups: gender, ability, SES, age?

13. How many hours a week do students spend watching TV? What types of shows do they watch? When are they most likely to watch? How might this affect their school performance? Are there any differences among any of the following groups: gender, ability, SES, age?

14. What is the average class size in your school or district? How does this compare with state or national averages? How does this compare with recommendations by the U.S. Department of Education or other national researched-based organizations?

15. What types of professional development activities does the teaching faculty in your school or district engage in? What new skills or types of knowledge are learned? How are these new skills implemented, or in what form does this knowledge appear in the curriculum? That is, what is the effect of teacher professional development? Can a case be made for a school or district paying for this?

16. What is the make-up of the teaching faculty? How many years of experience do they have? What levels and types of education do they have? Are their differences related to gender, age, or ethnicity?

17. How would students' perception of reading or reading class change if they were allowed to choose their own books to read?

18. Other than using test scores, how do you know learning is taking place in your classroom or school? What products or performances indicate growth, learning, curiosity, inquiry, exploration, and creativity?

19. In a particular subject, what do teachers think is important for students to know or be able to do? What products or performances might indicate this? Are students in a school or class able to do these things? To what degree or at what level?

20. Does students' writing change if they are allowed to choose their own writing topics? Use the writing assessment from in Figure 8.14 (p. 93) to note change. Do students' perceptions of writing change, or are there changes in self-efficacy if students are given autonomy in the choice of writing topics?

CHAPTER ELEVEN

DISCUSSION: YOUR PLAN OF ACTION

Although it may not be as long as the other parts of your paper, everything in your action research report leads up to the section in which you discuss your findings and make your conclusions and recommendations based on the data collected. This is followed by what most consider to be the most important part of an action research project—your plan describing the actions you will take based on your findings. Although they are described in three separate sections here, these items do not need to appear in this order or in this exact form and may even merge in your action research report.

Also, I am making the assumption that an action research project will result in some sort of written document or report. This report may vary in length and formality, depending on the purpose of your research. Even if you are doing action research simply for your own edification as a classroom teacher, I would encourage you to create a short written document of your findings and describe ideas for change. Writing helps to clarify and organize your thinking and enables you to see patterns or associations you may have missed. Also, a written report documents your professional development. In most states teachers periodically have to engage in some kind of continuing education to maintain their teaching license. An action research report can be used for this purpose. Finally, having a written account of your findings and ideas allows you to share them with others, either in oral or written form. In this way you can help to keep the field of education evolving and moving forward.

CONCLUSIONS AND RECOMMENDATIONS

A conclusion is a reasoned deduction. That is, you come to believe one thing based on another thing or series of things. Based on the data you have collected and reported, what does it all mean? What is it that you now know to be true? What can we deduce from the data you have presented? Your conclusion is often no more than a paragraph or two describing your current state of knowing or a list of things you have come to believe as a result of your study. It should bring together the important data and explain what they mean. As you write your conclusion be aware that it will be the basis for your recommendation. You are making a case for a particular plan of action.

A recommendation is a general suggestion for what is believed to be an effective choice or action based on your findings. You tell how your findings might be used or provide advice as to what should be done differently. Keep in mind, however, that the line between conclusions and recommendations is often blurred. Some action research papers have only conclusions; others have only recommendations. Still others, like those described next, have a combination of both.

Christina Stolfa, Nacogdoches, Texas

Christina Stolfa conducted an action research study to determine whether all students in her fourth grade multi-ability level inclusive classroom were receiving the writing instruction they needed to be successful writers. She did a case study focusing on three students who represented three ability levels in her classroom: Mark, Pat, and Nicole. Mark was a low ability student who left class during reading and math for special help in a resource room. Because of the severity of his disability, he spent the previous year in a self-contained special education classroom. Pat was identified as gifted and talented. Nicole was seen as an average student.

Conclusions

I found that if classes are to be successful, both in state assessments and in the minds of the students, classroom teachers must be given assistance or the class sizes must decrease. I know this is a difficult conclusion, but it is the most appropriate summarization. With a large gap between the levels of abilities in a fourth grade classroom it is difficult to use whole group instruction most of the time and actually reach and make an impact on students. The three children in this study represent the three major ability levels present in my classroom. If I am teaching the whole group, it is common that one of the groups will not be receiving the instruction that is most appropriate for them.

Because of the severity of emotional and social issues, I feel that Mark benefited the least from the instruction given. Much of this was out of our hands; however, there are other children like Mark who suffer from the lack of desperately needed one-on-one instruction. Children like Pat will excel in most situations, but they are also done an injustice when their minds are not stretched to their full capacity. Children like Nicole are often overlooked because they can stay afloat without calling attention to themselves. However, they deserve the attention and assistance that the others receive as well.

Recommendations

My recommendations include continuing writing conferences and structured writing lessons throughout the year. My hope is that all three students will be able to learn more strategies to help them complete and excel on the state-mandated writing tests and proceed successfully to fifth grade.

Also, all children deserve success, and it is important that they achieve it. Classrooms, both teachers and students, greatly benefit from smaller class sizes. It allows more time to communicate and use constructive criticism, which will help students become more involved, more confident writers in the end, no matter what the ability level ranking.

Jo Henriksen, St. Louis Park, Minnesota

Jo Henriksen is a gifted education teacher at Peter Hobart Elementary and Aquila Primary Center in St. Louis Park, Minnesota. Instead of the traditional parent–teacher conference, she studied student-led conferences involving identified gifted students in grades 1 through 3. Before their conferences, students were asked to synthesize and describe in writing their learning during the quarter. This information was shared with parents during the conference.

Jo's goals in this action research were to understand fully the process of student-led conferences and to see whether they were beneficial and worth continuing. To collect data, she created a survey for students (see Figure 11.1). Because she was conducting the conferences, she was able to record her thoughts and impressions following each conference. She created a checklist to guide her reflections (see Figure 11.2).

In the checklists in Figures 11.1 and 11.2, Jo Henriksen defined specific behaviors or attributes. The checklist allowed her to focus on these attributes consistently with each student. After presenting the data in her report, Jo wrote the following conclusion.

Name: _____ Grade: _____ Today's Date: _____

HOW DID YOUR CONFERENCE GO?

1. Who came to your conference besides you?	mom	dad	both
2. Were you glad you could come to your conference?	yes	no	not sure
3. Do you think your parents learned more about what you are doing in class?	yes	no	not sure
4. Did you learn more about putting facts into categories?	yes	no	not sure
5. Did you get to talk enough?	yes	no	not sure
6. Was the time long enough for the conference?	yes	no	not sure

7. What is the best part of getting to come to your own conference?

8. Could anything make the conference better next time?

FIGURE 11.1   Student Survey Form

Name: _____ Grade: _____ Today's Date: _____

REFLECTIONS ON THE CHILD-LED CONFERENCE

1. Who came to the conference?	mom	dad	both
2. Was the tone of the conference pleasant?	yes	no	comments:
3. Did parents seem to learn more about what happens in class?	yes	no	comments:
4. Did the child handle the vocabulary of the categorizing exercise?	yes	no	comments:
5. Did the child handle the categorizing exercise?	yes	no	comments:
6. Did the child get to talk enough?	yes	no	comments:
7. Was the time long enough for the conference?	yes	no	comments:

8. Do any points need to be remembered because of this conference?

9. Do you need to schedule another appointment for a conference without the child? Topic?

FIGURE 11.2   Teacher Reflection Form

Conclusions

I came to the following conclusions regarding student-led conferences:

1. They were a wonderful opportunity to meet with children in a pleasant situation.
2. Children learned more about what they have learned, thanks to this form of conferencing.
3. The conferences were energizing as opposed to energy draining.
4. Our district schedules the fall conferences very early. Since my gifted education program doesn't start until the second full week of school, I barely have time to get much work done with the children before it is conference time. I am going to have to do some thinking about the tightness of the schedule.
5. I will do more preconference planning with each child before the big night.
6. I routinely have a family night each spring. This is an opportunity for all to see what students have produced. I am thinking that I will have this night prior to spring conferences. That way, less time will be needed at conferences to explain the projects. More time can be devoted to discussion and assessment of projects.
7. Whereas I can't insist that parents schedule conferences, I am really determined to have conferences with virtually 100% of my students.
8. The conferences will still be only 25 minutes in length. Many of my students, being who they are, love to talk at length. I will have to think about how to reconcile the time allotment to still satisfy the desire of these children, if possible.
9. I absolutely will continue the practice.

Final Thoughts

Overall, I would have to say that my decision to conduct student-led conferences was good. I have worked in gifted education for 9 years, in regular education a lot longer. I know what makes children happy a lot of the time and what helps parents to feel secure some of the time. I also know what helps me to maintain zest for the job that I do. I designed the conferences to meet the needs of my students and families. I also designed the conferences to be a tool to help me to be more effective in my position. Conferences are an inherently difficult time for me; however, I look forward to making this time more positive and productive through the use of student-led conferences.

Cathy Stamps, Fifth Grade, Hopkins Elementary School

Cathy Stamps was interested in finding out if her fifth grade students learned better when they sat by their friends or when she assigned them seats. She collected data by (1) taking field notes focusing specifically on students' behavior, attitude, and production; (2) comparing samples of students' work that were completed in both settings; and (3) administering a student survey. She made the following conclusions and recommendations:

> Based on my observations and student responses, I would conclude that learning is positively affected when students have a say in where they sit. They feel more ownership in their learning; therefore, they are more excited about learning. I know when I am at conferences or workshops, I would much rather have my choice of people to work with versus being told who to work with. I think the saying, "Treat others the way you would like to be treated" applies to this situation. By giving students a chance to self-assign themselves, I discovered that students wasted less time working out differences that often hinder them when trying to complete a task in a minimal amount of time.
>
> My experience with this investigation has been beneficial. Students knew what was expected and also knew the consequences if they couldn't handle working in self-assigned groups. However, I did assign seats periodically in order to mix up the class and decrease cliques.

Delinda Whitley, Mt. Enterprise, Texas

Delinda Whitley conducted an action research project in a seventh grade classroom in a rural east Texas school. The purpose of her study was to determine whether working in pairs to discuss reading assignments would improve her students' reading comprehension. The conclusions and recommendations of her study are presented here.

Conclusions

Most students did perform better on vocabulary and comprehension assessments after working together in pairs on reading assignments. The mean for test scores increased 21.4 points from the first week to the sixth week's test. Students who did show improvement were those who seemed to struggle with homework. The ability to complete assignments quicker than by themselves reflected higher test score means. Assessment scores did not improve for the two students with the highest independent reading levels.

I discussed my findings with a colleague who taught math. My findings were consistent with studies that she has conducted in her classroom. I found that the really low and extremely high students did not benefit from paired reading, whereas the average and low average students gained tremendously. When students were given ownership and a voice, their learning became more meaningful and productive. Through the use of conversation and repeated readings, fluency increased, as did comprehension. For students who did not benefit from paired readings, the traditional instructional method is still needed. Students need to hear good literature read and modeled for them. I am grateful for this opportunity and definitely plan to incorporate paired readings in my classroom setting.

Recommendations

No method of reading instruction is the best. Balancing the traditional instructional method with paired students may allow greater gains for all students. Students will be focused and directed toward specific literary elements. They may also continue to benefit from modeled oral reading from the teacher through traditional instruction. Consequently, allowing students to complete some work in pairs should allow for a higher assessment test scores. Allowing students to work in pairs will also give them a voice in their learning and make it more enjoyable. Because some students are more vocal and learn auditorily, the repetition of novel information or vocabulary in a paired working assignment will also help them develop their literacy skills.

EVALUATION OF THE STUDY

There is no such thing as the perfect study. After reporting conclusions and recommendations, some researchers like to evaluate the effectiveness of their study, explain particular aspects of it, or describe how they might do it differently the next time.

Jim Vavreck, St. Peter, Minnesota

Jim conducted a study to see how his sixth grade students perceived intelligence and creativity. Data were collected by using a questionnaire and a self-rating scale

Name: _____

1. What is intelligence?
2. What is creativity?
3. How are intelligence and creativity related?
4. Is it possible to be creative without being intelligent?
5. Is it possible to be intelligent without being creative?

FIGURE 11.3   Student Survey

(see Figures 11.3 and 11.4). Jim evaluated his study as he reported the data. He did a nice job of letting us inside his head as he wrestled with various parts of his study. You can also see him thinking as a researcher in the way every question answered seemed to result in another question asked. I have included an excerpt:

> The students in this study generally seemed to feel that either creativity or intelligence was a personal strength. Only 13% rated their intelligence and creativity as equal. A follow-up question regarding what evidence each student could give for his or her personal ratings in intelligence and creativity would be helpful in identifying how students are differentiating between creativity and intelligence as they rate themselves in each.

> ### Other Implications
> It appears that I should have described the rating scale more clearly. It seems that either this group is exceptionally above average or else the students did not understand the concept of average. On the other hand, perhaps they have a good, albeit unrealistic, self-concept. Or maybe they pictured extremely low students to compare themselves with.
>
> I am also interested in exploring the differences in how the girls rated themselves and how the boys did using a much larger sample. The current indication is that the girls rated themselves higher in intelligence and creativity. A longitudinal study could be done to see if the self-ratings in creativity and intelligence change over time.

Staci Wilson, Irving, Texas

Staci Wilson conducted an action research project in her kindergarten classroom to see what skills her students were learning in the blocks center of her classroom. She

Name: _____

1. How creative are you on a scale of 0–10 where 5 is average?
2. How intelligent are you on a scale of 0–10 where 5 is average?

FIGURE 11.4   Student Self-Rating Scale

wanted to understand why blocks were important to the curriculum and in what ways children benefited from manipulating blocks. In describing the limitations of her study she describes not only how her study might have been changed, but also future research projects related to this area.

Summary of Findings and Conclusions

I found that students do learn important and useful skills from manipulating blocks on a daily basis. Students learn physical, cognitive, social/emotional, and language skills from working in the block center either individually or in groups. The kindergarten students also learned important skills in many different areas of the curriculum that will provide a base education to be built on later in their education.

Students developed skills in mathematics, science, language, social studies, the arts, and technology. By the teacher fostering an open environment for construction, the students are able to "build" their way to education. The teacher must facilitate the learning environment for these young students, but the children will be able to perform the necessary tasks that the teacher requests.

These young students do not realize that they are performing such detailed tasks because it comes so naturally to them. This is learning at its best because children are learning from doing. The teacher must facilitate these experiences because the children don't know how to do this on their own. Once the required objectives are explained or set out for the students, the development of many different skills can and will occur.

Recommendations

When utilizing a block center in my own classroom, I will make sure to foster experiences that cater to all areas of development. Keeping in mind the many different materials that can be placed in this center I will be able to achieve a fully rounded curriculum in my block center. Based on my observations I would recommend to other teachers to utilize blocks in their classrooms on a daily basis. My research indicates many positive benefits from using blocks in this way. Teachers could also benefit from working with their students and making observations on their own. I learned many different things about my students when interacting with them during this study. I feel it would give teachers an insight to students' thinking and creativity.

Limitations of the Study

The students in this study were allowed only 20 minutes each day to work in the blocks center. I feel that the depth of development would have been deeper and the results of this study more meaningful if more time were given to centers. I feel that children at this age level need more time for free movement and construction of their education.

If I could continue this study, I would observe the same block center in other classrooms in different areas of Texas. I would want to see the impact of development in many different economic areas of the state. I feel that the impact of the center for students might be different from that of my study. Also, students in different socioeconomic strata in the state would probably interact with one another differently. It would be interesting to make these observations and set up the same center in different schools to see the changes and differences across the board.

I would also like to extend this study even broader by examining older students in different subject areas. I would want to observe and question them on the importance of blocks and see whether playing here had a role in their understanding of their current curriculum. I feel that it would give a closing gap to what I and research indicate are great developmental measures started in kindergarten. Knowing the development over time would show how the basic fundamentals that research and my observations indicate are actually being used and extended.

DESIGNING A NEW PLAN OR PROGRAM

Designing a new plan or program is putting the action in action research. That means you have to do something or make a plan to do something. In some rare instances the results of an action research project will indicate that everything is just fine, in which case your action research plan is a plan to do nothing. However, most action research projects result in one of five possible outcomes.

1. *Greater understanding of the situation, child, or students in general.* In this case, you should describe how your interactions or instruction will change to reflect this greater understanding.

2. *The discovery of a problem.* Finding and defining a problem are the initial elements of the problem-solving process. If your action research project results in the discovery of a problem, use the problem-solving strategies described in Chapter 4 to create a plan of action. Once a plan has been created, it can be implemented and evaluated. This calls for another action research project, and thus action research becomes a vehicle for the continued growth and evolution of a classroom or school.

3. *A plan, program, or pedagogical method is found to be effective.* An action research report would describe why and how it is effective and allow you to make a case for its continued use. Also, even in an effective plan, program, or pedagogical method, some elements can be made more effective. Your research report should identify these.

4. *A plan, program, or pedagogical method is found to need modification.* Any new plan on paper rarely results in its perfect functioning in reality. Having to adjust and adapt is a normal part of doing anything new or innovative. An action research report is used in this situation to identify the elements that need to be modified and to describe how they will be changed.

5. *A plan, program, or pedagogical method is found to be ineffective.* Action research can be used to document the ineffectiveness of a program. Your research report can be used to support the change or elimination of the plan, program, or pedagogical method.

Creating a New Plan or Program

Sometimes as a result of your action research, you need to design or create a new plan or program. You will likely be more successful if the new plan or program contains the following three elements: (1) a school philosophy or mission statement, (2) goals, and (3) a rationale.

School Philosophy or Mission Statement. Each school or school district should have a school philosophy, a mission statement, or both. Putting this at the top of any new plan helps you align your objectives with the school's and provides support and justification for the ideas that follow.

A school philosophy is the general belief, policy, or set of ideas formulated by the educational system that reflects the values of the school and community. This may describe the nature of learning or how education and learning fit in a broader scheme of human endeavors. Consider the following example:

> The Anytown School District is a cooperative, democratic venture between students, parents, teachers, and community. It shall be the policy of this district to maintain the highest academic standards, to engage in the best practices in education, and to enable every child to reach his or her full potential.

Thus stated, the school philosophy can be used to support plans that would help maintain high academic standards, such as smaller class sizes, increased teacher development activities, and more books and computers in the classrooms. It can be used to justify change when current practices do not reflect what research describes as the best practices in teaching, such as when schools engage in an over-reliance on standardized tests to describe learning or educational progress. It also can be used to support new programs or the reallocation of resources when certain students are not able to reach their full potential, such as those with special learning needs, the intellectually gifted and highly creative, students with physical disabilities, and those from minority cultures. Thus, a school's philosophy can be used as an agent of change and continued growth.

A mission statement states what the school is trying to accomplish in a general sense. Consider the following example:

> The purpose of our education system is to help learners acquire the knowledge and skills necessary to become constructive world citizens, informed decision makers, and lifelong learners.

The mission statement is sometimes combined with or incorporated into the school philosophy. If your proposed plan or program meets resistance by colleagues, a building principal, or a school board, a mission statement can be used to justify or support what you want to implement.

Goals.   Goals define what you hope to accomplish with your new plan or program. They also help you in evaluation. That is, to determine success, you judge whether you have met some or all of your goals. Goals also help keep your plan focused and prevent you from wandering into unrelated areas. Again, you can create a better case for your new plan or program if your goals are aligned with the school philosophy and mission statement.

Rationale.   The rationale explains why the goals are important. You describe the benefit to the learner, the school, or society in general. Sometimes it helps to put your goals in a theoretical context.

A Less Formal Plan of Action

Depending on the nature and purpose of your action research project, sometimes it is appropriate to have an informal plan of action. This may be a simple description of your intentions or a list of specific steps that you plan to take. Action research is built on the premise that some type of action will result from your research. The final measure of your action research is the degree to which it clearly asks and answers your question, communicates your ideas, and serves to promote positive change.

A final word: I want to reiterate that the items described in this chapter should be adapted to your particular situation to meet the needs of your research project.

SUMMARY

- The final part of an action research report is making conclusions and recommendations, evaluating the study, and making a plan of action.
- A conclusion is a reasoned deduction based on your findings.
- A recommendation is a general suggestion for change based on your findings.
- An evaluation assesses the general effectiveness of your study and explains any interesting or important elements of it.
- A plan of action describes exactly what you intend to do as a result of your action research.
- Action research should result in some form of written document or report, which varies in length and formality.
- A new plan or program is more apt to be successfully implemented if it includes a philosophy or mission statement, goals, and a rationale.

QUESTIONS AND ACTIVITIES

1. Read your school district's philosophy or mission statement or use that of another school district. Do you agree with it? What would you include or eliminate? Can you find an instance in which practice does not align with this philosophy or mission statement?
2. Create your own philosophy or mission statement for your school district and for your classroom.
3. Find a plan, program, or piece of curriculum. Identify the goals. Do the goals align with the mission statement and rationale?
4. Describe a change you would like to see. Use your district's philosophy or mission statement to support your ideas.
5. Describe a class or a particular subject area. List three to eight general goals for that class or subject area. Provide a rationale for their importance.
6. Use the excerpts of one of the studies presented in this chapter to create a plan of action.

POSSIBLE RESEARCH QUESTIONS FOR ACTION RESEARCH PROJECTS

1. What types of interactions occur at parent–teacher conferences? Are parents generally satisfied? How might the interactions be improved?
2. Do report cards do a good job of describing learning? Are parents satisfied with the form currently used? Are teachers satisfied with the form currently used? Do students feel that this form describes their learning? What would students wish to include? What do parents wish were included?
3. Is learning affected in any way if students are allowed to work together?
4. Does being able to work in small groups to complete homework assignments increase understanding or learning?
5. Do advanced organizers used before a lecture or class session improve student learning? Used as a prereading activity does it seem to improve comprehension? What do students think?
6. What happens if students are asked to create concept maps as postreading experiences or homework assignments instead of the traditional comprehension worksheets or other types of homework? Does learning improve? Do students' attitudes change? What do students think?
7. What adaptations or accommodations are made for English language learners in your classroom, school, and district?
8. In the pause technique, you pause in the middle of a lecture or class session and ask students to work in pairs to highlight important ideas and to review notes. What effect might this have on students learning in elementary, middle, and high school? How do students perceive this? Are there differences related to gender or ability?
9. What would students like to include in a learning portfolio to demonstrate their learning? What happens if students are allowed to make some or all choices in this regard?

Notes	Ideas, Observations, or Associations

FIGURE 11.5 Two-Column Note-Taking System

10. What note-taking skills do students seem to lack? What are the results of instruction in this area? Does instruction here transfer to other academic areas?

11. The two-column note-taking system is one in which students draw a vertical line down their note-taking page that leaves about a two- to three-inch column on the right for their ideas, observations, or associations (Figure 11.5). Do students benefit from this type of note taking? Are they able to make personal connections? Do they seem better able to apply or extend concepts? Do they seem better able to transfer skills or concepts to real-life situations?

CHAPTER TWELVE

SAMPLE ACTION RESEARCH PROJECTS

This chapter contains nine short action research projects along with my comments. Most of these action research projects do not contain a literature review. Although the literature review adds an important dimension that connects your ideas to the literature, it is not always a necessary element.

SAMPLE 12.1
ALISON REYNOLDS, MINNEAPOLIS, MINNESOTA

Few action research projects have touched me as much as the one written by Alison Reynolds. She demonstrated how the domains of art and science might sometimes overlap. Indeed, both are ways of seeing and representing reality. Alison examined a small part of her world and brought it to life. She used words as an artist uses paint to create a picture on the canvas of our minds.

When Alison started this action research project, she was overwhelmed by the large quantity of data. She wanted us to understand the environment in which she worked but did not know where to start. She solved her dilemma by focusing on one student. You can see in her poignant picture a portrayal of the human spirit and an understanding of her teaching environment.

THE PAINTER
Sammy

There is a way that he comes into the classroom that is similar to the way that a storm blows into town. It is something akin to a little breeze that follows him through the doorway. By the end of class the furniture often lies toppled from his winds. At 12 years of age his anger is profound. He is verbally confrontational and is often "up in your face." Everyone is a "bitch" to him; he uses "fat ass" for men, "whore" and "slut" for women, and "fish" for girls his age.

Sammy has been at Greenwood Treatment School for 2 years. Greenwood School is one step above residential treatment. It is populated by students who have been unable to benefit from a slew of public schools throughout the Twin Cities area.

Sammy is a large boy weighing about 175 pounds. He possesses an artistic nature. Although he uses profanity for his daily interactions now, the rhythm of his speech often sounds a little delayed and awkward. It is as if he is not quite comfortable with this new persona of his. He acts like a tough guy who still has to think about his lines before saying them. His rage is real though. The expression of that rage is awkward and violent, but there is water in that well.

At School

When Sammy started at Greenwood School 2 years ago he was rambunctious, followed the classroom jokers, and did more fooling around than anything else. He was not verbally confrontational. He was not assaultive. He was not violent. Naturally, he did have conflicts with other students, but these conflicts had a different tone to them. They were conflicts about small student disputes such as taking someone else's chair, grabbing someone's pencil, or having a little too much fun at the expense of another.

Sammy was in the fifth grade when he started at Greenwood School, but his academic level was in the third to fourth grade range. I first met him because he started coming to my classroom to get his academic skills caught up. I had suggested to his fifth grade teacher that because of Sammy's academic delays, he might be better served in a lower level classroom. I was working in a third/fourth grade classroom at the time.

I worked with Sammy for a year and a half to try to get him caught up with his peers. He applied himself to learning addition, subtraction, and multiplication. He completed simple writing assignments. He read as many second and third grade–level books as possible in a given class period. At the end of each class, Sammy could see the math that he did, the writing that he completed, and the stack of books that he had read.

The purpose of all this work was not only to help him catch up academically with his peers but also to provide him with a visual pile at the end of every class that he could look at and say, "I did this much today." Helping Sammy to build his confidence relating to his academics was as important as his acquisition of academic skills. He became very focused on completing his work, often ignoring other classroom disruptions. He also became less vulnerable to the criticism of his fifth grade peers.

Painting

It was during this period that Sammy started painting watercolor pictures. He would title each one the same: "A Sunny Day." Because he would give these pictures to me, I acquired a large collection of Sammy's artwork.

I learned much about Sammy because he talked a great deal to me. He told me about his impoverished home life. He spoke about the violence in his neighborhood. He described the struggles of his family members. His father had come to "the States" from Mexico. His mother was African American. He had a 20-year-old brother in prison. He had an 18-year-old brother who was getting ready to marry his pregnant girlfriend. Sammy understood that his life and the lives of those in his family had troubles, but the troubles had not possessed his spirit and heart.

The Zoo

One day our school went to the Minnesota Zoo. Many of the students were doing tough guy clowning with each other while walking around the grounds. I broke off from the main group with a smaller group of these students. Sammy was with us. As we were walking, running, and bumping into each other, there on a grassy knoll was a flock of baby ducklings with their mother.

Sammy stood and watched the ducks for a long moment. Then he spotted an older duck approaching the group of ducklings. Sammy took off running after that duck. He chased it all over the grassy lawn, around trees and bushes. He never caught the duck, but if he had I am sure that it would have been safe in his care. He was still at that child's age where he would chase and capture something because of its freedom, and then tenderly care for what he had caught.

Life

On the Tuesday following the school's trip to the zoo, Sammy came to school, but I did not see him the entire day. The following day the same thing happened. I spoke with the school's therapy staff to ask why Sammy had come to school but was not participating in class or other activities.

Sammy's brother, the one who had been preparing to marry his pregnant girlfriend, had been killed. Sammy was at home on a Sunday evening and heard somebody knocking at the door. Sammy opened the door and saw his brother laying on his stomach with a trail of blood behind him. His brother had been shot and had crawled on his stomach up to his home. He died at the doorway.

Sammy's heart turned that night. He became the embodiment of his family's troubles. It is common to hear him banging against the lockers in the hall, yelling at the top of his lungs. The therapy staff working with him stated that they were trying to help Sammy find more appropriate ways of dealing with his anger.

Surprisingly, about 2 months after the murder of Sammy's brother, students at school started to use that tragedy and loss as a means of getting to Sammy. They made fun of him for having a brother who had been murdered.

Life at School

I don't see Sammy as much as I used to. He mostly stays with his sixth grade classmates. When I do see him, it is only to talk. We speak about how someone who has "passed" lives on in the hearts of those who were close to him. We speak about how to use the death of someone close to you to make you a stronger person on this earth. Periodically we speak about education and opportunity. When someone interrupts these conversations, Sammy immediately switches back into his aggressive and proving new self. I, along with everyone else, become the "bitch."

I don't expect to receive "A Sunny Day" picture ever again. Summer has passed for him. Yet, I know that he still holds a paintbrush in a hand behind his back. I don't know what his new pictures will look like. I don't know what will happen to him. I do know that if a student loses faith and strength in his soul, you lose the ability to teach him.

The desired action in the case of Sammy is a call for understanding. Alison enables us to see a human face and real-life problems behind the statistics and test scores.

SAMPLE 12.2
KAY DICKE, EDEN PRAIRIE

Kay Dicke created a nice, crisp introduction that draws the reader right into the paper. Her descriptions are precise, allowing us to see exactly what is happening at each stage.

MOTIVATING STUDENTS TO READ

Reading is an important part of a child's education. All subjects at any grade level include reading in many forms, whether it's nonfiction or a classic piece of fictional literature. There are many children who enjoy reading, but there are also many who do not. The benefits of reading are limitless, but what can be done to motivate all students to increase their time spent reading?

Action Research Question: How can I motivate my sixth grade students to increase their time spent reading?

Methods of Collecting Data

Collecting data was the first step of the action research process. The first method utilized was a general reading survey given to 27 sixth grade students. Questions asked pertained to the amount of free time out of school students spent reading and the types of books they read. Results of the survey showed that the majority of students like to read but most spent very little time outside of school doing it, usually 1 to 3 hours each week. Of the books read, adventure and humorous books were by far the most popular genres selected. The survey results supported a need for increased reading by these sixth grade students.

The next step of the research process was to begin observing and taking daily field notes during a 1-week period. These observations took place throughout the day during a variety of different subjects. Many questions from the student survey were considered as these observations were made, including, How often did students read during the school day? What types of reading did they do? What kinds of books do they select to read during their free reading time? What can be done to promote more reading by all students? Are students choosing books that are appropriate for their reading abilities?

Observations led to some general conclusions: Several students were observed reading and making great progress by completing one or more books throughout the week. At least seven students really did not seem to take an interest in the books they selected and spent more time looking around the classroom. Others had a different book each day, not actually reading one book completely. Students interested in reading often chose to read after completing assignments in class. There was definitely a wide variety of readers in this group.

From my field notes a checklist was created (see Figure 12.1). Each day for 1 week during silent reading time a small group of four or five students

STUDENT	DATE	TIME	TYPE OF BOOK	ON TASK	COMMENTS

FIGURE 12.1   Independent Reading Checklist

was observed. The checklist was used to look for the following behaviors: being on task, progress completing the same book, and the type of book being read. The checklist was an easy and useful method of collecting specific data.

After 2 weeks of collecting field notes and using my checklist, I asked students to begin using a log sheet to record the number of minutes and the genre of books read over a 2-week period both at home and at school. The number of minutes was totaled and written on a chart to track their progress.

Findings

Students responded positively to the reading log at school. They were very dedicated about tracking their minutes. As the study progressed, they took on more responsibility with their reading and began to make sure to track minutes spent reading their social studies book and other expository reading material encountered throughout the day.

At first, the number of minutes read at home was not as high as at school. Many students had very poor results here and quite a few did not return the log sheet from home. However, the minutes read at school and home were documented and would be used as a baseline to measure progress.

A high percentage of sixth grade students seemed to pick up on the importance of reading through their logs. A chart was posted in the classroom on which their minutes of reading were tracked. Many students compared their minutes to others' and seemed pleased with their results. They were always eager to get a new reading log sheet. Also, positive comments were made by parents at conferences. Here, goals were set to improve the time spent reading at home in order to increase students' total minutes.

The next log sheets were given for an additional 2 weeks. Again, these students took real initiative in tracking their reading minutes at school. However, the results of the home log were just as poor as the last time. Many still did not turn them in or if they did, they did little reading. However, 80% of the students in this class did improve their total minutes of reading (in school and at home) from the first reading log.

I realized that I needed to take more time discussing my expectations for the home logs. I talked with students and found that they read a lot of things at home such as web pages on the Internet, magazines, and even cereal boxes. I encouraged them to log those minutes and helped them to realize that they were reading more than they thought.

The results of the third reading log were improved again: 92% of the home logs were returned this time and the number of total minutes read (in school and at home) was increased.

Conclusions

Students took pride in their accomplishments here, and at the same time, they found that reading can be something enjoyable to do every day. Small gains were made in the amount of reading time. By the end of the school year my ultimate goal would be to get all students reading more and reading more independently without instruction.

SAMPLE 12.3
LOUANN STRACHOTA

LouAnn Strachota, a paraprofessional working in a classroom, was in the process of getting her teacher certification. I included her work to show how preservice teachers might use action research to analyze and reflect on their learning environments. LouAnn wanted to study the behavior of students in one of her classes; however, she did not know where to start. This is a common predicament among beginning action researchers. To provide more focus, she did a short pilot study to see what behaviors students were displaying. She used this initial observation to create a checklist (see Figure 12.2). Then, instead of trying to chart every student's behavior, she decided to look at one student each day. This made the task more manageable and helped her focus on specific behaviors over a predetermined time.

Student's Name: __Don N.__   Date: _____

Recorded at 5-minute intervals.

ON-TASK BEHAVIOR. THE STUDENT IS:	10:30	10:35	10:40	10:45	10:50	10:55	11:00
—Working							
—Listening to directions		x		x	x		
—Reading			x				
—Engaged in listening	x						
—Working with somebody else							
—Responding to the teacher							
—Other							

FIGURE 12.2 On-Task Behavior Checklist

ON- AND OFF-TASK BEHAVIOR IN A
HIGH SCHOOL HEALTH CLASS

This study was undertaken in order to examine the relationship between on- and off-task behavior in an Emotional Behavior Disorder (EBD) level 4 resource room in a high school health class. I work as a paraprofessional here and am in the process of getting my teaching certification. I was interested in finding out why there were differences in students' on- and off-task behaviors.

Collecting Data

Data were collected from observations using a checklist that indicated on- and off-task behavior at 5-minute intervals (Figures 12.2 and 12.3).

This health class was taught from 10:17 A.M. to 11:12 A.M. 5 days a week. I chose to study students' behavior in this particular class because there were only four students here: three boys and one girl. One of these students was observed each day over the course of 17 school days. The behavior of each student was noted at 5-minute intervals.

Recorded at 5-minute intervals.

OFF-TASK BEHAVIOR. THE STUDENT IS:	10:30	10:35	10:40	10:45	10:50	10:55	11:00
—Talking to somebody						x	x
—Doodling							
—Listening to another student							
—Looking in his/her desk							
—In a study carrel							
—Working on something else							
—Making noises							
—Walking around							
—Other							

OBSERVATIONS:

Don has not been to class for a few days—but while here he was working very well until the last 10 minutes of class. He then walked around the room and talked to other students in the room.

FIGURE 12.3   Off-Task Behavior Checklist

The first few times that students were told that they were going to be observed they kept watching to see what marks they were being given. After a few days, however, the stigma of being observed wore off and they acted in their usual manner.

The Classroom Setting

This EBD classroom contained 10 chair-desks placed in a half-circle surrounding a kidney-shaped table in front of the room. There were three study carrels in the back of the room and a teacher's desk in the front of the room on the far left side. Rules regarding behavior were posted on a chart in front of the room. The study carrels were used for students who displayed disruptive or inappropriate behaviors. If there were additional infractions, students were sent to an independent study room.

Other behavior management techniques included three forms of classroom contracts: limited, expected, and privileged. Each contract had varying levels of student privileges.

Findings

One noticeable observation was that students had a hard time staying focused around 11:00 A.M. because they were hungry. Students started watching the clock around this time, waiting for the bell to ring. Included here are the observations for each student (see Table 12.1).

Don

Don was observed only twice due to low attendance. When others were working on assignments, Don seemed to work well and stay on task. During the last 10 minutes of class he usually talked to other students.

Sally

Sally was observed four times. She seemed to spend most of her time working with an aide. She missed 3 days of class during this observation. When she returned, she worked hard to catch up on her assignments.

TABLE 12.1   **Total On-Task and Off-Task Behaviors**

STUDENT	ON-TASK BEHAVIOR	OFF-TASK BEHAVIOR
Don	85%	15%
Sally	90%	10%
Tom	80%	20%
Harry	83%	17%
Total Average	84.5%	15.5%

Tom

Tom was observed four times. He came every day but sometimes had to leave early to prepare for a choir concert that he was in. One day he was the only student in class and was able to work without distraction and stay on task. However, if somebody else was talking, Tom became easily distracted. When Sally was in the room, he often wanted to talk with her. He told another student that he had a crush on her. He was asked several times by the teacher or aide to stop talking. When Sally was not in class Tom's on-task behavior improved by 15%. Tom is a good student and can work very well in class when he wants to. However, it appears that he is easily distracted by Sally.

Harry

Harry was observed six times. His lowest percentage for on-task behavior was 40% and his highest was 100%. On his low day, Harry complained about being extremely tired and said he was not going to do any work. My observations also showed that he did not stay on task very well when he was tired. When he was tired, he complained that he was not feeling well and said he wanted to lie on the floor. If Harry appeared to be in a good mood, he worked very well and stayed on task. Harry also stayed on task much better if there was only one other student in class.

Conclusions

The high percentage of on-task behavior could be contributed to the small class size. My observations showed that when fewer students were in class they spent more time working. Also, students completed all assignments and stayed on task when they were working directly with the teacher or with me.

Off-task behavior resulted most often when (1) students were moody or tired, (2) students finished their assignments early and disrupted others, (3) there were more students in the class, and (4) one student liked another and preferred talking to work.

Recommendations

Based on these observations, I recommend the following:

1. Students should have something else to work on or read when they are finished with their work. They need preplanned assignments and other things to do to keep them occupied.
2. Students should be separated from other students if they keep talking.
3. Assignments should involve opportunities for hands-on experiences and allow students to interact. This would keep them involved and prevent boredom.
4. The units should be made more interesting by using content enrichment activities that keep students involved.

Things That Worked

These are some of the things that seemed to work in this health class:

1. Students recorded their ideas of what was interesting or important in each chapter (instead of using a study guide or worksheet).
2. A bingo game was created with the vocabulary words from each chapter.
3. Teams were used and a quiz game was created that used questions from the assigned chapters.
4. A visual organizer that showed the content covered during the unit seemed to help students understand.

Final Thought

Overall, I feel that a variety of methods should be incorporated into the curriculum to keep EBD students on task and interested in the subjects being taught.

SAMPLE 12.4
GEORGINA L. PETE

Georgina's action research project reads much like a staffing report (which it was). At the end of this report she outlines four things that she will try to implement to improve the situation.

HELPING BRANDON

Being the new talented and gifted (TAG) teacher in a suburban school district in the Twin Cities metro area, I had high hopes of starting the year off with a bang. However, I was approached not long after the school year started by a fourth grade teacher who had threatened one of her students with being taken out of the TAG program because of his low grades in her classroom. I decided this was an issue I needed to become involved with. This is a summary of the information I collected and the recommendations made for this student.

Data Collection

Information collected for this research was in the form of conferencing, observations with field notes, and interviewing. All data were collected over a 4-week period during the months of October and November.

The Conference

The first step was to set up a conference with the classroom teacher (Ms. Lee) and the principal (Ms. Kelly). Ms. Kelly was very familiar with this student, who I will refer to as Brandon, as she had him in her office several times to deal with discipline problems. In fact, she said that he had the most discipline offenses in the school. Ms. Kelly printed out a list of his infractions. These had to do mostly with being disrespectful and physical aggression.

The conference was very informative. Brandon's behavior in class, on the bus, and during recess was not what I saw when he was in my TAG classroom. I knew him to be polite, excited about learning, humorous, and well liked by his peers. Ms. Lee painted quite a different picture. She thought of him as very disrespectful and said he was not cutting it with his classroom assignments (he was not turning them in). Since he was not showing her his giftedness she felt he should not have the privilege of leaving the regular education classroom to go to the TAG classroom.

Ms. Kelly played a key role in this conference. She was very concerned about Brandon's future, as was I. She felt that the TAG classroom was something very important to him. Here he felt like he had some power and importance. She cautioned that taking away his TAG classes might make this troubled boy's situation more disastrous. I agreed.

We all agreed that something needed to be done to help Brandon steer his school career in a positive direction. His test scores indicated that he should have been operating at a much higher level; however, he was getting Cs and Ds in his classes. I agreed to make observations of him in the classroom and on the playground to see what might be done. The teacher and principal were going to stay in close contact with Brandon's mother (the father did not seem to play an active role in his son's education). All agreed that the mother needed to play a more active role in Brandon's education and help out with any action plan.

Observations

Brandon could be very sneaky and dishonest. He would look you in the eye and tell you he had all his work done when he did not. When I observed him in the classroom, he seemed to have a high level of on-task behavior if he was working with a partner in a situation in which both needed to cooperate in order to get the assignment done. However, when working by himself, he did not use his time very efficiently and became a distraction to others with his silliness. He also did not seem to put a great deal of effort into his assignments. Ms. Lee said that in the past, Brandon had claimed to have lost missing assignments or left them at home.

I also observed Ms. Lee to be very negative. In every discussion that I had with her, she never made one positive comment about him, whereas Ms. Kelly had made several positive comments and expressed concern for his future and seemed to have a real interest in turning his situation around.

Interviews

I interviewed Brandon and three of his peers in his TAG group. This gave me the impression that he has a history of being unorganized and irresponsible. They all agreed that they would not like to have Brandon in charge of getting something done for a group activity because "he never gets anything done." However, all looked favorably at him as a friend and seemed to enjoy working with him in TAG classes. They especially liked listening to him discuss and tell stories.

Brandon agreed that he needed to work hard in school at being more focused on his responsibilities. His attempts to be better organized and more responsible with his assignments usually lasted only a day at the most.

Recommendations

Based on the information collected here, I recommend the following:

1. Brandon should be placed in a different classroom. His mother also made this request, which Ms. Kelly granted. I believe that both the mother and Ms. Kelly felt as I did, that Ms. Lee was not a positive influence on Brandon and that he would be better matched with another teacher.

2. I will check in with Brandon on a regular basis. He is a very social person and likes an audience. I think that given an opportunity to express himself in an appropriate manner with somebody who is not continually pushing him to complete his homework with a higher quality, Brandon might feel less of an urge to act out by being silly in class and causing distraction. My goal here will be to encourage quality effort.

3. Communication with Brandon's mother must improve. He should get some positive calls home when he makes progress. His mother is used to getting calls home about discipline and late assignments, but not for positive behavior. I will be responsible for contacting her when Brandon and I have made some breakthroughs.

4. Brandon and his family should work on his organizational skills. I will recommend some reading for him and his family along this line.

Conclusions

I am hopeful that Brandon will benefit from these recommendations. I find him to be a very pleasant boy, but also someone who could end up being a leader in a negative way. I feel confident that he will enjoy having my interest in him so that he can express himself freely. He will be helped in all areas by a strong commitment at home to quality and organization.

SAMPLE 12.5

TERESA VAN BATAVIA, EISENHOWER ELEMENTARY, HOPKINS, MINNESOTA

Teresa Van Batavia's research shows the work of a master teacher carefully observing her students and making decisions based on students' needs. In this report she is able to create a good sense of being there. As you read the notes from her writing conferences, this classroom comes to life. Suddenly you can see exactly where her students are as writers. She also takes us inside her head, letting us overhear her thinking as she processes the information and makes decisions based on that information.

WRITING WORKSHOP

My first grade students at Eisenhower Elementary are involved in a writer's workshop setting at least three times a week. My concern is that children may be slipping through the cracks—doing little or no writing and not being noticed.

Data Collection

The first form of data collection that I used was that of a weekly checklist. As I circulated among students during the 2-week period from November 15 through December 3, 1999, I carried a clipboard and checked off each type of writing activity that I observed (see Figure 12.4). This checklist became an effective tool for helping me to choose minilesson topics for the children. I will continue to use this on an informal basis throughout the year.

In addition to the checklists, I met individually with each student and also collected their writing folders for further study of their writing habits. Following are my notes of these conferences.

Writer's Workshop Checklist, Week of November 15–19, 1999

Generating/prewriting	‖‖ ‖‖ ‖
Drawing/sketching	‖‖ ‖‖
Drafting	‖‖ ‖‖‖‖ ‖‖‖‖ ‖‖ ‖
Revising	‖‖ ‖
Editing	‖‖
Conference/talking	‖
Reading	‖
Other	‖‖ ‖

FIGURE 12.4   Writer's Workshop Checklist

Conference Notes—Individual Students

Joni is most comfortable starting with an illustration and then writing one or two sentences to accompany the picture. Her latest effort, however, is a story inspired by her neighbor's car accident. She is struggling with understanding how to expand it beyond two sentences.

Lynn and Valerie have regularly referred to their topic list and have created two to three stories each. Their writings have a solid beginning, middle, and end.

Tony, Walter, Jason, William, and Sonjia have accomplished very little over the past 2 months. Their folders contain very primitive drawings. All five students described frustration in choosing an idea and drawing or writing about it. Brainstorming ideas together failed to elicit a solid topic any of the five were willing to write about.

Tim has worked feverishly for the past five writing sessions on a story about his broken arm. He has included a great deal of detail on his surroundings as well as his emotions at the time.

Publishing has become Ryan's frantic goal. He worked diligently on a story titled "My World," a hodgepodge of facts and opinions about the world around him. We revised and edited together and now he is ready for publication.

Becky and Cassandra, two highly able students, have made little progress. The contents of their folders are simple drawings with little depth in writing.

Brian, Nancy, and Kirsten have successfully used the Five W's Web (who, what, where, why, and when) to generate ideas for their stories. They made a smooth transition from web to rough draft. All three found the web to be a useful tool and plan to use it again.

Picture books are the focus for Heather and Alicia as they sketch and then add the text to their drawings.

Unable to fathom the fact that he may choose topics for himself, Mitchell fluctuates between drawing and finding me to ask if his topic choice is acceptable. He is able to construct a very creative, oral story. These stories lose a lot in the recording process, which is difficult for Mitchell.

Conference Notes—Writing Difficulties

Two boys in my class are plagued by a need to spell each and every word perfectly. They are reluctant to put anything in writing without first verifying with an adult. This has had an adverse effect on the quality of their thoughts.

Another child has very poor fine-motor skills and several speech difficulties. He has been unable to function in this setting without an adult close by his side.

Conclusions

The two forms of data collection that I used supported each other in pointing out that I have a wide variety of stages of the writing process occurring on a daily basis. First of all, as I feared, five of my struggling students were frequently off task, frustrated by writer's block, unable to come up with a topic (even from their personal topic lists), and unable to sustain a 15–20 minute work period. As a result, I will begin a series of short minilessons with this small group. These lessons will begin with topic selection. This group of students seems to need a detailed step-by-step introduction and guided tour through the stages of the writing process. It will be necessary to bring them from start to finish through the entire process in a more structured setting.

I found the majority of my students to be in the drafting stage of their writing. These students varied widely in ability, but were similar in the fact that they could remain focused on their writing for a longer period than the three struggling writers mentioned previously. Seven of my students created a Five W's Web to generate ideas for their topic (a minilesson that was taught 2 weeks earlier). Of these seven, five were able to make the progression from the web to a piece of writing that had a beginning, middle, and end.

Given the results of the data I have collected, it seems sensible to proceed in the following manner: First, I need to address the needs of the struggling readers and writers by breaking the writing process down into more manageable steps. I plan to do this in the form of minilessons at the beginning of each writing period for this small group. We will choose a topic, brainstorm or generate ideas, and create rough drafts together. Students will be taught to work with a peer for revising and editing.

Second, I have a large group of children who are spending the majority of their time in the drafting and illustrating stages. I plan to revisit prewriting strategies regularly for a few weeks until I see a greater number of students applying these strategies. I believe that I have moved too quickly in expecting these children to pick up on brainstorming and webbing. I will need to do a great deal more modeling for it to transfer to their writing. When I am satisfied that this is a tool that the students understand and are able to use, I will move on to creating a first draft or sloppy copy of the web and brainstorming sessions that I have created as examples. I think that spending more time on each phase will lead to more children reaching the revising and editing stages.

Final Thoughts

This research has provided me valuable information in assessing the productivity and value of the writer's workshop model as it exists in my classroom. Although I found weak areas that need to be addressed, I also found children who greatly enjoy the freedom of choice. These children cannot wait to bring out their red folders and write about topics of utmost importance to them: broken arms, mothers with cancer, favorite pets, vacation trips, cherished holidays, and many others. One child recently reveled in the discovery that the red folder could be pulled out at any time during the day when he had a few extra minutes. The motivation to write exists. I now need to find the right combination of lessons to channel this desire through the stages of the writing process to publication.

SAMPLE 12.6
LINDA ROTH, ST. PETER SCHOOL DISTRICT, ST. PETER, MINNESOTA

This study was conducted by Linda Roth, a gifted education coordinator in St. Peter, Minnesota. She has included a short review of the literature at the beginning of her study. Notice how this serves to connect her observations with the ideas of others.

THE SOCIAL, EMOTIONAL, AND ACADEMIC ADJUSTMENT
OF AN ACCELERATED ELEMENTARY STUDENT

This action research study investigated the social, emotional, and writing development of a student who moved directly from a fourth to a sixth grade classroom.

Background

Grade acceleration can have a positive effect on the achievement of gifted students (Davis & Rimm, 1998). This strategy allows students to advance at an appropriate pace in order to meet their education needs. Researchers studying acceleration find that there are very few problems with social adjustment, academic achievement, or other effects (Colangelo & Davis, 1991). Advantages included improved task commitment, confidence, and academic advances.

On average, gifted students who are accelerated do as well as or better than older students in the same classroom, their social and emotional development is normally quite high, and they are more inclined to choose older students as companions (Clark, 1983). Therefore, the issue of age and maturity does not seem to be of consequence here.

Those who are apprehensive about the practice of grade skipping are concerned that skill gaps may surface in basic areas. Barbara Clark (1983) recommends that accelerated students be monitored and continually assessed. When considering a student for acceleration, it is important to have a thorough knowledge of the needs and abilities of that student with support from administration and staff at all stages (Gallagher & Gallagher, 1994).

Identification of the Action Research Problem

I work as a gifted and talented coordinator in the St. Peter, Minnesota, school district. A student in one of the elementary schools was accelerated from a fourth to sixth grade classroom. In this action research project I examined the social, emotional, and academic effects of this acceleration.

The Student

Bill was an 11-year-old male student. At the end of fourth grade he was going above and beyond the fourth grade tasks assigned to him. His fourth grade teacher described him as a good student, a nice person to talk to, and knowledgeable in many areas. He grasped concepts easily, finished assignments with time to spare, and completed extra assignments quickly. Other teachers who had worked with him gave him high praise for motivation, task commitment, and advanced knowledge. The hope was that by grade skipping, his enthusiasm would continue.

Behavior checklists completed by four teachers who had worked with him showed that he displayed many positive behaviors that might enable him to get along with his peers, function independently, and be successful academically.

On an academic achievement test Bill scored in the 95th percentile in reading and the 97th percentile in math. On a standardized ability test, he had an IQ score of 128, ranking him at the 97th percentile and classifying him in the superior range. On a standardized writing test it was found that his writing score was low because of the lack of sentence detail. Comments were made by the test facilitator and his fourth grade teacher that although his sentence structure, legibility, spelling, capitalization, punctuation, and sentence structure were good, Bill did not go into a great deal of detail in his writing.

Implementation of the Action Research

This study was begun during the fall of Bill's sixth grade year. The objective here was to find out how he was adjusting to skipping a grade, specifically in the area of writing. The social/emotional area was not a great concern to parents and teachers; however, for the well-being of Bill, I felt it important to also monitor this area of adjustment as it could have a bearing on the success of his acceleration.

Writing

Creative writing and expository writing samples were taken from Bill's sixth grade classroom portfolio. Other writing samples were taken from short answer tests and e-mail between Bill and me. These samples were evaluated using a writing rubric for middle school level performance. Format, mechanics, word choice, and organization were evaluated. In the creative writing samples, Bill's spelling, punctuation, and capitalization were of good quality. Words were used correctly and clearly; however, special or advanced vocabulary was not noted. In his expository writing, the introduction, paragraphs, and conclusions were present, but they were very brief and had little detail. No attempt was made to elaborate beyond what was being asked.

After an e-mail conversation with me and an interview with his classroom teacher regarding the importance of detail and elaboration, Bill was asked to write a creative story about a turkey. For this story, he was able to use his interest in technology and science. He wrote a four-page handwritten story about a turkey who lived in a space age city and visited a robot factory to obtain robot armor to protect himself from hunters of endangered species. This story ended with the explanation that it was all a dream sequence. This time more detail was evident, showing that Bill was capable of using detail and elaboration when writing about something that was of interest to him.

Social and Emotional Adjustment

Interviews with Bill were held weekly. In each of these he expressed great satisfaction with his new surroundings. Bill said that in sixth grade he was able to do whatever he wanted. He seemed to enjoy the freedom to make his own choices when assignments were completed. He also liked the responsibility of getting assignments done and turning them in on time.

Bill expressed concern about missing concepts in math; however, he felt that he generally got the ideas easily. His test results showed that he was not experiencing problems in this area. Bill also expressed concern about his art class. He felt he could put more effort into his drawings.

A goal Bill set at the beginning of the year was to get assignments in on time. He felt that he had met this goal. He also set a goal related to behavior, which was to not push people or interfere with their personal space. He felt this too had been met. Generally, Bill was pleased with his time management style and prided himself in completing his homework quickly.

Bill's sixth grade teacher was interviewed regarding his social and emotional adjustment as well as his academic performance. His teacher was pleased with all areas of adjustment. Bill had made friends in the class and had found others with similar interests. He had made two close friendships and was spending time with one of them outside of school. This teacher said that Bill was highly respected for his intellect and was sought after by classmates for information and help in academic areas. Academically, Bill was doing well. The teacher reiterated that he grasped new concepts in math quickly and needed little repetition to master them.

Conclusions

Overall, grade acceleration seems to have been successful here. Positive social interactions and academic achievement have been noted. Extra attention to his writing needs to be continued during the remainder of the year. Support from the classroom teacher and me will be important to the success of this student. Monitoring the support of Bill should continue throughout the year to ensure that problem areas do not develop.

References

Clark, B. (1983). *Growing up gifted*. Columbus, OH: Merrill.

Colangelo, N., & Davis, G. (1991). *Handbook of gifted education*. Boston: Allyn and Bacon.

Davis, G. A., & Rimm, S. B. (1998). *Education of the gifted and talented* (4th ed.). Boston: Allyn and Bacon.

Gallagher, J. J., & Gallagher, S. A. (1994). *Teaching the gifted child* (4th ed.). Boston: Allyn and Bacon.

SAMPLE 12.7
ANGELA HASSETT BRUNELLE GETTY, MARTINEZ, CALIFORNIA

This study by Angela Hassett Brunelle Getty looks at gender and special education referrals. She does a nice job of connecting her findings to the research literature. Notice how she keeps things as simple as possible to create a report that is easy to read. Also, she uses tables to display her findings. This creates a visual action research report that also enhances the readability. A simple, well-written report like this is much more apt to be read than one that is long and unorganized.

GENDER IMBALANCE IN SPECIAL EDUCATION
Purpose

This action research project was conducted to examine the relationship between gender and teacher referrals for special education services in our school. Do teachers possess certain biases toward males because of their behavior? Are males referred to student study teams (SST) more often than females? How many of the students referred actually qualify for special education services?

Participants

Participants in this study were students from kindergarten through fifth grade in an elementary school with high state academic achievements. The student population at this school consisted of 66% White, 19% Asian, 6% Hispanic, 4% Other, 3% Black, and 2% Filipino. Instructional staff provided support to students through special programs such as reading specialist, counseling, special education, library, vocal and instrumental music, gifted and talented education, physical education, and science and computer education.

Procedures

In our school, teachers refer students who they suspect have special needs to an SST. The SST then looks at various classroom data and that from psychoeducational assessment. This study examined the files of students who had been referred by their teacher to the SST during the 2002–2003 school year. There were 35 total files; 23 of them were active SST files and 12 had been resolved or were in process of a psychoeducational assessment. Figure 12.5 shows the grade and gender breakdown.

After obtaining the permission of the vice principal, who is in charge of the SST process, student SST files and cumulative files were collected for those students whose teacher had initiated the SST process during some part of the 2002–2003 school year. Each student's file was then reviewed. Data were collected using a student data sheet. This was a data sheet designed to collect the following information: grade level, gender, month they were referred, reason for referral to the student study team, and whether they qualified for special education services.

Files were reviewed to see if students were referred for behavior, academics, or both. In order to be consistent throughout the data collection

GRADE	TOTAL	MALE	FEMALE
Kindergarten	3	1	2
1st	8	4	4
2nd	8	4	4
3rd	5	3	2
4th	9	5	4
5th	2	2	0
Total	35	19	16

FIGURE 12.5   Files Examined for SST

process, *behavior* was the term used to indicate those instances in which classroom teachers described a student using the terms "difficulty staying focused," "lacks motivation," "off task," "not independent," or "easily distracted." *Academics* was the term used to indicate when a student was below grade level in specific academic areas.

Analysis

Data were analyzed by noting the referral totals and separating them by gender into the following three categories: behavior only, academics only, and behavior and academics. Also noted were the number of students referred to special education versus those who qualified for special education services. This too was broken down into gender categories.

Findings and Conclusions

Reasons for Referral

In our school, slightly more males than females were referred (see Figure 12.6). Slightly more males were referred for both behavior-only reasons as well as behavior and academics. Slightly more females were referred for academics-only.

Because of the limited numbers in this action research project, no strong conclusions can be made; however, the results seem to reflect the results of Phipps's (1982) study of 165 special education students. Phipps examined the differences between males and females in academic achievement and behavior and looked at how this affected the referral process. In her study, behavior was the reason for referral in 83% of the cases for boys, but in only 45% of the cases for girls. She concluded that boys might be overplaced in special education classes to relieve the pressures of behavior management in the regular education classroom. Further, she posited that girls may be excluded from referral to special education programs because of their passive and more manageable behaviors. Lloyd, Kauffman, Landrum, and Roe (1991) have also reported that boys outnumber girls in special education referrals by a ratio of more than 2:1. Higher referral rates have also

	TOTAL	MALE	FEMALE
Behavior Only	11	7	4
Academics Only	11	4	7
Behavior and Academics	13	8	5
Total Number of Students	35	19	16

FIGURE 12.6   **Reasons for Referral to Student Study Teams**

	TOTAL	MALE	FEMALE
Number of Students Referred for Special Ed. Services	14	7	7
Number of Students Who Qualified for Special Ed. Services	4	1	3

FIGURE 12.7   Students Referred Versus the Number Qualified for Special Education Services

been reported by Anderson (1997), Flynn and Rahbar (1994), MacMilliam, Gresham, Lopez, and Bocian (1996), McIntyre (1988), Shinn, Tindal, and Spira (1987), and Ysseldyke, Vanderwood, and Shriner (1997).

Qualifying for Special Education Services

This study found that of the students referred, there were slightly more females than males who actually qualified for the special education services (see Figure 12.7). Of these, one female qualified was for academics only and two females for behavior and academics. One male qualified for academics and behaviors. This may reflect the study by Flynn and Rahbar (1994), who found that girls seemed to be less likely to be referred and thus, underidentified for remedial services.

Plan of Action

Based on the information found in this study, I will be making the following suggestions to our school principal:

1. Teachers should be made aware of the general tendency to overidentify boys for referral to special education programs. I will recommend teacher inservices be conducted to inform teachers of this and provide instruction on behavior management techniques that would work specifically with the male population. Also, we may want to provide inservices on teaching practices that are less likely to cause behavior problems.

2. Because there are often fewer behavior problems, girls may be underidentified for referral. This is something that needs attention in the coming year. Again, teacher inservice and training should be made available to inform teachers of female learning styles.

3. Our school needs to have more prereferral interventions that are documented before students are referred for psychoeducational assessments. We should probably set up some procedures for this, with a variety of intervention strategies that could be used by classroom teachers.

4. We need to keep our eye on this issue. A study like this should be conducted every year.

References

Anderson, K. G. (1997). Gender bias and special education referrals. *Annals of Dyslexia, 47,* 151–162.

Flynn, J. M., & Rahbar, M. H. (1994). Prevalence of reading failure in boys compared with girls. *Psychology in Schools, 31,* 66–71.

Lloyd, J. W., Kauffman, J. M., Landrum, T. J., & Roe, D. L. (1991). Why do teachers refer pupils for Special Education? An analysis of referral records. *Exceptionality, 2,* 115–126.

MacMillian, D. L., Gresham, F. M., Lopez, M. F., & Bocian, K. (1996). Comparison of students nominated for prereferral interventions by ethnicity and gender. *Journal of Special Education, 30,* 133–151.

McIntyre, L. (1988). Teacher gender: A predictor of special education referral? *Journal of Learning Disabilities, 21,* 382–383.

Phipps, P. A. (1982). The LD learner is often a boy—Why? *Academic Therapy, 17,* 425–430.

Shinn, M. R., Tindal, G. A., & Spira, D. A. (1987). Special Education referrals as an index of teacher tolerance: Are teachers imperfect tests? *Exceptional Children, 54,* 32–40.

Ysseldyke, J. E., Vanderwood, M. L., & Shriner, J. (1997). Changes over the past decade in special education referral to placement probability: An incredibly reliable practice. *Diagnostique, 23,* 193–201.

SAMPLE 12.8

MICHELLE BAHR, SHAKOPEE, MINNESOTA

As part of my Literacy Methods graduate course that I teach at Minnesota State University, Mankato, I have my students conduct short action research projects related to literacy. I have found that these often serve to reinforce many of the ideas that I try to get across during class (the importance of choice and holistic teaching strategies). Also, these projects present a portrait of students that you simply would not get by looking at a series of scores. And perhaps most important, these projects all serve to inform teaching. Michelle Bahr's action research project provides a sense of adolescents' attitudes about reading. Although her findings cannot reasonably be generalized to a larger population, they do help in understanding this population.

This was a powerful educational exercise for me. In doing this action research project I noticed some interesting things related to students' attitudes toward reading. I surveyed 10 students who were friends of my 17-year-old son to get a sense of their attitude toward reading (see Figure 12.8). They were in grades 11 and 12 and ages 16 and 17. At least two that I know of have some learning difficulties.

Date: _____   Your age: _____   Grade: _____

READING ATTITUDE SURVEY

Reading and Interest Inventory
(yes or no answers here please)
1. _____ I borrow books from the library or school for educational reading.
2. _____ I borrow books from the library or school for pleasure reading.
3. _____ I buy books for educational reading.
4. _____ I buy books for pleasure reading.
5. _____ My parents used to (or still do) read to me.
6. _____ I read before I go to bed.
7. _____ I read magazines.
8. _____ I read only when I have to.
9. _____ I read for enjoyment.
10. _____ I read the newspaper sometimes.
11. _____ I like to read poetry.
12. _____ I like to read song lyrics.
13. _____ I like to receive books as gifts.
14. _____ I would like to hear my teacher read out loud more.

What are your top three favorite books
1.
2.
3.

Reading Questions
(please fill in the blanks)
1. I think books are . . .
2. I think reading . . .
3. Reading is hard when . . .
4. Reading is easy when . . .
5. My favorite magazine is . . .
6. I think the newspaper is . . .

Information Questions
(please fill in the blanks)
1. School is . . .
2. I wish teachers . . .
3. When I finish high school . . .
4. When I get my report card . . .
5. I'd read more if . . .
6. I cannot read when . . .
7. I like reading about . . .
8. I don't like to read about . . .
9. When I read out loud . . .
10. To me books are . . .

I read because . . .

I write because . . .

Are there any other comments about reading you'd like to share?

FIGURE 12.8   Michelle Bahr's Reading Survey

Findings

Reading and Interest Inventory

Under Reading and Interest Inventory only one statement received a unanimous "Yes" by all respondents. That was item 12, "I like to read song lyrics." Also, most of these students borrow and buy books for both pleasure reading and educational reading. All except one student were read to by their parents when they were young. And they definitely did not like reading poetry. From this set of questions I learned that song lyrics seemed to be a hot item for reading. I'm thinking that this might be an excellent source to use to get adolescent students reading.

Five of the teens mentioned a sports-related book as one of their favorite books to read. The Bible was mentioned by five students.

Reading Questions

These kids seemed to like books that are fun. Their definition of fun was "a good book that isn't too hard to read." In response to item 3 under Reading Questions, "Reading is hard when . . . ," all said that reading was hard when they didn't like what they were reading. This makes perfect sense. Choice, choice, choice! Even if students don't like a textbook used in school, I will try to supplement their reading with related books that would be defined as "fun." There are many alternatives to using only a textbook in my classes.

Information Questions

The most interesting and important insights came from the Information Questions. School is boring for most of these students. They wish their teachers were not so crabby, peppier, and that they understood them better. They also wished that teachers would make assignments more fun and would take more time in going over lessons and assignments. They seemed to be genuinely frustrated when there wasn't enough time for an assignment or when they didn't understand the assignment and they got a bad grade. These are all things that are relatively easy to fix.

The majority of these students have difficulty reading when there is noise and lots of distractions like people talking or hearing noises from another classroom. A quiet classroom environment when reading seems to be important. The kinds of books they liked reading included biographies and war and murder stories. The kinds of books they didn't like to read included romance, history, and any English textbook.

In response to the prompt, "I read because . . . ," most responded, "Because I have to" or "it's something to do when I'm bored." In response to the prompt, "I write because . . . ," student responses included "Because it's fun," "it's an easy way to express myself," "I can put my thoughts on paper," and "I can list pros and cons to help me make decisions."

Ideas

The sample size was small in this survey, but still it gave me some important new insights. I will certainly be much more careful about my choice of reading selections for my students. I want to make sure that I find books that students want to read. Also, I will make sure that in regard to selecting reading material, students have choice, choice, and choice!!!

SAMPLE 12.9
KIM SCHAFER, MINNETONKA, MINNESOTA

Kim Schafer was also a student in my graduate literacy methods class. She conducted a reading interest inventory in her second grade class that she followed up with individual interviews. To extend her research she then compared her results with a reading miscue analysis that she had done previously. At the end of her report she describes how she would like to extend this project to look for change over time.

My second grade classroom includes wide range of abilities, from emergent readers to truly independent readers. Included here are children who receive reading support services, although most students are at the expected second grade level for our school.

Before administering my reading survey to the whole class (Figure 12.9), I went over each question to make sure they could read it and understand it. I followed up this survey with individual interviews in order to get a better feel for at-home reading experiences. After analyzing the survey results I compared them to a miscue analysis I had done earlier. I wanted to see if there were any trends or correlations.

Name: _____   Age: _____   Date: _____

1. When I read I feel . . .
2. I enjoy reading books that are: facts/stories
3. I like to read about . . .
4. I don't like to read about . . .
5. At home I am read to. Yes/No
6. At home I read to myself. Yes/No
7. When I read at home I am usually . . .
8. When I go to the library I like to get books about . . .
9. This year I would like to learn to read . . .
10. I read things in the newspaper. Yes/No

Other things you want me to know about your reading:

FIGURE 12.9   Kim Schafer's Reading Survey

Findings

Interestingly, those students who were more able readers (had fewer mistakes in their miscue analyses) thought about reading in a more global sense. For example, many wanted to learn how to read maps or how to read mysteries. They also seemed to have broader reading experiences with magazines and newspapers. These more able readers also said they lost themselves in books or liked reading because they used their imaginations.

Those students who were less able readers (had more mistakes in their miscue analyses) tended to like to read fact books about specific subjects. They did not see reading as a viable entertainment option. Almost every one of these students said he or she wanted to learn to read chapter books—not about anything special, just chapter books. Being able to read chapter books is considered a milestone by most second graders, although those who do read them think it is no big deal and will often read picture books.

I would like to redo and extend this survey in February or March and then compare answers. My hope is that all students will begin to take a more global view of reading and see themselves as capable readers. In addition, I am hoping that they will be able to express a greater knowledge of genre and be able to elaborate further when explaining their likes and dislikes in reading.

A FINAL WORD

The length and complexity of an action research project do not always increase its rigor and insight. Many short action research projects provide important insight and information. The goal of action research is to increase understanding in order to improve teaching practice. All the reports in this chapter meet this criterion.

CHAPTER THIRTEEN

PRESENTING YOUR ACTION RESEARCH

If a teacher has a good idea in the middle of the forest but nobody is there to hear it, does that idea make a noise? This chapter talks about venues for sharing your action research.

THE EDUCATIONAL ENVIRONMENT

Your Colleagues

The most appreciative audience for presentations of your action research might be your colleagues. These presentations can take the form of a formal staff development inservice, a short talk at a regular faculty meeting, or simply a continued dialogue with colleagues. Whatever the form, these presentations promote conversation among teachers about the dynamics of their classrooms and various pedagogical methods and are essential for promoting reflection and growth in our profession.

When presenting action research projects, your findings are more apt to be attended to by your audience if you keep the presentation short and focused and include only those ideas that other teachers might use in their classroom. Presentations are also enhanced by including some kind of visual aid in the form of a poster, overhead, PowerPoint presentation, or handout. Always leave time for discussion at the end. Aspects of a short presentation include the following:

1. *Your purpose.* Why did you choose to study what you did? Did a particular problem, special interest, or question lead you to your research? Describe your reasons for engaging in the action research project.
2. *Theoretical background.* Keep this short. If available, include some research or basic theoretical ideas related to your question, then link this to classroom practice.

3. *Data collection.* Describe the various forms of data and tell how you collected them.
4. *Findings.* Tell what you found. If your findings lend themselves to visual display, create a poster or handouts with the information in the form of a list, graph, or table.
5. *Conclusions.* What do your findings mean? What do they imply? What might be some of the reasons you came up with your findings? Again, keep this short.
6. *Your plan of action.* Tell what you plan to do or what you might do as a result of your findings. You might also ask teachers to brainstorm ideas for possible actions or possible solutions. This creates dialogue and allows teachers to share their ideas.
7. *Time for questions and discussion.* Finally, always leave time at the end of a presentation for questions and discussion.

Your Students

Your students will be interested to know what you found. After all, they have a vested interest in what goes on in your classroom. Also, action research mirrors the inquiry process, a powerful learning technique that you might consider using in your class. Inquiry is the process of designing learning activities that incorporate methods of science (Johnson, 2000). In doing inquiry, students are taught to ask a question and then to collect data to answer that question. In sharing your action research with your students you will be modeling the inquiry process as well as demonstrating methods for collecting and presenting data. Just as with teachers, allow and encourage questions and discussion. Students' thoughts and observations at the end of an action research study are often apt and might even be included as a form of data in your final report.

School Boards, Principals, and Administrators: Making a Case

Decisions in education are sometimes made apart from a theoretical context or without considering any of the research related to learning and education. This can result in bad educational practice or educational malpractice. Action research can be used to enable your school or district to make informed decisions. It can also be used to make a case for employing a particular methodology or program. However, when doing action research to make a case, the onus is on you to keep an objective perspective during all phases of your research. That is, you must allow for the possibility that the literature or the data collected might disprove your original thesis.

Your Classroom: Evaluating New Programs

If you are piloting a new program, action research can be used as formative evaluation to see how things are going and what needs to be changed and as summative evaluation to judge the program's effectiveness. The key in using action research for evaluation is to keep the data collection simple and manageable. Do not let data collection get in the way of implementing the new program.

To illustrate how action research might be used in program evaluation, at Minnesota State University, Mankato, I piloted a new approach to my under-graduate literacy methods course. Students spent less time in my class listening to me speak (1 day a week) and more time in an elementary classroom practic-ing their teaching skills (3 days a week). Before I implemented the program, I made a plan to collect four types of data: (1) a pre- and poststudy survey of the undergraduate students, (2) a poststudy survey of teachers, (3) observations recorded using field notes, and (4) an analysis of students' reflections collected at eight points during the course of the semester. My goal was to see what was happening with this new approach, what was working, and what needed to be changed.

When the study was completed and the data compiled, I found that overall the new plan was fairly successful in helping to create knowledgeable, skillful teachers. My students could see how the ideas I presented in my methods classes applied to a classroom setting. But like any new program, it needed some tweaks and changes. The data collected were extremely useful in helping to pinpoint the changes that needed to be made. As a final step, I made a short presentation to the dean and to my colleagues at a faculty meeting. There I was able to make recom-mendations about future programs based on some solid data.

Parent Conferences

I remember as a beginning teacher feeling that I never had enough to say to parents at parent conferences. I was able to describe the child in terms of numbers using scores on standardized tests and homework assignments, but that was about it. As stated previously, many of the data collection methods described in Chapter 8 are forms of authentic assessment. The individual data related to each child can be used to provide a much clearer picture of who that child is as well as his or her strengths and interests.

Also, parents like to know what is happening in your classroom. Sharing your action research in a short newsletter gives them a sense of what is happening. It lets them know that your classroom is an intellectually vibrant place, and it shows that you are always looking for the best methods to use in helping their chil-dren grow and learn.

As Part of a Master's Thesis

In the Department of Educational Studies: Special Populations at Minnesota State University, Mankato, one of the options we have used as part of our master's the-sis is to require that students present their research project to an audience. After all, why should they do all the work for a thesis and have it read only by the members of their graduate committee? We want this new knowledge to move out into the teaching field where it can be used and applied.

1. The presentation should be between 30 and 45 minutes in duration.
2. Enter a teacher mode. Remember, the audience knows nothing about your topic.
3. Describe the problem, topic, research question, or area of investigation as well as what brought you to it.
4. Include a short synthesis of related research or the theoretical background (review of the literature).
5. Briefly describe how you collected your data.
6. Describe your results or what you found. Along with your recommendations, this should be the heart of your presentation.
7. Include your recommendations, practical application, or plan of action. Make sure there is a strong connection between your results and your recommendations, application, or plan of action.
8. Be clear and concise. Include only what will be of interest to your audience. What you choose not to include is as important as what you choose to include in a presentation.
9. Use a visual aid of some kind (overhead, poster, PowerPoint, video clip, or handouts).
10. Include 5 to 10 minutes for questions at the end.

FIGURE 13.1   Guidelines for an Action Research Presentation

Presentation venues may include a district or school inservice as described previously, a professional conference (described in the next section), a parent organization, a graduate class, or a university-sponsored conference consisting of action research projects by other graduate students. General guidelines for the research presentation are in Figure 13.1.

The Presentation Response Form in Figure 13.2 is used to assess and give feedback to presenters. This form can also be downloaded from our website. If action researchers make their presentations in their districts, at a conference, or in some other off-campus location, we give them self-addressed stamped envelopes and ask that three people present evaluate their presentation. We also ask that they turn in an audiotape of their presentation so that we can listen and evaluate.

THE PROFESSIONAL ENVIRONMENT

Professional Conferences and Conventions

These days most researchers in education recognize the importance of including teachers' voices in the conversation. Professional conferences and teachers' conventions are a good place to create this conversation. I would recommend contacting local or state organizations that hold conventions and ask them to send you a proposal form. The proposal form you receive describes exactly what you need to include and usually needs to be returned 4 to 6 months before the conference date.

Academic Journals

You might consider sending your study to an academic journal. This is a good way to get your ideas out there for others to see and use. Start with state journals or

Action Research Project
Presentation Response Form

Presenter: _____ Date: _____

Session title or topic: _____

Name and position of person completing this form: _____

Directions: This is a presentation of his/her Master's Thesis. Please rate this presenter's session on the following items using this scale: 5 = excellent, 4 = good, 3 = average, 2 = fair, 1 = poor

Content
1. Relevance of action research project to its intended application: _____
2. Importance of this action research project: _____
3. Connection of action research project to practice: _____
4. Ground in the literature: _____
5. Appropriately rigorous, sheds new light in an area/application: _____

Scholarship
6. Action research project enhanced professionalism of presenter: _____
7. Demonstrated knowledge directly linked to research literature: _____
8. Quality of content and methods reflects graduate level work: _____
9. Limitations acknowledged: _____
10. Credible work, lacking in bias: _____
11. Used data to answer a question: _____
12. Made recommendations based on data collected: _____

Communication and Presentation
13. Ability to convey ideas/meaning: _____
14. Familiarity/ease with topic/study: _____
15. Clarity of presentation: _____
16. Ability to respond to questions and address concerns: _____
17. Professional quality of handouts/materials/visual aids: _____
18. Overall professional quality of presentation: _____

Specific comments regarding strengths and weaknesses of this presentation
(use the back side if necessary):

FIGURE 13.2   Presentation Response Form

smaller publications that are focused on areas related to your study. You can get addresses and submission requirements for these as well as other important information at the following websites:

1. National Science Teachers Association Journals and Publications: www.nsta.org/journals
2. National Council for the Social Studies: www.socialstudies.org
3. International Reading Association: www.reading.org
4. National Council of Teachers of Mathematics: www.nctm.org
5. National Council of Teachers of English: www.ncte.org

To find other possible academic journals to submit your action research studies, do an Internet search using terms such as *education, teachers, publishing, academic journals,* or some variations of these.

Academic journals are peer reviewed, which means that two or more people look over your writing, make comments and suggestions (not always pleasant), and recommend whether to publish. Do not get discouraged, however, if you get your action research report back with a rejection or many suggestions for improvement. It is quite common for writers to have to revise several times before an article is finally accepted for publication. Although this process may seem a little intimidating at first, getting feedback and specific comments is one of the best ways to improve your writing.

ERIC

ERIC stands for the Educational Resources Information Center. Sponsored by the National Library of Education at the U.S. Department of Education, it is a massive database containing information on all imaginable subjects related to education. ERIC has evolved since the second edition of this book. It now accepts fewer types of material but of higher quality. Accepted types include research reports, dissertations, and conference papers and presentations. You can submit your action research projects online at www.eric.ed.gov.

LOCAL COMMUNITY ORGANIZATIONS

In most communities people outside education appreciate hearing about the latest teaching trends and ideas. Often, the perceptions these people have of education are based on their own experiences (which can be 20 to 40 years old) and what they read about in newspapers and magazines. Neither of these are very accurate sources. Presenting your action research at functions such as Rotary lunches, social and professional groups, religious organizations, parent organizations, or other types of gatherings provides people in your community with an updated version of the latest trends in education and, at the same time, generates good public relations for your school.

SUMMARY

- Your colleagues and students are often interested in hearing about the findings of your action research project.
- Action research can be used to make a case of a particular methodology or program or for evaluating new programs.
- The data collected in action research can be used to provide a more complete picture of your students.

- Professional conferences, academic journals, and the Education Resources Information Center are all viable venues for sharing your action research projects.
- Local community organizations are often interested in hearing of the latest trends in education and may also be a good place to present your action research findings.

QUESTIONS AND ACTIVITIES

1. Visit the ERIC website. Find five articles or reports related to an area of interest.
2. Do an Internet search to find possible journals to submit an action research report. List three journals you might consider.
3. List three other places besides a journal where you might present your action research report.

CHAPTER FOURTEEN

WRITING AN ACTION RESEARCH REPORT

Unless you are making an oral presentation or conducting action research only for your own edification, you need to create some sort of written document describing your observation and findings. This chapter contains suggestions for writing an action research report.

An action research report is written using an academic writing style. Academic writing enhances the credibility of your report and increases the likelihood that it will be read. It is not within the scope of this book to describe at length the many parts of academic writing; however, a few tips concerning tone and style, length, and clarity are offered in the following sections.

TONE AND STYLE

Academic writing is different from creative writing in that it is more concise and written as objectively as possible. The prime directive in academic writing is clear communication, thus, ideas are presented in a logical, orderly manner so that the reader is able to gain a maximum amount of understanding with a minimum amount of time and effort.

Traditionally, experimental research is written in an objective style. You will not find any *I*, *you*, or *me* pronouns—only the facts described in third person. Personal observations are saved for a special section at the end of the report and are also written in third person. The goal in experimental research reports is to eliminate any bias or subjectivity on the part of the researcher and allow only the data to speak.

Action research, however, is written in a more subjective style. It is recognized that you are part of the research; thus, your thoughts and observations are valued and are recorded along the way. (You can see this personal, reflective writing style in the sample research reports in Chapter 12.) But keep in mind that an action research report is not a letter to the editor. Pronounced biases or hidden agendas are fairly easy to spot and detract from your accuracy and credibility.

In your action research report, you must demonstrate that your descriptions are fair and honest if your research is to be given credence. Consider the following examples:

Less Effective

I really believe that schools should throw away those disgusting state standards that require that certain things be taught in a certain way. These outrageous mandates are an insult to our hard-working, knowledgeable teachers who know best how to meet the needs of students. It also sucks all the joy and creativity out of teaching.

More Effective

Teachers can become more effective when they have a certain amount of freedom in determining what is taught, and when they are able to design learning experiences in a way that best matches their teaching style and the needs of their students. State mandates do not always allow teachers to make the best choices or to utilize their creativity.

Avoid using value statements, highly charged language, and emotional buzzwords:

Less Effective

In my opinion, using invented spelling is the best strategy I have ever seen for helping young children learn to write. I really like the way that students in this study thought about the message instead of worrying about correct spelling. And don't forget all the excitement that was generated as students eagerly shared their wonderful new creations with each other. And of course, there was the pride of taking home a finished product to share with parents. Using invented spelling helped to produce elaborate and imaginative ideas, helped children organize their writing, and created an environment that is very productive and enjoyable. Invented spelling is a must for primary students.

More Effective

Invented spelling seems to have been effective in helping young children learn to write. Children in my classroom were able to concentrate on communicating their ideas rather than worrying about spelling. They seemed to create writing that was more elaborate and better organized than when they were using conventional spelling. They also seemed to enjoy sharing their ideas in these settings. It seems that invented spelling is an effective technique to use in moving children toward mature writing.

LENGTH

How long should your action report be? Long enough to say it; short enough so as not to bore or confuse the reader. This means using as few words as possible. There is nothing more frustrating than having to sort through a thick forest of words to try to find an author's point. If you use too many words, your ideas are obscured and you lose the reader. Using fewer words increases the likelihood of your report being read and understood. In your action research reports, always consider what does not need to be there. Good writers know how to state their ideas using a minimum number of words.

Less Effective

I believe that writing is extremely important because it helps my students organize their thinking. This is helpful. All people, students as well as adults, should try to develop their writing skills. This will help in their school lives as well as in their careers. Writing forces you to think through your ideas before you begin writing. You have to record your ideas to see what it is you believe about a thing. Also, the very act of generating ideas helps you to see the relationships between more things. This is what creativity is. Creativity has to do with seeing connections, associations, and relationships. Thinking also shapes our writing. Sometimes you do not know exactly what it is you are going to say. When you write, you see your thoughts hung out in space, frozen in time. The advantage of writing is that you can go back and tweak it to get it just right before you deliver the message.

More Effective

Writing shapes thinking by helping the writer to generate ideas, see relationships, and put ideas in an organized form. However, thinking also shapes writing. With writing, we can see our thoughts, organize them, and edit them to get them just right before we deliver them.

CLARITY

The clarity of your final report should be such that another person could read it and duplicate your steps. As stated previously, clarity can be enhanced by using as few words as possible. It can also be enhanced by entering a teaching mode; that is, you assume that the reader knows nothing and you must explain to them what you did and what you saw. Clarity can also be enhanced by the organization of your report. To organize your thoughts, first create an outline so that you are able to see the logical structure of your report. Then, use headings and subheadings to let the reader see the structure and to show when you move from one major idea to the next.

▌ HEADINGS

Following is an example of a short section I wrote that enters into a teaching mode but does not use headings.

CONSCIOUSNESS

Consciousness is that which we choose to be aware of, both internally and externally. Consciousness is a composite of those thoughts and images that we attend to. Jungian theory describes four levels of consciousness.

Collective consciousness is the outer world of values and perceptions that a society shares. Here every stimulus has a response. Machines have gears, springs, and levers, all operating according to the laws of physics. All physical effects spring from physical causes, and time is conceived of in strictly linear terms. This is the objective outer world where reality is determined by repeatability and the laws of cause and effect.

The collective unconscious is a part of the human psyche that is shared by all. An illustrative metaphor might be to think of it as psychic cyberspace to which every human is connected. Here, every thought, action, and emotion ever experienced by humanity is embedded and available to us in the form of archetypal images. Archetypal images are those images formed around patterns within the collective unconscious and birthed into human consciousness as symbols and motifs.

Personal consciousness or ego is the thinking with which we are consciously aware. This can include logical reasoning as well as emotions and intuition. To expand personal consciousness, one becomes aware of a wider variety of stimuli, both internal and external. This can be done through meditation or simply slowing the mind and concentrating on being aware.

The personal unconscious is the layer of thinking not readily accessible to our conscious mind. Contained here is material that has reached consciousness and been forgotten, such as repressed memories, emotions, and personal experiences. It also contains material that has not yet reached consciousness, such as archetypal images. This is the subjective inner world where reality is determined by meaning. That is, the images perceived here are real in so far as they have some meaning or significance for us.

Now here is the same piece of writing with the headings inserted. Notice the difference in the clarity and understanding.

CONSCIOUSNESS

Consciousness is that which we choose to be aware of, both internally and externally. Consciousness is a composite of those thoughts and images that we attend to. Jungian theory describes four levels of consciousness.

Collective Consciousness

Collective consciousness is the outer world of values and perceptions that a society shares. Here every stimulus has a response. Machines have gears, springs, and levers, all operating according to the laws of physics. All physical effects spring from physical causes, and time is conceived of in strictly linear terms. This is the objective outer world where reality is determined by repeatability and the laws of cause and effect.

The Collective Unconscious

The collective unconscious is a part of the human psyche that is shared by all. An illustrative metaphor might be to think of it as psychic cyberspace to which every human is connected. Here, every thought, action, and emotion ever experienced by humanity is embedded and available to us in the form of archetypal images. Archetypal images are those images formed around patterns within the collective unconscious and birthed into human consciousness as symbols and motifs.

Personal Consciousness

Personal consciousness or ego is the thinking with which we are consciously aware. This can include logical reasoning as well as emotions and intuition. To expand personal consciousness, one becomes aware of a wider variety of stimuli, both internal and external. This can be done through meditation or simply slowing the mind and concentrating on being aware.

Personal Unconscious

The personal unconscious is the layer of thinking not readily accessible to our conscious mind. Contained here is material that has reached consciousness and been forgotten, such as repressed memories, emotions, and personal experiences. It also contains material that has not yet reached consciousness, such as archetypal images. This is the subjective inner world where reality is determined by meaning. That is, the images perceived here are real in so far as they have some meaning or significance for us.

For specific information related to both the process of academic writing and the form that product should take, I direct you to *A Short Guide to Academic Writing* (Johnson, 2003a) published by University Press of America. This text will teach you the basics of academic writing using the APA 5th edition style manual (American Psychological Association, 2001).

Figure 14.1 contains a checklist that can be used for your action research reports. This checklist can be downloaded at the following website: www.ablongman. com/JohnsonAR3e.

Key: 4 = Outstanding, 3 = very good, 2 = average, 1 = below average

Criteria	Rating

1. **Topic:** The research investigates an interesting, relevant, or important topic.

2. **Asks a question:** The researcher puts the topic in the form of a question. The question can be answered by collecting data. The question is clear and answerable.

3. **Systematic plan for collecting data:** The researcher describes a systematic plan for collecting data under the Methods section (see Chapter 15). The descriptions of the methods for collecting data are clear, understandable, and easy to follow. (The rule of thumb is that somebody should be able to replicate your action research study by reading your Methods section.) The plan for collecting data is sufficient to answer the question.

4. **Data-based conclusions:** The researcher uses data to answer the question.

5. **Credibility:** The research demonstrates credibility by providing multiple data sources. The researcher demonstrates an unbiased approach. The language used is as objective and value free as possible.

6. **Sentences:** The research uses complete sentences. The sentences (1) are concise yet descriptive, (2) are consistent with tense and plurality, (3) avoid repetition, and (4) make sense and are easy to read.

7. **Paragraphs:** The researcher uses paragraphs to break up and organize larger ideas. The paragraphs (1) make sense, (2) avoid conceptual leaps, and (3) are used to explore or support an idea.

8. **Word choice:** The researcher (1) uses an academic style, (2) avoids speechisms or colloquialisms, and (3) makes pragmatic choices about the quantity and quality of words.

9. **Headings:** The researcher uses headings to organize the paper and make it reader-friendly (see Chapter 17). All the information under a particular heading is germane to that section.

10. **Quotes and citations:** The researcher uses APA form as described here. The quotes and citations are used intelligently to support the writer's ideas.

11. **Fluency:** The piece flows and is easy to read. Ideas are described and supported.

12. **Structure/Organization:** Structure is used to help carry the ideas (see Chapter 17).

13. **Form/Mechanics:** The piece looks presentable. The spacing, margins, font, and headings are correct. Spelling, grammar, and punctuation have been attended to.

14. **Strengths of this research report:**

15. **Questions or areas to reconsider:**

FIGURE 14.1   **Criteria for an Action Research Report**

SUMMARY

- Using an academic style of writing in your action research report enhances its credibility and makes it more likely to be read.
- Academic writing is an objective style of writing in which as few words as possible are used in describing data and ideas.
- The clarity of your action research report is enhanced by entering a teaching mode and by using headings and subheadings.

QUESTIONS AND ACTIVITIES

1. Select a letter to the editor from a newspaper. First, list the facts presented, then report the author's ideas using a purely subjective tone.
2. Find a paragraph in a textbook, newspaper, or magazine. Lengthen it by adding words to it while retaining the original meaning. Then, trade your paragraph with a partner and take out all the words that do not need to be there.
3. Go on a treasure hunt. Find the following: (1) a concise, well-written paragraph, (2) a confusing paragraph, (3) a paragraph with a lot of extra words and sentences, and (4) a paragraph that seems overly biased or subjective.

CHAPTER FIFTEEN

ACTION RESEARCH AS MASTER'S THESIS

I would encourage those of you who are in graduate programs in education to consider doing an action research project for your master's thesis. In advising graduate students over the years, I have found that writers tend to find these projects more interesting and enjoyable to do. Action research projects are also more likely to affect their classroom practice. Not coincidentally, these projects usually seem to be more interesting to read and of better quality.

BEFORE YOU START

The graduate thesis represents the culminating experience of a graduate program. In it you must demonstrate that you are able to utilize academic sources to come to a conclusion in a way that will move the field forward. Following are nine tips and a flexible guide to use in structuring your action research thesis. Note, however, that colleges and universities have varying requirements for the master's thesis.

Nine Tips for Writing Your Master's Thesis

1. *See your advisor before beginning your graduate paper.* It is recommended that the first consultation occur at least 1 year and not less than 6 months before the projected completion. It takes a great deal of time to comprehend and synthesize all the ideas necessary for a graduate thesis. Your goal is to create a professional paper that contributes to the field, and this cannot be done in a few weeks.

2. *Decide on a topic or area of research first, then put it in the form of a question or questions.* A clear focus saves you much time in your research and results in a tighter and more coherent paper.

3. *Keep your thesis proposal short and flexible.* Most graduate programs ask students to write a thesis proposal. This is a very short description of your research project with 5 to 10 literature sources used to put your research question into a theoretical context. Proposals usually have to be preapproved by a graduate committee and the department of graduate studies at your school before you begin. Your initial proposal is a flexible guideline of your intended research project. It is common for the final product to look somewhat different from the proposal. Figure 15.1 contains an action research proposal form. This form can be downloaded at our website, www.ablongman.com/JohnsonAR3e.

4. *Do not expect your advisor to be an editor.* The onus is ultimately on you to write in a logical, coherent, objective style that can be easily understood by all who read your paper. An advising professor will provide feedback and some editorial comments, but this is much different from taking on the role of an editor.

5. *Start collecting journal articles for your literature review as soon as possible.* All master's papers contain a review of the literature related to the topic or research question. A number of sources are needed. (I tell my graduate students that a minimum of 25 is needed.) These sources must be from current texts or juried academic journals (see your advisor if you have questions here). It takes time to read, take notes, and synthesize all the material you read; thus, allow plenty of time for this stage. Some graduate students try to take shortcuts at this stage; however, I have found that these shortcuts always end up being "long cuts."

6. *Create a preliminary outline for your literature review.* An outline is used to help you find a logical structure. This structure is like the frame of a house and is used to hold your ideas together. Some like to use an inverted triangle that goes from most general to most specific. For example, if I were writing a paper on gifted learners and reading in the elementary school, I would use the following sections: (1) gifted learners, (2) reading in the elementary school, and (3) gifted learners and reading in the elementary school.

7. *Begin to plan how you will collect data.* Teachers often use a pilot study in their class to experiment with and refine several data collection methods before selecting those they will use. Keep in mind that your data collection must be well planned and systematic.

8. *Plan on revising each chapter at least four times.* Revision is what separates good writing from average writing. Revision is at the heart of writing of any kind.

9. *Assume the reader knows nothing.* Adopt a teaching, describing mode. The reader should know exactly what you are doing and why, and be able to replicate your procedures.

THE ACTION RESEARCH THESIS

Described next are the parts that might make up a master's thesis using action research. This is not meant to be a recipe; rather, it is a flexible guideline. The order and parts to be included may vary depending on your research topic and the requirements of your college or university. Your advisor may also ask for slight variations of this form; thus, it is imperative that you meet with your advisor before you begin. This will save you both a great deal of time and help you avoid frustration.

Action Research Proposal

Name: _____   Date: _____

I. Topic or Problem

What are you interested in? What problem do you see in your school or classroom? What do you want to investigate? Your topic should not describe what you wish to find; rather, it should simply indicate an area of interest to you. Example: Meeting the needs of gifted elementary readers in a general education setting.

My topic is _____.

II. Question

Put your topic in the form of one to three questions. The question or questions are used to help guide your search for data or articles. Do not start with the answer as this will make your research much more difficult. Example: (1) What special needs do gifted readers have in the elementary grades? (2) How can general education teachers best meet these needs within the confines of reading instruction?

My question/s is/are:

1.

2.

3.

III. Methodology

Briefly describe your initial plan for collecting data. For a qualitative study you should use at least two sources. This should be considered a flexible plan at this point.

IV. Advisor's Signature

Check with your advisor and get his or her signature before continuing.

_____   _____
                Advisor's Signature   Date

V. Sources

You will need a minimum of 15 sources for the literature review. These sources could be journal articles or chapters in academic textbooks. For the purpose of the proposal, you will need to see whether there is enough written on your proposed topic. Therefore, list at least eight possible journal articles or book chapters that may be of use to you (use correct APA form here).

VI. One Empirical Study

For your proposal, find one empirical study related to your topic. *Empirical* means that it uses data or systematic observation. In the proposal, use one or two sentences to describe each of the following:

1. Purpose:
2. Subjects or participants:
3. Treatment or conditions:
4. Measures, instruments, or ways of collecting data:
5. Results (data collected):
6. Conclusions (what do the data mean or imply?):

VII. Initial Literature Review

Using correct APA form, write an initial review of the literature using three of the book/article sources and the one empirical study source described above. This initial literature review should be between four and eight pages in length and should contain an introductory paragraph and a reference page, all in correct APA style (fifth edition).

FIGURE 15.1   Action Research Proposal Form

CHAPTER 1
INTRODUCTION

1. Introduction to the topic (no heading for this section)
   A. Identify the problem or area of interest.
   B. Provide background information.
2. Purpose Statement (heading, centered)
   A. State purpose of paper/study. Example: *The purpose of this paper was to examine the writing workshop in my second grade and to describe effective implementation practices.*
   B. Put the purpose in the form of one or more questions. Example: *The specific research questions are . . .*
      1. *What is happening during my writing workshop?*
      2. *Is the writing workshop effective in developing my students' writing skills?*
      3. *If so, how should the writing workshop be implemented in a primary grade setting?*
3. Importance of the Study (heading, centered)
   A. Tell why this study is important.
   B. Example: *The information here will be of value to . . . It will also provide elementary teachers with a plan to . . .*
4. Definition of Terms (heading, centered)
   A. List important terms.
   B. Briefly describe each term using one or two complete sentences.

CHAPTER II
REVIEW OF THE LITERATURE

1. This builds the foundation for your thesis. Here you provide background information to support your question or to put your research topic in a theoretical context. Also, you want to see what others have found related to your topic that may be of use in your action research.
2. Gather material. Consider using 25–40 sources. Use current, peer-reviewed journal articles whenever possible.
3. After reading each piece, take notes listing the citation at the top and only those items of importance below. Use headings whenever possible. This will make it easier to organize your notes.
4. Begin thinking about the structure. Some people like to web or outline to find structure initially. As data in the form of your notes are gathered, begin to look for categories. Your initial structures should be very flexible because they most likely will change.

5. As you write this chapter, use headings and subheadings to break up the text. It is very hard to read several pages of text without headings.
6. Describe empirical research related to your topic. When describing research studies, try to use one or two sentences to describe each of the following: (1) the question or purpose of the study, (2) the number and type of participants, (3) the treatment or conditions involved, (4) the type of measures, and (5) the results and conclusions.
7. This chapter ends with a brief summary of the major points covered that is generally about one paragraph in length. Sometimes the summary is put in list form with each point cited.

CHAPTER III
METHODOLOGY

1. Participants (heading, centered)
   A. Describe the people involved. The reader should know ages, number, gender, ethnic makeup, and anything else you feel is pertinent to your research.
   B. Describe the environment: classroom, school, or community.
2. Materials (heading, centered)
   A. Describe any materials used in your research. If you are using a particular curriculum, product, or procedure, describe it fully. Include relevant examples in an appendix. Remember that the reader knows nothing.
   B. Describe all types of measuring devices. If surveys, checklists, rubrics, or rating charts are used, describe them briefly, then include a sample in the appendix.
3. Procedures (heading, centered)
   A. Describe the length of the study.
   B. Describe how you collected the data, how much, and how often.
   C. Use past tense in describing all aspects of your methodology and findings. Research always exists in the past, in a specific time and place.
   D. If you use a special curriculum, technique, or procedure, let the reader know exactly what it is. This section should be described in such a way that one could pick up this chapter and replicate your procedures.
4. Analysis (heading, centered)
   A. Describe how you will organize and analyze your data. Inductive analysis will most likely be used for your field notes and other qualitative data.
   B. Quantitative data will generally be analyzed using totals and mean scores. Here a simple comparative analysis will be made. It is outside

the scope of this book to talk about statistical methods; however, statistical analysis is also an option.

CHAPTER IV

FINDINGS

1. Restate your research questions.
2. Describe the data that answer that question (this chapter is often the longest chapter in an action research thesis).
3. Describe the themes, categories, and patterns.
4. Use illustrative examples for each category.
5. Use tables, graphs, figures, and artwork as necessary.
6. Use headings and subheadings to make the structure readily apparent.

CHAPTER V

DISCUSSION

1. Overview of the Study (heading, centered)
   A. Restate the general purpose of the study.
   B. Briefly describe how the results were obtained.
2. Summary of Findings (heading, centered)
   A. Provide a brief summary of the findings.
   B. This may be one to two paragraphs.
3. Conclusions (heading, centered)
   A. Move beyond the data. Tell what these results mean.
   B. Describe possible implications of the results.
4. Recommendations (heading, centered)
   A. Describe how the results might be used in your classroom.
   B. Describe how the results may be used to bring understanding to other classrooms or situations.
   C. Sometimes the conclusions and recommendations merge.
5. Limitations of the Study (heading, centered)
   A. Describe things that may have hindered or affected your findings.
   B. Describe things that you needed to change during the study, or things that did not go as expected. Remember, a good study is not one that proves your particular point; rather, a good study is one that looks carefully, reports accurately, and fairly represents the bit of reality that you experienced.
   C. Describe the limitations or applicability of the findings. For example, your recommendations might be applied only to a certain segment of the population. Also, were you able to look at all facets of the problem?
   D. Describe ideas for future research related to your research.

EXAMPLES OF FULL MASTER'S THESES

Readers have asked that I share some examples of full-length master's theses. Space precludes me from doing that here; however, I have included two excellent examples of master's theses at our website, www.ablongman.com/JohnsonAR3e. Brief descriptions of these theses are provided.

Christine Reed, Educational Specialist Degree, Nerstrand Elementary School, Nerstrand, Minnesota

Christine Reed conducted an action research study to determine whether an embedded spelling program was more effective than the traditional approach in helping students learn to spell. She looked at students enrolled in multiage classes for grades one through three. Spelling instruction was embedded in their literacy program and taught throughout the day rather than being taught as a single subject. Among other things, she found that students learned to spell through meaningful reading and writing experiences instead of the traditional test method.

Jackie Royer, Master's Thesis, Trimont Schools, Trimont, Minnesota

Jackie Royer conducted an action research study to observe and analyze the responses and perceptions of 22 high potential fifth grade students as they received weekly direct and structured creative thinking instruction. Here, students were introduced to the four creative thinking factors of fluency, flexibility, originality, and elaboration and were then given doodles and writing activities to encourage the development of their creative thinking. Among other things, she found that students quickly learned and used creative factor terminology and that choice, flexible grouping, and student self-esteem and self-confidence were key factors that affected student performance and perception.

THE LAST WORD

I have found that graduate students like to have some idea of what goes into a thesis; however, I once again reiterate: The structure described in this chapter is a flexible guideline that should be adapted to meet the needs of your particular research question.

CHAPTER SIXTEEN

THE LITERATURE REVIEW

A THEORETICAL CONTEXT

As described previously, a literature review is used to set your ideas in a theoretical context. You synthesize what the literature says about your research topic, then report it in an organized fashion. Chapter 7 identified the possible sources for the literature review as: academic journals, the Internet, books, and nonprint sources. Again, the number of sources used is dictated solely by your question and the purpose of your study.

Steps for a Literature Review

It is common to spend a great deal of time during the beginning stages of an action research project reading articles and taking notes. Although this may seem time consuming initially, it makes the research and writing process more efficient and effective. Steps to use in gathering data for your literature review follow.

Step 1: Find a Good College Library or Journal Database. Public libraries usually do not have the academic journals and books needed to complete a literature review. Most college libraries do have a wide variety of academic journals as well as recent books published in the area of education. As indicated in Chapter 7, it is possible to find peer-reviewed academic journals on the Internet. Many sites require a subscription of some sort; however, if you are a great distance from a collage library this will be far less than the time and expense required for travel. Also, most universities now provide off-campus access to journal databases to students who are currently enrolled.

Step 2: Locate Possible Sources. The library or Internet site will have some sort of database system in which all its journal articles and books are entered by subject, author, and key words. It sometimes takes a little detective work using a variety of different key word terms to find exactly what you are looking for. When you enter your topic in the search engine, the database provides you with one or more entries that look something like this:

> Johnson, A. (1998). What exactly are comprehension skills and how do I teach them? *Reading, 32*(2), 22–26.

This entry tells you the author (Johnson, A.), the year the article was published (1998), the title of the article ("What Exactly Are Comprehension Skills and How Do I Teach Them?"), the name of the journal (*Reading*), the volume (32), the journal number within that volume (2), and the page numbers on which it can be found (pages 22–26).

If you are in a library you will have to physically find the journal article. Most libraries organize their journals and magazines alphabetically by journal title. Once you locate the journal, the year and volume number should be listed on the front cover. When journals are 2 years old or older, libraries usually take all the journals from a particular year or volume and bind them in book form. This makes the journals easier to find and helps them last longer.

For example, to find the article above, go to the R section of the journals and magazines until you find the journal *Reading*. Then look for volume number 32 (several *Reading* journals will be listed as volume 32), and find the second journal (number 2) published within that volume. The article will be found on page 22 of that journal.

Sometimes, journals are organized by Library of Congress number. On the computer screen the number will look something like this:

> LB 1101. R2

Go to the journals found in the L section (these will all be journals of similar topics). Then move down until you find the LB section, then the 1101s, and, finally, 1101.R2. In another database, all the books contained at that library are categorized and described. To locate relevant books, enter the title, author, or subject. Books may be organized either by Library of Congress numbers or the Dewey decimal number. In all cases, if you are lost or confused (a common experience), find a librarian. They are usually glad to help. I recommend using journal articles instead of books for the majority of your sources because they are more current and more focused, and they allow you to get a great amount of information from a variety of sources in a short amount of time.

Step 3: Peruse Your Sources.   After you get a pile of books or journals, take a few minutes to see whether your sources provide information related to your question. For books, look at the table of contents and the index and skim a few chapters. For journal articles, read the abstract and scan the headings, subheadings, and final paragraph. A few minutes here saves you much time later on. It also prevents you from having to carry around a pile of books and journals.

Step 4: Take Careful Notes.   When taking notes, first record the full reference citation at the top of the page. Having the citation here saves you the task of looking up the articles again when creating the reference page. Next, record your notes using only one side of the page. This allows you to spread all your notes out in front of you when you begin to write your first draft. Record only information that is directly related to your research question. To illustrate this process, I have included some of the notes that I used in writing an article about using literacy techniques to attend to the emotional needs of gifted students (Johnson, 2003b). In taking notes, I recorded only the information that was needed to support the question: How can we use literacy to attend to the emotional needs of gifted students? These notes were written using short sentences that were often incomplete. The goal during note taking is not to create grammatically correct writing; rather, it is to restate and remember the author's ideas in a way that makes them readily accessible to you.

NOTES FOR ARTICLE

Shaker, P. (1982). The application of Jung's analytical psychology to education. *Journal of Curriculum Studies, 14,* 241–250.

1. Jung was empiricist, studying the subjective psyche objectively.
   A. Used objective to study the subjective.
2. Political structure of academia has led to neglect of Jung's work.
3. Process of development = individuation or self-realization.
   A. Birth and transformation of ego.
4. Myth provides a means for analyzing issues of existence.
5. Process of development: individuation or self-realization.
   A. Transformation of ego.
6. Educators can employ elements of analytic psychology.
   A. Attend to concepts of multiple realities.
   B. Look at symbols in literature.

Lovecky, D. V. (1998). Spiritual sensitivity in gifted children. *The Roeper Review, 20,* 178–183.

1. Many gifted children appear to explore spiritual concepts.
2. Take delight in exploring spiritual questions.

Russel-Chapin, L. A., Rybak, C. J., & Copilevitz, T. B. (1996). The art of teaching Jungian analysis. *Journal of Humanistic Education and Development, 34,* 171–181.

1. For Jung, life is a process of becoming more fully and wholly one's self (self-realization).
   A. Opposing parts of personality become more integrated.
2. Need to recognize and address the influence of the unconscious.
3. Ego = part of person they permit themselves to be consciously aware of.
   A. The process of individuation, ego shifts inward.
   B. Toward subjective perspective.

> **Smith, C. D. (1990). Religion and crisis in Jungian analysis.** *Counseling and Values, 34,* 177–186.
> 1. Underlying cause of meaninglessness is psychic fragmentation.
>   A. Arises when individual is cut off from unconscious content.
>   B. Cure is also found in unconscious.
> 2. Analytical process = establishing contact with unconscious.
>   A. Dream analysis, active imagination, artistic experiences.

Step 5: Create a Rough Draft and Start the Revision Process. The next step is to look for groups of ideas and begin writing a rough first draft. This is followed by a series of revisions in which you revisit your notes and continue refining your document.

Using an Objective Writing Style

Your literature review is much more convincing when you use objective language and let the ideas speak for themselves. This means avoiding value statements and highly charged language in your writing.

Avoiding Value Statements. A value statement states what you believe without offering support. You can avoid these by creating sentences that state an idea and then support it.

Less Effective
Teachers really need to learn how to differentiate the curriculum so that they can meet the needs of highly able and less able learners.

More Effective
Learning how to differentiate the curriculum will help teachers meet the needs of both highly able and less able learners.

Less Effective
A study by Jones (2002) reveals a startling statistic: Low ability readers spend the majority of their reading class engaged in mindless skills instruction apart from any meaningful context and do very little reading for pleasure. Is it any wonder that these students hate to read?

More Effective
A study by Jones (2002) showed that low ability readers spend the majority of reading class time engaged in isolated skills instruction with very little time spent on pleasurable reading. Doing more free reading for pleasure in reading class may increase the amount of voluntary reading done outside of class.

You can also avoid creating value statements by not using value words such as *must, should,* and *needs to be.* Instead, say what you mean and support it.

Less Effective

It is important for educators to use real literature in their reading courses. They should also utilize an aesthetic response whenever possible.

More Effective

Using real literature in reading courses enhances a reading program. This type of material more closely reflects authentic reading experiences and allows for an element of choice by both teachers and students. And instead of utilizing an efferent response to literature in which students are asked to recount story details, requiring an aesthetic response allows students to respond with their ideas and emotions. This too is a closer approximation of authentic reading experiences.

Less Effective

Educators need to recognize other forms of intelligence.

More Effective

Recognizing other forms of intelligence will help educators develop the full potential of all their students.

A SAMPLE LITERATURE REVIEW

Following is a sample of part of an article written to describe how elementary teachers might incorporate classroom computers into their reading curricula when they only have one or two in their classrooms. I used eight sources here to set my ideas in a theoretical context.

INTEGRATING CLASSROOM COMPUTERS INTO A READING CURRICULUM

Most elementary classrooms today also have one or two computers; however, these computers are often used only for administrative purposes or for playing games, instead of being used for learning (McCannon & Crews, 2000). Teachers sometimes feel they do not have the time, resources, or knowledge necessary to effectively integrate computers into teaching and learning (Hoffman, 1997; Smith-Gratto & Fisher, 1999). This article describes some several very simple ideas and activities that can be used to integrate two classroom computers into a reading curriculum.

Computer-Integrated Learning in the Classroom

This article describes how one or two classroom computers can be integrated into a reading curriculum. There are four benefits of integrating computers into a classroom curriculum.

1. *Computer-based learning allows students' individual learning needs to be met* (Bagui, 1998; Chisholm & Wetzel, 1997; Ertmer, Addison, Lane,

Ross, & Woods, 1999). With computer-based learning, students can work at their own rate in a nonthreatening environment. This frees up the teacher to spend more time with students who need extra help. Also, students can work to improve specific content area skills and knowledge.

2. *Computers enhance students' writing skills* (Chisholm & Wetzel, 1997). Writing on the computer does not seem to be as permanent as writing on paper; therefore, students are more willing to take risks and write more creatively. Editing and revising are easier to do on the computer than on handwritten stories. It is much easier to move things around and change the order of your words, sentences, and paragraphs. Students who have difficulties with handwriting due to fine motor skills can overcome them by writing with a keyboard.

3. *Computers create opportunities for students to do meaningful work and make connections with things outside of school* (Peck & Dorricott, 1994). Students can create products that have value outside of the school such as web pages, presentations, brochures, and flyers for a multitude of purposes. They might also write stories and poems and submit them for publication or post them on the Internet and receive feedback.

4. *Students have access to a wide variety of up-to-date information through the Internet and CD-ROMs.* Access to the World Wide Web provides students with unlimited information on almost any subject instantly. Information here can be used to enhance or provide background information on stories, books, or various class topics. Also, e-mail correspondence allows students to have direct contact with people, schools, and businesses around the world.

Computer Labs

Most schools have some sort of computer lab; however, this is not always the most effective method for integrating computers into classroom instruction for two reasons. First, instruction in the computer lab may not be related to learning that is happening in the regular classroom. Instruction here is often taught by a specialist teacher and as a result, the activities done during this period are often isolated computer skills lessons that do not integrate ideas and skills from the classroom (Ely, 1993).

Second, computer labs provide limited access to computers. Because computer labs are shared by many classrooms, fairly rigid schedules must be prepared in advance. This creates restricted opportunities for teachers to use the computer lab. Also, the hassles involved in scheduling a computer lab and marching students down to a separate facility often prevent teachers from integrating computers into their daily lessons. As a result, students may have access to computers only once or twice a week for 30 to 50 minutes. In this situation, computers have minimal impact on learning.

THE REFERENCE PAGE

Any article or book that is referred to in your text must appear on the reference page at the end of that text. This informs readers as to what sources were used and allows them to locate these sources if necessary. Following is the reference page for the previous article.

References

Bagui, S. (1998). Reasons for increased learning using multimedia. *Journal of Educational Multimedia and Hypermedia, 7*(1), 3–18.

Chisholm, I. M., & Wetzel, K. (1997). Lessons learned from a technology-integrated curriculum for multi-cultural classrooms. *Journal of Technology and Teacher Education, 5*(4), 293–317.

Ely, D. (1993). Computers in schools and universities in the United States of America. *Educational Technology, 33*(9), 53–57.

Ertmer, P. A., Addison, P., Lane, M., Ross, E., & Woods, D. (1999). Examining teachers' beliefs about the role of technology in the elementary classroom. *Journal of Research on Computing, 32*(1), 54–72.

Hoffman, B. (1997). Integrating technology into schools. *The Education Digest, 62*(5), 51–55.

McCannon, M., & Crews, T. B. (2000). Assessing the technology training needs of elementary school teachers. *Journal of Technology and Teacher Education, 8*(2), 111–121.

Peck, K., & Dorricott, D. (1994). Why use technology? *Educational Leadership, 51*(4), 11–14.

Smith-Gratto, K., & Fisher, M. (1999). An aid to curriculum and computer integration: Prototypes for teachers. *Computers in the Schools, 15*(2), 61–71.

SUMMARY

- A literature review sets your ideas in a theoretical context.
- The number of sources used for a literature review varies depending on the question and the purpose of your study.

- Possible sources to use for a review of the literature include academic journals, the Internet, books, and nonprint sources.
- The steps in creating a literature review are to (1) find a good college library, (2) locate possible sources, (3) peruse your sources, (4) take careful notes, and (5) begin the draft and revision process.
- Using an objective writing style that avoids value statements creates a more convincing document.
- Any book or article that you cite in your text must be listed on your reference page at the end of your report.

QUESTIONS AND ACTIVITIES

1. Find an example of an article in an academic journal that has a well-written literature review. What traits or attributes lead you to believe this review is well written?
2. Identify a topic that interests you. Find two articles related to this topic. Synthesize the information and report it in an organized fashion using no more than two double-spaced pages.
3. What is an effective practice or program that you support or that you believe should be instituted in your classroom or in schools. Find an article in an academic journal that supports your view and write one to two paragraphs to make your case using objective, academic language.
4. Find in a newspaper a letter to the editor with which you agree. Take out all the value statements and list only the facts. Make a case to support the position using objective, academic language.
5. Find in a newspaper a letter to the editor with which you disagree. Take out all the value statements and list only the facts. Make a case to support the position using objective, academic language.

CHAPTER SEVENTEEN

FINDINGS: REPORTING QUALITATIVE DATA

Presenting the data you collected in your action research project may comprise the bulk of your report. You use your data to create a picture that describes what you found. The goal is to transform your field notes and other data into a form that can be easily digested (Taylor & Bogdan, 1998). Do not try to recount and report every bit of data collected because you will overwhelm and bore your reader. Instead, describe the meaningful trends, patterns, and categories you found and include representative samples so that the reader gets a sense of what you discovered. In this sense you are representing a particular view of reality (yours).

PRESENTING QUALITATIVE DATA

You can be creative in how you present the data as long as you describe your experiences fairly and adequately. Five tips can help you create an effective writing tone and style.

1. *Try to be an impartial reporter.* Action researchers realize that it is impossible to be totally impartial; however, you should fairly represent all aspects of what you are studying. In your writing tone, avoid letter-to-the-editor syndrome. As described previously, you create a more credible document when you simply state and support your ideas and avoid using value statements.

Less Effective
The observations in this study clearly demonstrate the absurdity of those misinformed educators who insist that time spent reading good books in reading class is wasted time.

More Effective
The observations showed that allowing time for voluntary reading in reading class has some very positive effects.

2. *Include yourself when it is warranted.* It is acceptable to use the I pronoun when describing something that you did or observed (McNiff, Lomax, & Whitehead, 1996). You are, after all, a part of the study; thus, you should refer to yourself in a personal way instead of using an impersonal form, such as "the researcher."

Less Effective

For this study, the researcher spent 7 weeks observing students in a second grade classroom.

More Effective

For this study, I spent 7 weeks observing students in my second grade classroom.

3. *Take readers along with you in all phases of your study.* Let them inside your head so they know exactly what you did and why you did it. To do this, your action research report should describe some or all of the following: (1) your question or focus, (2) the present environment or conditions, (3) what data you plan to collect, (4) the methods used to collect the data, (5) the data, (6) your thoughts along the way, and (7) how the data might be applied or used to understand other situations. The rule of thumb is that a reader should be able to replicate your procedure.

Teresa Van Batavia wrote in such a way that we knew exactly what she was doing (her complete project is included in Chapter 12):

WRITING WORKSHOP

My first grade students at Eisenhower Elementary are involved in a writer's workshop setting at least three times a week. My concern is that children may be slipping through the cracks—doing little or no writing and not being noticed.

Data Collection

The first form of data collection that I used was that of a weekly checklist. As I circulated among students during the 2-week period from November 15 through December 3, 1999, I carried a clipboard and checked off each type of writing activity that I observed (see Figure 12.4). This checklist became an effective tool for helping me to choose minilesson topics for the children. I will continue to use this on an informal basis throughout the year.

In addition to the checklists, I met individually with each student and also collected their writing folders for further study of their writing habits. Following are my notes of these conferences.

4. *Write clearly and precisely.* As stated previously, too many words are as damaging to comprehension as too few words. Be selective in what you choose to report. The goal is to achieve maximum communication using a minimum of words. A clear, concise paper is more apt to be read. A long, rambling paper is more apt to be ignored.

5. *Organize your paper.* You have a certain amount of freedom in the structure or form of your research report. That is, you are not bound by the same confines that dictate empirical research studies; however, the onus is on you to create a paper that can be easily understood. One way to do this is to organize your paper so that the structure is readily apparent to the reader. The next section describes this.

THE IMPORTANCE OF STRUCTURE

Structure is the essence of all things. In writing, structure is the skeleton used to carry your ideas.

Structure and Inductive Analysis

One way to create structure for your paper is to use the process of inductive analysis described in Chapter 9:

1. Gather data and collect notes.
2. Spread out your notes in front of you.
3. Look for common ideas.
4. Move common ideas into groups to create sections.
5. Within each section, look for similar items to create paragraphs or subsections.

Using Headings to Create Structure

Using heads makes a report easier to read. Following is a writing sample that does not use headings. To the reader it appears as a large blob of text. Large blobs like this are less reader friendly because the structure is indistinct.

MS. BAKER'S WRITING WORKSHOP

In November 1996, I spent 2 weeks in Ms. Baker's second grade class-room watching her writing workshop. Here writing was taught as a process consisting of five stages: prewriting, first draft, revising, editing, and publication. Student choice was integral to this process. Ms. Baker said that allowing students to choose their own writing topics seemed to result in a better quality of writing. Students' writing often reflected events going on in their lives, thus increasing feelings of ownership and emotional attach-ment. They seemed eager to share their ideas and experiences using writing.

Conversation was an integral part of the writing workshop. Students talked about possible writing topics, about their current writing projects, and about things happening in their lives. More formal conversations related directly to students' writing occurred in individual and small-group conferences and in large-group sharing sessions.

Skills identified in language arts manuals and unit tests were taught using explicit instruction in short minilessons lasting 5 to 10 minutes. After each skill was presented, students moved into small groups to create examples of that skill. This allowed students to help each other generate ideas and hear the thinking processes of others. For documentation, checklists were created that listed each skill and the date it was taught. Students' work was also used to determine those skills used in minilessons. When unit tests were given, it was found that these students performed just as well on tests of basic skills as students in other second grade classrooms. Thus, it appeared that students in this writing workshop were learning literacy skills using far less instructional time than did other classes while more time was spent writing and composing.

Ms. Baker said that management was going better than she had expected. She put more responsibility on students for correcting tests, organizing the classroom, and choosing writing topics. This made the room more student centered and resulted in her having fewer behavior problems. The time spent teaching routines and procedures led to fewer distractions and helped her workshops run smoothly. Also, creating writing experiences that tapped into students' interests and valued their ideas seemed to contribute to much of her success with classroom management. My observations showed few incidents of off-task behavior during writing workshops. Ms. Baker created structure while giving students choices and a sense of autonomy within this structure.

Notice how the same large blob of text becomes more reader friendly when I insert some headings and add a short introductory paragraph at the beginning. The structure becomes readily apparent and, thus, comprehension is enhanced.

MS. BAKER'S WRITING WORKSHOP

In November 1996, I spent 2 weeks in Ms. Baker's second grade classroom watching students in her writing workshop. Following are described (1) the writing process, (2) student talk, (3) teaching skills, and (4) behavior management.

Writing

Here writing was taught as a process consisting of five stages: prewriting, first draft, revising, editing, and publication. Student choice was integral to this process. Ms. Baker said that allowing students to choose their own writing topics seemed to result in a better quality of writing. Students' writing often reflected events going on in their lives, thus increasing feelings of ownership and emotional attachment. They seemed eager to share their ideas and experiences using writing.

Talk

Conversation was an integral part of the writing workshop. Students talked about possible writing topics, about their current writing projects, and about things happening in their lives. More formal conversations related directly to students' writing occurred in individual and small-group conferences and in large-group sharing sessions.

Skills

Skills identified in language arts manuals and unit tests were taught using explicit instruction in short minilessons lasting 5 to 10 minutes. After each skill was presented, students moved into small groups to create examples of that skill. This allowed students to help each other generate ideas and hear the thinking processes of others. For documentation, checklists were created that listed each skill and the date it was taught. Students' work was also used to determine those skills used in minilessons. When unit tests were given, it was found that these students performed just as well on tests of basic skills as students in other second grade classrooms. Thus, it appeared that students in this writing workshop were learning literacy skills using far less instructional time than did other classes while more time was spent writing and composing.

Behavior Management

Ms. Baker said that management was going better than she had expected. She put more responsibility on students for correcting tests, organizing the classroom, and choosing writing topics. This made the room more student centered and resulted in her having fewer behavior problems. The time spent teaching routines and procedures led to fewer distractions and helped her workshops run smoothly. Also, creating writing experiences that tapped into students' interests and valued their ideas seemed to contribute to much of her success with classroom management. My observations showed few incidents of off-task behavior during writing workshops. Ms. Baker created structure while giving students choices and a sense of autonomy within this structure.

Using Subheadings to Create More Structure

Subheadings can be used to further organize large sections of text. Subheadings are italicized, flush left, with the first letter of the principal words capitalized. Example:

SKILLS

Teaching

Skills identified in language arts manuals and unit tests were taught using explicit instruction in short minilessons lasting 5 to 10 minutes. After each skill was presented, students moved into small groups to create examples of that skill. This allowed students to help each other generate ideas and hear the thinking processes of others.

Assessment and Evaluation

For documentation, checklists were created that listed each skill and the date it was taught. Students' work was also used to determine those skills used in minilessons. When unit tests were given, it was found that these students performed just as well on tests of basic skills as students in other second grade classrooms. Thus, it appeared that students in this writing workshop were learning literacy skills using far less instructional time than did other classes while more time was spent writing and composing.

CASE STUDIES OR REPRESENTATIVE SAMPLES

Including samples of students' products, quotes, or excerpts from your research journal makes your data come alive. Again, the goal is to convey to the reader a sense of being there.

It's Alive!

When I was doing my doctoral work at the University of Minnesota, I taught writing courses in the composition department. To inform my teaching practice, one quarter I used a technique called dialogue journaling (Watts & Johnson, 1995). I recorded and analyzed my thoughts and feelings after each class on a computer disk (journal). Michelle, a colleague, did the same. At the end of each week we exchanged disks and responded to what the other had written. This had three positive effects: (1) it provided a good sense of what was going on in our classes; (2) it gave us another viewpoint; and (3) we could see how the other was organizing and teaching the writing course. This is an extremely informative practice and one that I would highly recommend to all teachers.

Notice in the following sample how the inclusion of just a few journal entries gives you a sense of what I was seeing and experiencing. My entries are in lowercase. Michelle's responses are in uppercase. We both agreed to write without worrying about spelling, grammar, punctuation, or word choice.

1/2/99

Good to start this journal. It is very helpful for me to communicate with somebody else what does and doesn't work and also to hear the triumphs and tribulations of another. It helps also to know what other instructors are doing in their classes and also what they're thinking and feeling. We are human beings dammit!

Also, as teachers of writing we will be practicing what we preach. We will write to see what it is we have to say. We will write to extend and analyze our thoughts. Writing will affect our thinking.

ANDY—THANK YOU FOR ASKING ME TO DO THIS. JUST READING THROUGH YOUR COMMENTS ABOUT THE FIRST WEEK MAKES ME PLEASED TO BE INVOLVED IN THIS VENTURE. I AM LEARNING ALREADY FROM HEARING ABOUT EXPERIENCES YOU'RE HAVING IN YOUR CLASS. THIS IS A GOOD THING.

1/5/99

They're so quiet. Not like my other class at all. I miss the busy bustle of voices when I come into the room. I love to hear students chattering away. I like when students tell me things, tease me gently, or ask me questions. I like when there's a gosh darn relationship. Teaching starts with a relationship. Until then I'm just some clown dancing in front of the classroom.

I have to remember that it's only week 1. It will take me awhile to get there. Students have to learn to trust me and to trust each other. Like petting a strange dog: you have to let him/her smell your hand before you pet him/her.

"Arf!"

Building community—I can't demand instant community. Trust is earned.

ANDY—IT'S THE THIRD WEEK AND MY STUDENTS ARE STILL QUIET AT THE BEGINNING OF THE HOUR. THIS BOTHERS ME. I LIKE WALKING INTO A ROOM WHERE EVERYONE IS TALKING, SHARING STORIES ABOUT OTHER CLASSES OR THE COMMUTE TO SCHOOL. LAST QUARTER WHEN MY STUDENTS WOULD FALL SILENT AS I CAME INTO THE ROOM, I WOULD SAY, "TALK, TALK. THERE'S NO REASON TO BE QUIET JUST BECAUSE I'M HERE. I WANT TO HEAR YOUR VOICES!" I WOULD SAY THIS LIGHTLY AND IT OFTEN WORKED. BUT LAST QUARTER I TAUGHT IN A SMALL ROOM WITH ONLY THREE ROWS OF DESKS, SO STUDENTS WERE ALREADY CLOSE TO ME AND TO ONE ANOTHER. THIS QUARTER I'M IN A FISH BOWL (302 LIND HALL) WITH MANY ROWS AND A GREAT DEAL OF DISTANCE BETWEEN ME AND THE STUDENTS WHEN I FIRST WALK IN THE ROOM. SOMEHOW I HAVE A LESS EASY TIME MAKING JOKES OR LIGHTENING THE TONE AT THE BEGINNING OF CLASS. ARE YOUR STUDENTS TALKING MORE NOW?

1/9/99

In group work I allow for chatter-time. Groups are more expensive in terms of time, but the payoff is great in terms of tapping into a diversity of ideas and talents and creating a positive social climate.

My all-female group has done a great job of getting to know each other. I looked up to see them passing pictures around. One of my all-male groups is having a hard time with this. You can insert your own gender generalizations here:

ANDY—I'M EAGER TO KNOW MORE ABOUT HOW YOU BUILD COMMUNITY IN GROUPS. I HAVEN'T STARTED ANY PARTICULAR COMMUNITY BUILDING EXERCISES, ALTHOUGH MOST OF MY GROUPS ARE WORKING OKAY. I'D BE EAGER TO HEAR ABOUT ANY ACTIVITIES YOU HAVE UP YOUR SLEEVE.

PERHAPS YOU COULD ASK YOUR ALL-MALE GROUP TO BE RESPONSIBLE FOR REPORTING BACK TO THE CLASS ON SOME ASSIGNMENT OR FOR MAKING A PRESENTATION? MAYBE THEY WOULD BOND THROUGH THE EXPERIENCE OF HAVING TO ASSUME A MORE PUBLIC ROLE IN THE CLASS? I'M NOT SURE.

1/12/99

Ryan is a male student. I read faces pretty well. I got anger from him. He gave me stone face. Sullen, almost challenging at times. I'm beginning to see this as a defense mechanism. He's scared, wondering if he measures up. I know I've sometimes put on a tough exterior to protect my soft inner core . . . Funny the things we do to protect our inner core.

ANDY—I REMEMBER ONE STUDENT FROM LAST QUARTER WHO LITERALLY GLOWERED AT ME. I THINK HE HAD REASON TO BE FRUSTRATED, BUT I COULDN'T FIGURE OUT HOW TO MAKE THINGS BETTER. DON'T YOU WANT TO INTERVENE WHEN YOU SEE A STUDENT LOOKING SO ANGRY? I WANT TO ASK HIM OR HER WHAT'S THE MATTER? BUT THEN I WORRY THAT IT WOULD NOT BE THE PROFESSIONAL THING TO DO.

1/29/99

So its Monday . . . I'm sure every writing instructor has the same feelings that I'm having this week. Am I doing any good? Are students learning anything? Am I just standing up here wiggling my arms, getting excited for nothing? Are they just nodding their heads like dogs in the back of car windows just so they can get their five credits and move on down the road?

ANDY—IT'S INTERESTING THAT WE'RE BOTH HAVING THESE SAME WORRIES THIS WEEK. IN MY JOURNAL THIS PAST WEEK I MENTIONED THAT TEACHING IS HARD WORK PRECISELY BECAUSE IT IS DIFFICULT TO MEASURE HOW "GOOD" WE ARE. WE DON'T SEE A BUSINESS DEAL GO THROUGH OR CURE A PERSON OF A RASH. INSTEAD, WE HOPE THAT WE'LL PLANT SEEDS . . . OR, EVEN MORE INDIRECTLY, THAT WE'LL FOSTER SOME SORT OF EXCITEMENT ABOUT LEARNING.

Inductive analysis was used to analyze the wealth of data in my dialogue journal. I went through and found the patterns emerging in the types of responses and reported the categories and their frequency. I was then able to report these data in terms of numbers (see Chapter 18). I mixed this with my insights and representative samples to create a good sense of being there.

APPENDICES

Appendices (plural form of appendix) contain information that interrupts the flow of the text. These are placed at the end of your report and comprise information such as data retrieval charts, surveys, questionnaires, tests, interview questions, detailed descriptions that may be too distracting if inserted in the body of your report, or longer samples of your data. Information should be indicated in the body of your text by a reference within parentheses.

SUMMARY

- Reporting your findings usually comprises the bulk of your action research report.
- Your data should be converted into a form that can easily be read and understood.
- In writing your action research report the onus is on you to be fair and impartial.
- You are part of the research and should include your thoughts and actions in your report.
- When you write your report, let the readers hear your thoughts as you go through all phases of your research.
- Write as concisely as possible.
- Creating structure using headings and subheadings improves the comprehension of your report.
- Important information that seems to interrupt the flow of your report should be put in an appendix.

QUESTIONS AND ACTIVITIES

1. Find and share a piece of qualitative research related to an area of interest. What do you notice about the writing style?
2. Find and share a piece of quantitative research related to an area of interest. What do you notice about the writing style?

CHAPTER EIGHTEEN

FINDINGS: REPORTING QUANTITATIVE DATA USING TABLES AND FIGURES

QUANTIFYING REALITY

In an action research report, you may want to describe quantifiable data. In these instances, when do you use numbers and when do you use words to express these arithmetic concepts? The following information is taken from the Publication Manual of the American Psychological Association (2001).

Using Numbers

Use numerals to express arithmetic concepts in the following cases:

1. Numbers 10 and above

   The class generated 27 different ideas in the space of 5 minutes.

2. Dates

   This study took place on May 5, 1999.

3. Ages

   She is 7 years old.

4. Time

   The subjects reported to the laboratory at 1:00 P.M. They stayed there for 2 hours and 7 minutes.

5. People in a study

   There were 15 students in this study: 8 males and 7 females.

6. Grade level

   Most children begin grade 2 with a thorough knowledge of consonant sounds.

   (*Note:* It is grade 2 but second grade.)

7. Chapters

   Most would agree that Chapter 17 is the most fascinating chapter of the book.

8. Pages

   Page 1 of this text begins with a fascinating review of the writing process.

9. Scales or rating systems

   He scored a 7 on a 10-point scale.

10. Money

    The subjects in this study were paid $8 for participating.

11. Numbers grouped for comparison with other numbers 10 and above

    The study showed that 9 of 15 students were able to improve their grade averages significantly by learning how to read critically. Of the 15 students participating, 6 received a grade of A, 5 received a grade of B, and 4 received a grade of C.

Using Words

Use words to express arithmetic concepts in the following cases:

1. Numbers below 10

   He sank three of seven free throws.

2. Numbers that begin a title

   Mr. Higgins read the book *Seven Silly Swans* to his second grade class.

3. Numbers that begin a sentence

   Fourteen children fell asleep during the story.

   (Try to avoid starting sentences with numbers.)

4. Numbers grouped for comparison with other numbers below 10

   In reading class, seven out of the nine boys preferred action stories.

5. Numbers in a hyphenated word

   The Minnesota Vikings are four-time Super Bowl losers.

Reporting Arithmetic Data

Four rules apply for arithmetic data numbers.

1. Arithmetic data are reported in descending order (from greatest to least). In the following example, in which some numbers are above 10 (27 walruses), I used numbers instead of words throughout to remain consistent even though some numbers are below 10 (9 kangaroos and 3 white-tailed deer).

   The mosaic contained 27 walruses, 14 elephants, 9 kangaroos, and 3 white-tailed deer.

2. Tell what you are observing first.

   This study was designed to determine the types of movie genre that were popular among elementary students.

3. Tell the total number before you report categories. Both the examples below are correct. The second one, however, seems a little less repetitive.

   Of 99 total responses, 47 preferred action movies, 31 preferred comedies, 14 preferred science fiction, and 7 preferred historical movies.

   Respondents in this study reported their favorite movie genre. Of 99 total responses, the following preferences were noted: 47 action movies, 31 comedies, 14 science fiction, and 7 historical movies.

4. Stay consistent with the order of gender or other categories. Always report numbers in descending order; however, when reporting gender or other categories, the order of the first example must remain consistent throughout. In the following example, I start with the largest total category (Caucasians). The order is 9 males and 2 females. In the categories that follow (Black and Asian), even though the number of females is greater than the number of males, they are reported second to maintain a consistent order.

   There were 28 students in the class: 14 males and 14 females. Nine males and 2 females were Caucasian, 3 males and 7 females were Black, and 2 males and 5 females were Asian.

TABLES

Tables are a quick, visual way to organize and report information. They are especially useful if you have a great deal of numerical data to report. Tables are meant to replace information written in the text. Thus, you might refer to data in the text, but do not duplicate table information in the text. For example, in a study looking at the leisure reading habits of high school students, the following data could appear in the text in written form:

A study was conducted to determine the leisure reading preferences of high school students. Of the 250 students surveyed, 140 were females and 110 were males. The responses were as follows: action or adventure was preferred by 35% of the males and 5% of the females; mysteries were preferred by 10% of the males and 25% of the females; histories were preferred by 0% of the males and 35% of the females; biographies were preferred by 5% of the males and 20% of the females; fantasies were preferred by 20% of the males and 0% of the females; comedies were preferred by 15% of the males and 3% of the females; technical reading was preferred by 5% of the males and 10% of the females; and science fiction was preferred by 10% of the males and 2% of the females. Total responses were as follows: 40% preferred action or adventure, 35% preferred mysteries, 35% preferred history, 25% preferred biography, 20% preferred fantasy, 18% preferred comedy, 15% preferred technical reading, and 12% preferred science fiction.

This paragraph is certainly correct; however, it is not easy to digest this amount of information in this form. A table can be used to report the same information (see Table 18.1). For each gender, the preference is listed from greatest to least. Use parentheses to refer to a table in the text (see Table 18.1). Because it is a title, the word Table is capitalized. In the actual table, the table number should be listed above the table, flush left. The title should be listed on the next line, also flush left. This lets readers know quickly and easily exactly what they are reading. If you are using chapters, merge the table and figure numbers with the chapter numbers. For example, Table 18.1 means Chapter 18, Table 1.

In Table 18.2 the leisure reading preferences of high school students are again reported; however, the data are grouped and listed in descending order according to the genre totals. (*Note:* Because I referred to Table 18.2 in the sentence, I did not have to put "see Table 18.2" in parentheses.)

Tables help organize information and make it readily available to the reader. Consider the following example:

TABLE 18.1 **Percentages of Leisure Reading Preferences of High School Students**

MALES		FEMALES	
Action/adventure	35	Historical	35
Fantasy	20	Mystery	25
Comedy	15	Biography	20
Science fiction	10	Technical	10
Mystery	10	Action/adventure	5
Biography	5	Comedy	3
Technical	5	Science fiction	2
Historical	0	Fantasy	0

TABLE 18.2   **Percentages of Leisure Reading Preferences of High School Students**

GENRE	MALE	FEMALE	TOTAL
Action/adventure	35	5	40
Mystery	10	25	35
Historical	0	35	35
Biography	5	20	25
Fantasy	20	0	20
Comedy	15	3	18
Technical	5	10	15
Science Fiction	10	2	12

This study was conducted to see what kind of footwear middle school students wear. For this study 127 middle school students were observed. The findings are shown in Table 18.3

FIGURES

Figures include lists, graphs, diagrams, or pictures. Figures are labeled differently than tables. The figure number is italicized, flush left, and followed by a period. In the title, only the first letter is capitalized and the last word is followed by a period (see Figure 18.1). Figures are not the same as tables and should be counted differently. For example, I have used three tables thus far in this chapter, but this is the first figure, so it is labeled Figure 18.1.

Graphs

Graphs are listed as figures. Bar graphs are used to show comparison. Most word processors have options that allow you to make high-quality graphs quickly and easily. The Vision Quest data described in Chapter 9 is displayed in Figure 18.2. Line graphs are used to show change over time. Figure 18.3 shows how the types of responses in my Vision Quest study changed over time.

TABLE 18.3   **Type of Footwear Worn by Middle School Students**

TYPE OF SHOE	MALE	FEMALE	TOTAL
Athletic or court shoes	25	20	45
Hiking boots	20	21	41
Sandals	10	20	30
Dress shoes	5	6	11

PLAYGROUND GAMES
1. Jump rope
2. Soccer
3. Playground equipment
6. Football
7. Chasing games
8. Softball
9. Other

FIGURE 18.1   Playground Games

Other Visuals

Pictures, photographs, maps, illustrations, or sample products are all examples of figures and should be referred to in the same way as those figures just described. If you have an abundance of these, they should be included in an appendix at the end of your report and simply referred to in the body of your text.

SUMMARY

- Numbers and words are both used to express arithmetic concepts.
- Tables are an effective way to organize information and are especially useful in reporting a large amount of arithmetic data.
- Do not duplicate table information in the text of your action research report.
- Figures are different from tables and include lists, graphs, diagrams, pictures, photographs, maps, illustrations, and various kinds of examples.

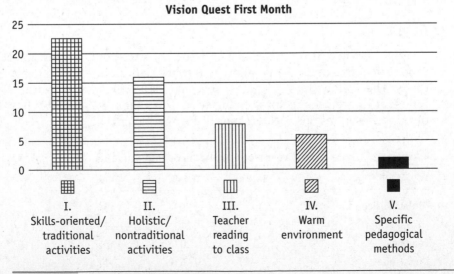

Vision Quest First Month

| | I. Skills-oriented/ traditional activities | II. Holistic/ nontraditional activities | III. Teacher reading to class | IV. Warm environment | V. Specific pedagogical methods |

FIGURE 18.2   Vision Quest Bar Graph

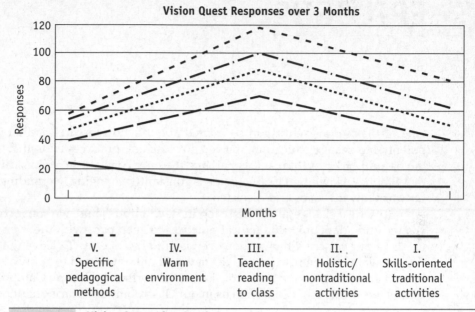

FIGURE 18.3   Vision Quest Line Graph

QUESTIONS AND ACTIVITIES

1. Do a quick survey asking at least 25 people to name their favorite book or books. Use inductive analysis to find groups and numbers within each group. Report your data using a table or figure.
2. In the activity above, report your data without using a table or figure.
3. Do a quick survey of at least 25 people to determine their preference for movie genre. Report your data. In your report, describe how the data were collected, what you found, possible differences related to gender, and what those data might mean or how they might be applied.
4. Repeat the previous activity, except compare adults' preferences to adolescents' (ages 12–19) and children's (ages 6–11).
5. Find an area where you can observe many people. Observe to get a feel for the different kinds of shoes people wear, then find categories and use a data retrieval chart and tally marks to determine what kind of shoe is most often worn. Report your data. In your report, describe how the data were collected, what you found, possible differences related to gender, and what those data might mean or how they might be applied.
6. Repeat the previous activity, except find a different place to collect the same information. Compare the kinds of shoes worn at the two places.

EPILOGUE

One of the reasons why I am so excited about action research is that it has the potential to change education, to keep our teaching practices evolving. Change is the natural order of things. It is perhaps the only constant in a physical universe that Stephen Hawking (1988) tells us is constantly changing, expanding, moving outward toward chaos and disorder.

To refuse change is the first step in devolution. Thus, we must continue to change and adapt our pedagogical practices to keep pace with the ever-changing needs of our society. Change, however, is not always easy. To leave the safe confines of what is known, to go into the new and unknown, and to allow ourselves to be transformed is to take the heroic journey described by Joseph Campbell (1968). This is the journey that confronts us in our classrooms and throughout our lives.

GLOSSARY

academic journals—journals that contain articles written by specialists in the field who describe their research, secondary research, novel applications of existing theories, or interesting new ideas set in a theoretical context. Before acceptance, each article is peer reviewed, which means it is critiqued by a jury of three to six experts in the field to check for accuracy and validity.

academic learning time (ALT)—time spent by a student actively engaged in a task that is directly related to the teacher's desired outcome and during which the student is able to successfully complete the task. Academic learning time is different from engaged time in that students are able to successfully complete the task. It is positively correlated with achievement.

academic writing style—a writing style that uses concise, objective language. This is the style of writing preferred for action research reports. Ideas are presented in a logical, orderly manner so that the reader is able to gain a maximum amount of understanding with a minimum amount of time and effort. This writing style creates a more readable and credible report.

accuracy—a quality in action research in which the data collected creates a fairly true picture of the bit of reality being observed.

action research—a systematic and orderly way for teachers to observe their practice or to explore a problem and a possible course of action.

allotted time—the time allotted during the school day to teach a specific subject.

analysis of variance (ANOVA)—statistical procedure used to compare the difference in mean between or within three or more groups.

archival data—data sources that include past grades, test scores, cumulative folders, health records, parental occupation, or attendance records.

attitude scales—a series of statements given to respondents who must then choose from a set of responses for each statement. Their choice for each statement indicates their level of agreement or disagreement.

best practice—informed, thoughtful teaching that is supported by research and research-based theory.

brainstorm and list—a method of generating ideas where, given a problem or a prompt, you list ideas without evaluating them. The nonevaluative aspect of this method is important, as it gets you thinking outside of conventional boundaries.

causal–comparative research—a type of research designed to find the reason for existing differences between two or more groups. It is used when the random assignment of participants for groups necessary for the true experiment cannot be met, which is certainly the case in most classrooms. Like correlational research, it is used to describe an existing situation. It is called causal–comparative research as it compares groups in order to find a cause for differences in measures or scores.

checklist—a list that specifies certain attributes, such as behaviors, traits, assignments, or skills. When that attribute is seen, some method is used to check it off or indicate the number of times it was present.

checklist for collecting data—a checklist used to record which data were collected and when. This ensures that data are collected systematically and that all types of data are equally represented.

chi square—statistical procedure used to compare frequencies of two or more groups.

closed-ended questions (also called **closed response questions**)—questions for which there is a specific answer or response.

conclusion—found at the end of an action research report, the conclusion is a paragraph or two that describes your current state of knowing or a list of things you have come to believe as a result of your study. It should bring together the important data and explain what they mean. The conclusion will be the basis for your recommendation or plan of action.

conference—a data source in which one or more students talk about their work or some aspect of classroom functioning. Prompts may be used to get students talking about a particular topic; however, lists of planned questions are not used. Conferences can be conducted individually or in small groups known as focus groups.

consciousness—thoughts, images, emotions, and other stimuli (both internal and external) of which we are aware.

constructivism—an educational philosophy that posits that knowledge is not passively received; rather, it's actively built up or constructed by students as they connect their prior knowledge and past experiences with new information and experiences.

control group—in an experiment, a group as similar as possible in all characteristics to the treatment group that is not exposed to the particular treatment for the purposes of comparison.

correlational research—a type of research designed to determine whether and to what degree a statistical relationship exists between two or more variables. It is used primarily to describe an existing condition or something that has happened in the past.

correlation coefficient—a numerical value that describes the degree or strength of a relationship between two variables. A positive correlation means that when one variable increases, the other one also increases. A negative correlation means that when one variable increases, the other one decreases. A correlation coefficient of 1.00 would indicate a perfect one-to-one positive correlation. This rarely happens. A correlation coefficient of .0 means that there is absolutely no correlation between to variables. A correlation coefficient of −1.00 would indicate a perfect negative correlation. This also rarely happens.

creative problem solving (CPS)—a problem solving strategy in which you define the problem,

generate as many ideas as possible, then chose one or two to refine and test.

credibility—a quality in action research that indicates it is trustworthy or capable of being believed. This quality enables you and others to use your data with confidence.

data retrieval charts—visual organizers that are used to help collect and organize information. These can come in a variety of forms.

dependent variable—the particular result or the effect of the treatment or condition. The dependent variable depends on the treatment or independent variable.

descriptive statistics—statistical analyses used to describe an existing set of data. There are three major types of descriptive statistics: measure of central tendency, frequency distribution, and measures of variability.

discussion—the part of a thesis or action research report where you provide an overview of the study and a summary of the findings. It may also include some or all of the following: conclusions, recommendations, and an evaluation of the study.

dualism or a dualistic perspective—a view of reality that posits that the universe comprises two distinctly different kinds of stuff: physical and metaphysical. The physical dimensions consist of matter and energy and are studied using the traditional tools of science. The metaphysical (beyond the physical) dimensions are made up of meta-energy in the form of consciousness.

ego-consciousness—awareness and interpretation of the outer physical world.

equivalent time-sample design—a quasi-experimental research design in which the treatment is presented at irregular intervals; however, the measures or observations are made at regular intervals. This allows the researcher to account for and control outside influences.

ERIC—the Educational Resources Information Center, sponsored by the National Library of Education at the U.S. Department of Education, it is a massive database containing information on all imaginable subjects related to education (www.eric.ed.gov).

evaluation of the study—after reporting conclusions and recommendations, this section of a thesis or action research report evaluates the effectiveness of the study, explains particular aspects of it, or describes how it might be done more effectively the next time.

experimental research—a mode of inquiry in which a hypothesis is proposed and tested by examining relationships between independent and dependent variables. In experimental research the researcher creates an artificial environment in order to maintain control over all factors that may affect the result of the experiment. True experimental research uses random sampling of subjects.

explicate reality—the physical world.

field notes—a data source that includes written observations of what you see taking place as you conduct your action research project.

figures—information found in visual form such as lists, graphs, diagrams, or pictures.

focus group—a small-group conference used to gather data. The moderator uses questions as prompts and guides. The goal is to get participants to carry the conversation as much as possible.

frequency distribution—a way of organizing information that tells the scores or numbers that were attained and the frequency, or how many times each score or number was attained.

holism—the idea that the universe is made up of integrated wholes that cannot be reduced to the sum of their parts.

holistic education—an educational philosophy based on holism and construction around the principle of interconnectedness. A holistic approach to education seeks to integrate multiple levels of meaning and experience and strives to help students realize their full potential in multiple dimensions: intellectual, creative, spiritual, physical, social, and emotional.

holomovement—the underlying flow between implicate and explicate realms in which reality can be experienced.

hypothesis—a tentative statement that can be supported or rejected depending on the outcome of an experiment.

implicate reality—a reality deeper than physical reality that is beyond our senses; the metaphysical world.

independent variable—the treatment or factor that the researcher manipulates to determine a particular effect. It is what is done or not done to a group of people, animals, plants, or things in an experiment or other types of research.

inductive analysis—the process of looking at a field or group of data and inducing or creating order by organizing what is observed into groups.

inferential statistics—statistical analyses used to determine how likely a given outcome is for an entire population based on a sample size. These analyses allow the researcher to make inferences to larger populations by collecting data on a small sample size. The most common inferential statistical analyses are the t-test, analysis of variance (ANOVA), and chi square.

instructional time—the time during a class in which you are actually engaged in instruction.

interview—a data source in which students respond to a series of planned questions.

levels of significance—the level at which we can be reasonably certain that the differences in scores or other measures are due to something other than chance or sampling error. In educational research, two different levels of significance or probability are generally used: $p = .05$ and $p = .01$.

literature review—an examination of journal articles, research, research reports, ERIC documents, books, and other sources related to a particular topic.

materialistic monism—a view of reality that posits that the universe consists only of matter and energy. The only things said to exist are those that can be weighed and measured.

mean—the arithmetic average of a set of scores or numbers.

means-end analysis (MEA)—a problem-solving strategy in which you first describe the desired outcome or end state and then list the goals necessary to reach the end stage.

measures of central tendency—a way of describing a set of data with a single number. The three measures of central tendency are the mode, the median, and the mean.

measures of variability—a measure that describes the spread of scores or how close they cluster around the mean. There are three measures of variability: range, variance, and standard deviation.

median—in a set of scores or numbers it is the point at which 50% of the scores are above and 50% are below.

meta-energy—energy in the form of consciousness.

metaphysical dimensions—dimensions that are beyond the physical dimensions (implicate reality) that are not readily accessible to our normal five senses.

mission statement—a statement that defines the core purpose of a school or district. It often contains some or all of the following: goals, a defining philosophy, a statement of beliefs related to teaching and learning.

mode—in a set of scores or numbers, it is the score or number attained most frequently.

Moses effect—a situation in which researchers hand down research edicts to teachers with the expectation that they will be passive receivers of these edicts.

negative correlation—a relationship between variables in which one variable increases at the same time as the other one decreases.

ontological perspectives—what one believes to be real and true in regard to the nature of reality.

open-ended checklist—a checklist that contains a list of skills with enough space for students to describe their ability, understanding, or usage of each skill.

open-ended questions—questions for which there are no set answers or responses.

paradigm—a common framework from which to view reality. It includes a set of beliefs or assumptions that (1) establishes boundaries and principles within a particular field, (2) guides perception, and (3) describes a particular view of reality.

personal consciousness—the consciousness of an individual that includes both ego-consciousness and self-consciousness.

plan of action—the plan describing the actions you will take based on the findings of your action research.

positive correlation—a relationship between variables in which one variable increases at the same time as the other one also increases.

positivism—a philosophy that emphasizes observable, measurable facts as the only way to come to know the world in which we live. Here the scientific method is the final arbiter of truth.

pretest–posttest design—a quasi-experimental research design in which a group is given a pretest, a treatment, and a posttest. Pretest and posttest scores are compared.

Product and Performance Assessment Form (PPAF)—a rating checklist that is used to analyze and evaluate any type of product or performance, such as science projects, inventions, dramas, dances, or experiments.

pseudoscience—any inquiry that starts with the answer and looks only for data that supports that answer. Whereas science uses data to determine reality, pseudoscience uses beliefs to determine a perceived reality.

qualitative research—research that uses some type of systematic observation to understand a phenomenon, condition, situation, or environment. Qualitative researchers take the world as they find it instead of trying to manipulate conditions to isolate variables. The research questions are more open ended and less defined, with plenty of room to collect a variety of data through collateral observations.

quantitative research (also called **experimental research**)—the researcher takes an active role in setting up an observation or experiment to isolate a variable. The goal is to determine the effect (dependent variable) of a particular approach or treatment (independent variable). The strength of effect is determined by measurable (quantifiable) data.

quasi-action research—quasi-experimental research used in an action research setting.

quasi-experimental research—experimental research without random assignment to groups.

range—in a set of scores or numbers, the difference between the highest and lowest score or number.

rating checklist—a checklist that specifies traits you are looking for in a product or performance and allows the observer to assign levels of performance to each trait. This is similar to a rubric;

however, whereas a rubric uses a sentence or more to provide a description of each level, a rating checklist uses one-word indicators.

rating scales—a scale used to determine the strength of a response. These are often used to determine how much, how often, or how many times something occurs.

recommendation—found after the conclusions in an action research report, the recommendation section describes what is believed to be an effective action based on the findings. You tell how your findings might be used.

reference page—a list of the books, journal articles, and other sources cited in your thesis action research report. This informs readers as to what sources were used and allows them to locate these sources if necessary.

reliability—the degree to which a study or experiment can be repeated with similar results.

research—a variety of procedures that are used to view and review the world to understand it. Research is the systematic method used to collect data to answer questions.

research journal (also known as a **log**)—a notebook used to record thoughts and observations related to all parts of your research. A variety of data may be included here such as insights, analyses, interpretations, impressions, ideas, diagrams, sketches, quotes, student comments, scores, questions, or chronology of your research project.

research question—the purpose of a research study put in the form of a specific question for which the researcher seeks to find an answer.

science—the processes used to objectively examine and organize the world around us. To engage in the process of science means to look, to seek to understand or know, to guess and test guesses, to create order from chaos, and to develop concepts. True science does not start with an answer.

self-consciousness—one's awareness and interpretation of the inner world of feelings, memories, intuition, and impressions.

small-group conference—a focus group used to gather data. The moderator uses questions as prompts and guides. The goal is to get participants to carry the conversation as much as possible.

standard deviation—the square root of the variance. It is the most frequently used index to describe variability or the dispersion of scores. Whereas variance tells you how tightly the scores are clustered, standard deviation tells you how tightly the scores are clustered around the mean in a set of data.

statistical significance—a measure that describes the likelihood that differences in mean between two or more scores or numbers were caused by chance or sampling error.

student checklist—checklists that are completed by students to evaluate their own performance or the performance of the group in which they are working.

students' products or performances—samples of students' work that are used as data sources.

surveys—a data source that enables you to get a variety of information from respondents fairly quickly. Surveys contain a predesigned list of questions that can be either open ended or closed response.

teacher checklist—checklists designed for use by teachers to indicate exactly what skills have been introduced or mastered and when. Checklists can often be used to indicate the level of student performance for each skill.

theory—an interrelated set of concepts that is used to explain a body of data. A theory is a way to explain a set of facts.

time on task—in a class it is the time students are actively engaged in relevant learning tasks.

time series design—a quasi-experimental research design in which a group is examined over time, both before and after the treatment. This is essentially an elaborate pretest–posttest design except that here the researcher collects an extensive amount a data to look for patterns over time.

transcendental monism—a view of reality that posits that the basic essence of the universe is consciousness. Here consciousness is primary, and matter and energy materialize from this. From this perspective ultimate reality is not found solely in the physical world as we know it; rather, it lies in a metaphysical dimension.

transition time—the time in a classroom between one class or activity and the next.

transpersonal research methodology—research methodologies or ways of collecting data that allow an individual to move beyond personal consciousness (ego-consciousness and self-consciousness) to approach universal-consciousness.

treatment group (also called **experimental group**)—the group of subjects, participants, or objects that are exposed to the particular treatment.

triangulation—using different kinds of data to look at something from more than one perspective.

t-**test**—statistical procedure used to determine whether the difference between two means is statistically significant.

universal-consciousness—a type of consciousness that is shared by all individuals past and present. It also refers to dimensions described by religious and spiritual thinkers and also now being explored by some in quantum physicists.

validity—the degree to which a thing measures what it reports to measure.

variable—the thing that is changed or varied in an experiment. In a qualitative study the variable is the category or thing to be examined.

variance—a mathematical procedure that describes the amount of spread among a set of numbers or test scores. If the variance is small, the scores are bunched together. If the variance is large, the scores are spread out.

wait time—the time between asking a question and answering a question. This gives students time to think about and fully process the question. About 7 seconds is usually recommended for most questions; however, higher-level and more complex questions require longer wait time.

REFERENCES

Aamidor, S., & Spicker, H. H. (1995). Promise for the future: Gifted education in rural communities. *Rural Special Education Quarterly, 14*(2), 39–46.

Al-Khalili, J. (1999). *Black holes, worm holes & time machines.* London: Institute of Physics Publishing.

Alkove, L., & McCarty, B. (1992). Plain talk: Recognizing positivism and constructivism in practice. *The Journal of the Association of Teacher Educators, 14,* 16–22.

Allington, R. (2006). *What really matters for struggling readers: Designing research-based programs.* Boston: Pearson.

American Psychological Association. (2001). *Publication manual of the American Psychological Association* (5th ed.). Washington, DC: American Psychological Association.

Armbruster, B. (1993). Science and reading. *The Reading Teacher, 46,* 346–347.

Atwell, N. (1997). *In the middle: New understandings about writing, reading, and learning* (2nd ed.). Portsmouth, NH: Heinemann.

Barone, T., Berliner, D. C., Blanchard, J., Casanova, U., & McGown, T. (1996). A future for teacher education: Developing a strong sense of professionalism. In J. Sikula (Ed.), *Handbook of research on teacher education* (4th ed., pp. 1108–1149). New York: Macmillan Library Reference USA.

Bereiter, C., & Scardamalia, M. (1992). Cognition in curriculum. In P. W. Jackson (Ed.), *Handbook of research on curriculum* (pp. 517–542). New York: American Educational Research Association.

Berliner, D. (2002). Educational research: The hardest science of all. *Educational Researcher, 31*(8), 18–20.

Birman, B. F., Desimone, L., Porter, A. C., & Garet, M. S. (2000). Designing professional development that works. *Educational Leadership, 57,* 28–33.

Bohm, D. (1980). *Wholeness and implicate order.* London: Routledge.

Book, C. L. (1996). Professional development schools. In J. Sikula (Ed.), *Handbook of research on teacher education* (4th ed., pp. 194–210). New York: Macmillan Library Reference USA.

Braud, W., & Anderson, R. (1998). *Transpersonal research methods for the social sciences.* Thousand Oaks, CA: Sage.

Campbell, J. (1968). *The hero with a thousand faces* (2nd ed.). Princeton, NJ: Princeton University Press.

Chase, W. G., & Simon, H. A. (1973). Perceptions in chess. *Cognitive Psychology, 4,* 55–81.

Chi, M. T., Feltovich, P. J., & Glaser, R. (1981). Categorization and representation of physics problems by experts and novices. *Cognitive Science, 5,* 121–152.

Craik, F. I. M., & Lockhart, R. S. (1972). Levels of processing: A framework for memory research. *Journal of Verbal Learning and Verbal Behavior, 11,* 671–684.

Creswell, J. W. (2002). *Educational research: Planning, conducting, and evaluating quantitative and qualitative research.* Upper Saddle River, NJ: Pearson Education.

Csikszentmihalyi, M. (1990). *Flow: The psychology of optimal experience.* New York: HarperPerennial.

Danielson, C. (1996). *Enhancing professional practice: A framework for teaching.* Alexandria, VA: ASCD.

Davis, G. A. (1997). Identifying creative students and measuring creativity. In N. Colangelo & G. A. Davis (Eds.), *Handbook of gifted education* (2nd ed., pp. 269–281). Boston: Allyn & Bacon.

Davis, G. A., & Rimm, S. B. (1998) *Education of the gifted and talented* (4th ed.). Boston: Allyn & Bacon.

de Groot, A. D. (1965). *Thought and choice in chess.* The Hague: Mouton.

De Lieon, J., Argus-Calvo, B., & Medina, C. (1997). A model project of identifying rural gifted and talented students in the visual arts. *Rural Special Education Quarterly, 16*(4), 16–23.

Detert, J. R., Louis, K. S., & Schroeder, R. G. (2001). A culture framework for education: Defining quality values and their impact in U.S. high schools. *School Effectiveness and School Improvement, 12,* 183–212.

Dinkelman, T. (1997). The promise of action research for critically reflective teacher education. *The Teacher Educator, 32*(4), 250–257.

Eisner, E. (1983). The art and craft of teaching. *Educational Leadership, 40*(4), 4–13.

Eisner, E. (1998). *The enlightened eye: Qualitative inquiry and the enhancement of educational practice.* Upper Saddle River, NJ: Prentice-Hall.

Erickson, F. (1986). Qualitative methods in research on teaching. In M. Wittrock (Ed.), *Handbook of research on teaching* (3rd ed., pp. 119–161). New York: Macmillan.

Feldman, A., & Atkins, M. (1995). Embedding action research in professional practice. In S. Noffke & R. Stevenson (Eds.), *Educational action research.* New York: Teachers College Press.

Feldman, D. H., Csikszentmihalyi, M., & Gardner, H. (1994). *Changing the world: A framework for the study of creativity.* Westport, CT: Praeger.

Foshy, A. W. (1998). Action research in the nineties. *The Educational Forum, 62,* 108–112.

Gallagher, J. J., & Gallagher, S. A. (1994). *Teaching the gifted child* (4th ed.). Boston: Allyn & Bacon.

Gambrell, L. B., & Mazzoni, S. A. (1999). Principles of best practice: Finding the common ground. In L. B. Gambrell, L. M. Morrow, S. B. Neuman, & M. Pressley (Eds.), *Best practices in literacy instruction.* New York: The Guildford Press.

Gardner, H. (1983). *Frames of mind.* New York: HarperCollins.

Gardner, H. (1996). Reflection on multiple intelligence: Myths and messages. *Phi Delta Kappan, 77,* 200–209.

Gay, L. R., & Airasian, P. (2003). *Educational research: Competencies for analysis and applications* (7th ed.). Upper Saddle River, NJ: Pearson Education.

Gentry, R. J. (1992). *Teaching kids to spell.* Portsmouth, NH: Heinemann.

Glaser, R. (1984). Education and thinking: The role of knowledge. *American Psychology, 15,* 93–104.

Good, T., & Brophy, J. (1995). *Contemporary educational psychology* (5th ed.). White Plains, NY: Longman.

Goodman, K. (1986). *What's whole in whole language?* Portsmouth, NH: Heinemann.

Graves, D. H. (1983). *Writing: Teachers and children at work.* Portsmouth, NH: Heinemann.

Graves, D. H. (1992). *A fresh look at writing.* Portsmouth, NH: Heinemann.

Guyton, E., & McIntyre, J. D. (1990). Student teaching and school experiences. In W. Houston (Ed.), *Handbook of research on teacher education* (pp. 514–534). New York: Macmillan.

Hansen, J. (1987). *When writers read.* Portsmouth, NH: Heinemann.

Harman, W., & Rheingold, H. (1984). *Higher creativity: Liberating the unconscious for breakthrough insights.* Los Angeles: Tarcher.

Harman, W. (1998). *Global mind change* (2nd ed.). San Francisco: Berrett-Koehler Publishers.

Hawking, S. W. (1988). *A brief history of time: From big bang to black holes.* New York: Bantam Books.

Hensen, K. T. (1996). Teachers as researchers. In J. Sikula (Ed.), *Handbook of research on teacher education* (2nd ed., pp. 53–66). New York: Macmillan.

Herbert, N. (1985). *Quantum reality: Beyond the new physics.* New York: Doubleday.

Hodson, D. (1988). Toward a philosophically more valid science curriculum. *Science Education, 72,* 19–40.

Hunsaker, S. L., Abeel, L. B., & Callahan, C. M. (1991). *Instrument use in the identification of gifted and talented children.* Paper presented at the meeting of the Jacob Javits Gifted and Talented Education Program Grant Recipients, Washington, DC. ERIC Document Reproduction Service No. Ed 334 732.

Hunter, M. (1982). *Mastery teaching.* El Segundo, CA: TIP Publications.

Hursh, D. (1995). Developing discourse structure to support action research for educational reform. In S. Noffke & R. Stevenson (Eds.), *Educational action research.* New York: Teachers College Press.

Imag, D. G., & Switzer, T. J. (1996). Changing teacher education programs: Restructuring collegiate-based teacher education. In J. Sikula (Ed.), *Handbook of Research on Teacher Education* (2nd ed., pp. 213–226). New York: Macmillan.

Johnson, A. (2000a). It's time for Madeline Hunter to go. *Action in Teacher Education, 22,* 72–78.

Johnson, A. (2000b). *Up and out: Using creative and critical thinking skills to enhance learning.* Boston: Allyn & Bacon.

Johnson, A. (2003a). *A short guide to academic writing.* Lanham, MD: University Press of America.

Johnson, A. (2003b). *Gifted students and the inner curriculum: Seven literacy techniques to attend to inner dimensions.* Denver, CO: Institute for the Development of Gifted Education.

Johnson, A. (2006a). I am a holistic educator, not a dancing monkey. *Encounter: Education for Justice and Social Meaning, 18,* 36–40.

Johnson, A. (2006b). *Making connections in elementary and middle school social studies.* Thousand Oaks, CA: Sage Publications.

Kessler, R. (2000). *The soul of education: Helping students find connection, compassion, and character at school.* Alexandria, VA: ASCD.

Knight, S. L., Wiseman, D. L., & Cooner, D. (2000). Using collaborative teacher research to determine the impact of professional development school activities on elementary students' math and writing outcomes. *Journal of Teacher Education, 51,* 26–38.

Krishnamurti, J. (1953). *Education and the significance of life.* San Francisco: HarperCollins.

Leedy, P. D., & Ormrod, J. E. (2001). *Practical research: Planning and design* (7th ed.). Upper Saddle River, NJ: Merrill Prentice-Hall.

Marks, H. M., & Louis, K. S. (1997). Does teacher empowerment affect the classroom? The implication of teacher empowerment for instruction, practice and student performance. *Educational Evaluation and Policy Analysis, 19,* 245–275.

Marzano, R. J., Pickering, D. J., & Pollock, J. E. (2001). *Classroom instruction that works: Research-based strategies for increasing student achievement.* Alexandria, VA: ASCD.

Marzano, R. J. (2003). *What works in schools: Translating research into action.* Alexandria, VA: ASCD.

Maslow, A. (1971). *The farther reaches of human nature.* New York: Viking Press.

McIntrye, D. J., Byrd, D. M., & Foxx, S. M. (1996). Field and laboratory experiences. In J. Sikula (Ed.), *Hand of research on teacher education* (2nd ed., pp. 171–193). New York: Macmillan.

McNiff, J., Lomax, P., & Whitehead, J. (1996). *You and your action research project.* New York: Routledge.

McTaggart, R. (1997). Reading the collection. In R. McTaggart (Ed.), *Participatory action research* (pp. 1–12). Albany, NY: SUNY Press.

McQuillan, J. (1998). *The literacy crisis: False claims, real solutions.* Portsmouth, NH: Heinemann.

Metcalf, K., Hammer, R., & Kahlich, P. (1996). Alternative to field-based experiences: The comparative effects of on-campus laboratories. *Teaching and Teacher Education, 12*(3), 271–283.

Miller, J. P. (1996) *The holistic curriculum.* Toronto: OISE Press.

National Center for Educational Statistics. (1998). *NAEP 1996 trends in educational progress: Addendum.* Jessup, MD: U.S. Department of Education.

Nichol, L. (2003). *The essential David Bohm.* New York: Routledge.

Noffke, S. (1995). Action research and democratic schooling. In S. Noffke & R. Stevenson (Eds.), *Educational action research* (pp. 1–11). New York: Teachers College Press.

Patterson, L., & Shannon, P. (1993). Reflection, inquiry, and action. In L. Patterson, C. Santa, K. Short, & K. Smith (Eds.), *Teachers are researchers: Reflection and action* (pp. 7–11). Newark, DE: International Reading Association.

Perkins, D. N. (1987). Thinking frames: An integrative perspective on teaching cognitive skills. In J. B. Baron & R. J. Sternberg (Eds.), *Teaching thinking*

skills: Theory and practice (pp. 41–61). New York: W. H. Freeman.

Piirto, J. (1994). *Talented children and adults: Their development and education.* New York: Macmillan.

Recht, D. R., & Leslie, L. (1988). Effect of prior knowledge on good and poor readers' memory. *Journal of Educational Psychology, 80,* 16–20.

Renzulli, J. S., & Reis, S. M. (1997). The Schoolwide Enrichment Model: New directions for developing high-end learning. In N. Colangelo & G. A. Davis (Ed.), *Handbook of gifted education* (2nd ed., pp. 136–154). Boston: Allyn & Bacon.

Richert, E. S. (1997). Excellence with equity in identification and programming. In N. Colangelo & G. A. Davis (Eds.), *Handbook of gifted education* (2nd ed., pp. 75–88). Boston: Allyn & Bacon.

Rogers, K. (1993). Grouping the gifted and talented: Questions and answers. *Roeper Review, 16,* 8–12.

Routmann, R. (1996). *Literacy at the crossroads: Crucial talk about reading, writing, and other teaching dilemmas.* Portsmouth, NH: Heinemann.

Santrock, J. W. (2004). *Educational psychology* (2nd ed.). New York: McGraw Hill

Savage, T., & Armstrong, D. (1996). *Effective teaching in elementary social studies* (3rd ed.). Englewood Cliffs, NJ: Prentice Hall.

Schmuck, R. A. (1997). *Practical action research for change.* Arlington Heights, IL: IRI/Skylight Training and Publishing.

Shulman, L. S. (1986). Those who understand: Knowledge growth in teaching. *Educational Researcher, 15*(2), 4–14.

Smith, F. (1985). *Reading without nonsense* (2nd ed.). New York: Teachers College Press.

Stanovich, K. (1992). *How to think straight about psychology* (3rd ed.). New York: HarperCollins.

Sternberg, R. (1996). *Successful intelligence: How practical and creative intelligence determine success in life.* New York: Plume.

Sternberg, R. J., & Williams, W. M. (2002). *Educational psychology.* Boston: Allyn & Bacon.

Sweetland, S. R., & Hoy, W. K. (2002). School characteristics and educational outcomes: Toward an organizational model of student achievement in middle schools. *Educational Administration Quarterly, 36,* 703–729.

Talbot, M. (1991). *The holographic universe.* New York. HarperPerennial.

Taylor, S. J., & Bogdan, R. (1998). *Introduction to qualitative research methods: A guidebook and resource* (3rd ed.). New York: John Wiley & Sons.

Thelen, J. N. (1984). *Improving reading in science* (2nd ed.). Newark, DE: International Reading Association.

Thomas, K., & Kjelgaard, P. A. (1998). Professional development schools: A review of experiences in eight pioneer sites in Texas. *ERS Spectrum, 16*(1), 41–46.

Tomlinson, C. A. (1995). Action research and practical inquiry: An overview and an invitation to teachers of gifted learners. *Journal for the Education of the Gifted, 18*(4), 468–484.

Tomlinson, C. (1995). *How to differentiate instruction in mixed-ability classrooms.* Alexandria, VA: ASCD.

United States Department of Education. (1993). National excellence: A case for developing America's talent. Retrieved from www.ed.gove/pubs/DevTalent/part3.htrr.

Watts, S., & Johnson, A. (1995). Toward reflection in teacher education: The role of dialogue journals. *Journal of Reading Education, 21,* 27–38.

Woolfolk, A. (2004). *Educational psychology* (9th ed.). Boston: Allyn & Bacon.

Zeichner, K., & Liston, D. (1996). *Reflective teaching: An introduction.* Mahway, NJ: Lawrence Erlbaum.

Zemelman, S., Daniels, H., & Hyde, A. (2006). *Best practice: New standards for teaching and learning in America's schools* (3rd ed.). Portsmouth, NH: Heinemann.

INDEX